THE ULTIMATE BOOK OF DESIGNER
DREAM HOMES

Over 475
Best-Selling Plans

PRESENTED BY

PRESIDENT	Angela Santerini
PUBLISHER	Dominic Foley
WRITER	Jennifer Bacon
GRAPHIC ARTIST	Bishana Shipp
CONTRIBUTING EDITORS	Shannon Addis Jennifer Emmons Laura Segers
CONTRIBUTING GRAPHIC ARTISTS	Kim Campeau Emily Sessa Joshua Thomas Diane Zwack
CONTRIBUTING WRITERS	Paula Powers Claire Ulik
ILLUSTRATORS	Architectural Art Allen Bennetts Greg Havens Holzhauer, Inc. Dave Jenkins Kurt Kauss Barry Nathan
PHOTOGRAPHERS	Walter Kirk Matthew Scott Laurence Taylor Happy Terrebone Doug Thompson Bryan Willy

A DESIGNS DIRECT PUBLISHING® BOOK

Printed by Toppan Printing Co., Hong Kong
First Printing, August 2006
10 9 8 7 6 5 4 3 2 1

TABLE OF
CONTENTS

FEATURE PLANS

Stunning Statement

Longleaf

- UDHFB01-3782
- 1-866-525-9374

Right: The master bedroom features a window seat and a tray ceiling for both vertical volume and added luxury.

Making a statement about form, function and flair, *Longleaf* presents a timeless façade of brick stone and cedar shake. But perhaps the most dramatic element is the incredible front entry crowned with a cathedral gable and framed by two sets of columns, which directs eyes to stunning doors that soften the gable with their curved tops.

A stunning front staircase flows into the open foyer, while a transom and columns frame the study and dining room.

While the metal roof further distinguishes the entry and front porch, the rear is just as beautiful with arched and ladder transoms, and French doors that lead to a large deck. Continuing the metal accents of the front, metal underscoring on the rear gables provides an element of cohesiveness, similar to how details on the box-bay windows correlate with architectural details found on the columns.

A stone archway and fireplace become focal points in the family room, while the coffered ceiling lends drama.

Frank Betz Associates, Inc.

The second floor pays just as much attention to detail as the first with walk-in closets in two of the three secondary bedrooms and a spacious room dedicated to family entertainment. A master suite that rivals all master suites includes a sophisticated tray ceiling, large sitting room, window seat that overlooks the backyard and a dream of a master bath. And who could ignore that divided walk-in closet!

With a basement level that awaits interpretation, *Longleaf* makes a statement indeed and does so with grace and comfort.

Below: The elegant dining room is crowned with a coffered ceiling, and accented by decorative wainscoting and custom molding for a formal appearance.

Above: The rambling kitchen features more than ample cabinetry and counter space, and also includes French doors that bathe the room with natural light.

Interior columns mark entry to the dining room, while it's no coincidence that double doors lead to the study. From the foyer, a guest receives a good idea of how the home is – with glimpses into every common area.

A number of features make this home extraordinary – from three garage bays with close proximity to the kitchen to the remarkable coffered ceiling that distinguishes the family room. There's also a walk-in pantry in the kitchen and a stone floor-to-ceiling fireplace in the family room, but another wonderful element is the first-floor guest/in-law suite.

Frank Betz Associates, Inc.

Longleaf

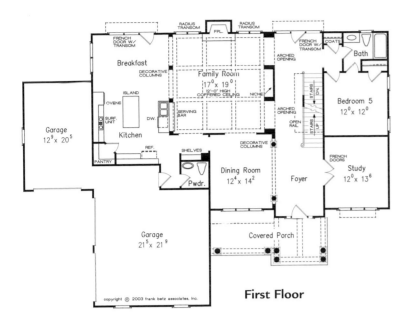

First Floor

copyright © 2003 frank betz associates, inc.

Second Floor

Rear Elevation

UDHFB01-3782 — 1-866-525-9374

Home photographed may differ from actual construction documents.

Total Living	First Floor	Second Floor	Opt. Bonus	Bed	Bath	Width	Depth	Foundation	Price Category
4066 sq ft	1773 sq ft	2293 sq ft	N/A	5	4-1/2	69' 0"	54' 4"	Basement or Crawl	J

Frank Betz Associates, Inc.

www.ultimatehomeplans.net

Royal Roots

Cedar Court

- UDHAL01-5004
- 1-866-525-9374

Right: The large master bath features dual sinks, a grand arched window and pot lights overhead for an enchanting look.

Stone and stucco combine with a cupola and finials to add a touch of European elegance to the *Cedar Court*. A towering stone wall--topped with a gable--creates the perfect frame for an impressive front entry, while arched windows and vents soften this hillside walkout's strong exterior. Perfect for lakeside lots or those who want to capitalize on the seclusion of the mountains, the *Cedar Court* is true luxury.

Windows, transoms and French doors invite the views inside.

Above: A large center island features additional storage and a gas range.

Outdoor living is accommodated in grand style. With a decorative chimney cap, a massive fireplace highlights the screened-turret porch, extending outdoor enjoyment time. The wrapping rear porch, along with the basement-level patio, provides an abundance of recreation space.

The common area is filled with rooms that are open to each other, and the rear wall is almost entirely made up of floor-to-ceiling windows and French doors that enhance the airiness with natural light and pristine views.

High, decorative ceiling treatments in the great room, study and dining room increase volume and partition the common rooms without enclosing

Accented by a tray ceiling and sitting area, the master bedroom lives even larger than its size indicates.

space. Wood pillars edge the foyer and dining room, and the fireplace hides the descending staircase, yet a railing--by its side--allows you to look down to the lower level.

An art niche complements the hall leading to the master suite. Truly stunning, the master suite features a bayed sitting area and tray ceiling that grant striking architectural interest in the bedroom. Making up the rest of the suite are two walk-in closets and an elegant master bath with twin vanities, private privy and separate bathtub and shower.

The basement level features two bedrooms and a rec room with fireplace. Each secondary bedroom has its own walk-in closet, and the unfinished storage areas leave room for growth.

For those who appreciate sophistication and comfort, the *Cedar Court* is designed to please. It blurs the line between indoor and outdoor living, while making the most of both.

Left: Rich textures and neutral-colored furniture accent the hardwood floors and natural elements throughout the home.

Donald A. Gardner Architects, Inc.

Cedar Court

First Floor

Within the floor plan:
- SITTING
- MASTER BEDROOM 18 - 0 X 15 - 0 (TRAY CEILING)
- PORCH
- SCREEN PORCH 13 - 0 X 14 - 10
- BRKFST. 10 - 0 X 13 - 0
- GREAT ROOM 22 - 0 X 20 - 0 (CATHEDRAL CEILING)
- KITCHEN 14 - 0 X 14 - 8
- MASTER BATH
- STUDY 13 - 0 X 14 - 0 (TRAY CEILING)
- FOYER 7 - 0 X 12 - 0
- DINING 15 - 0 X 12 - 0 (TRAY CEILING)
- PD. RM.
- UTIL. 8 - 0 X 9 - 0
- PORCH
- GARAGE 24 - 0 X 39 - 2

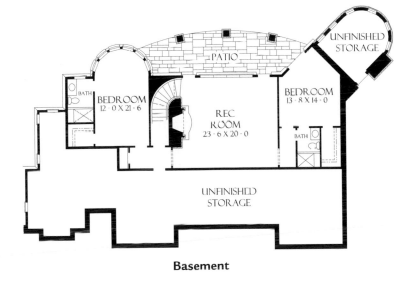

Basement

Within the basement plan:
- PATIO
- UNFINISHED STORAGE
- BATH
- BEDROOM 12 - 0 X 21 - 6
- REC ROOM 23 - 6 X 20 - 0
- BEDROOM 13 - 8 X 14 - 0
- BATH
- UNFINISHED STORAGE

Rear Elevation

UDHAL01-5004 — 1-866-525-9374

Total Living	First Floor	Basement	Bonus	Bed	Bath	Width	Depth	Foundation	Price Category
3820 sq ft	2446 sq ft	1374 sq ft	N/A	3	3-1/2	82' 4"	95' 10"	Hillside Walkout	O

Donald A. Gardner Architects, Inc.

© The Sater Design Collection, Inc.

Visual Feast

Sunningdale Cove

- UDHDS01-6660
- 1-866-525-9374

Right: The rambling lanai creates an optimal space
for outdoor entertaining and relaxation.

This spectacular home steps beyond tradition
to offer a stunning floor plan crafted around a
large center courtyard. The main house — with
its generous master suite, dramatic grand salon
and well-crafted family living spaces — flank the
courtyard on two sides, while an extended
garage and full guest suite border the third.

The grand salon, just inside the foyer, captivates with a two-story coffered ceiling, bayed glass wall and arched transom windows.

A private wall completes the area. A pool and spa, built-in planters and a fireplace take the courtyard to a level seen only in the most discriminating homes.

The visual feast begins just inside the exterior door, which leads to a long entryway lanai adjacent to the courtyard. The interior front door opens into a two-story foyer with views straight ahead through an impressive grand salon, where oversized bay windows and half-moon transoms lure an expansive view into the home. The foyer also offers just a few short steps to the staircase and the family rooms.

Right: Arches frame the entryway into the kitchen and dining room, creating an open feel throughout the home.

The Sater Design Collection, Inc.

Above: The two-story foyer highlights the drama of the home, with a stepped ceiling and sweeping staircase.

Above: A grand arch leads into the dining room from the great room, and uses French doors to bathe the room with natural light to create a warm room for meals.

Above: The leisure room includes a built-in entertainment center and access to the lanai, making outdoor refreshment just a step away.

Flanking the courtyard on one side, and embracing the space with bay windows and sliding glass walls, are a large leisure room/kitchen/breakfast nook. The kitchen features a center island, an angled serving bar and a niche for a desk, while the family room boasts a built-in media wall.

The guesthouse includes a generous bedroom, full bath and walk-in closet, as well as its own lanai with portico entry and built-in grill. The partial second story completes the home, with two bedrooms, a full bath and two observation decks overlooking the courtyard and the back lanai.

The Sater Design Collection, Inc.

Sunningdale Cove

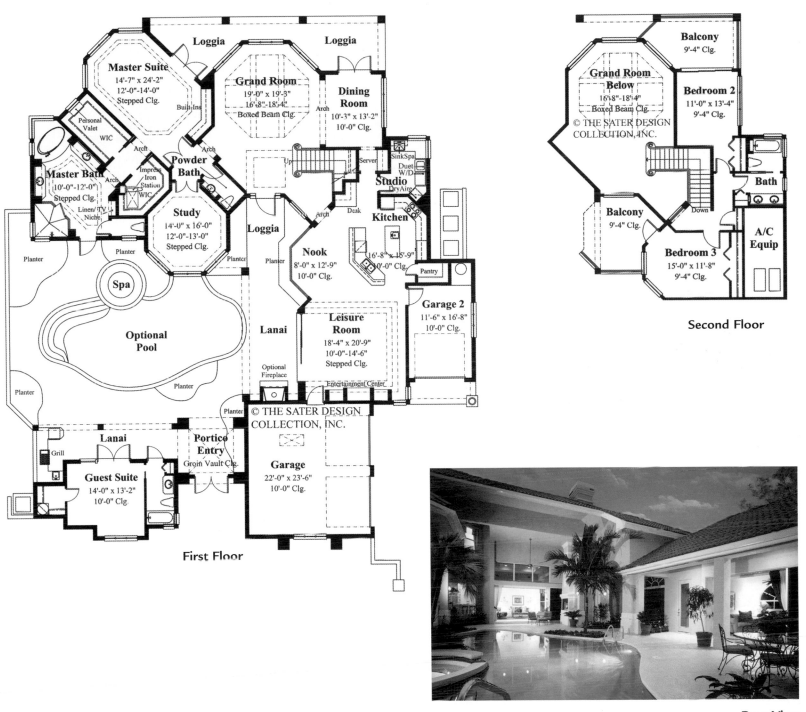

First Floor

- Loggia
- Loggia
- Master Suite 14'-7" x 24'-2" 12'-0"-14'-0" Stepped Clg.
- Grand Room 19'-0" x 19'-3" 16'-8"-18'-4" Boxed Beam Clg.
- Dining Room 10'-3" x 13'-2" 10'-0" Clg.
- Personal Valet
- WIC
- Built-Ins
- Server
- Sink Spa
- Duet W/D
- Master Bath 10'-0"-12'-0" Stepped Clg.
- Powder Bath
- Impress Iron Station
- WIC
- Up
- Studio DryAire
- Arch
- Linen/TV Niche
- Study 14'-0" x 16'-0" 12'-0"-13'-0" Stepped Clg.
- Loggia
- Desk
- Kitchen 16'-8" x 15'-9" 10'-0" Clg.
- Planter
- Planter
- Nook 8'-0" x 12'-9" 10'-0" Clg.
- Pantry
- Spa
- Optional Pool
- Lanai
- Leisure Room 18'-4" x 20'-9" 10'-0"-14'-6" Stepped Clg.
- Garage 2 11'-6" x 16'-8" 10'-0" Clg.
- Planter
- Optional Fireplace
- Entertainment Center
- Planter
- © THE SATER DESIGN COLLECTION, INC.
- Lanai
- Grill
- Portico Entry Groin Vault Clg.
- Garage 22'-0" x 23'-6" 10'-0" Clg.
- Guest Suite 14'-0" x 13'-2" 10'-0" Clg.

Second Floor

- Balcony 9'-4" Clg.
- Grand Room Below 16'-8"-18'-4" Boxed Beam Clg.
- © THE SATER DESIGN COLLECTION, INC.
- Bedroom 2 11'-0" x 13'-4" 9'-4" Clg.
- Bath
- Balcony 9'-4" Clg.
- Down
- Bedroom 3 15'-0" x 11'-8" 9'-4" Clg.
- A/C Equip

Rear View

UDHDS01-6660 — 1-866-525-9374

Total Living	First Floor	Second Floor	Guest Suite	Bed	Bath	Width	Depth	Foundation	Price Category
3744 sq ft	2822 sq ft	610 sq ft	312 sq ft	4	3-1/2	80' 0"	96' 0"	Slab	J

© 2002 Donald A. Gardner, Inc.

Craftsman Collage

Satchwell

■ UDHDG01-967

■ 1-866-525-9374

Right: Dual sinks, a private privy and separate shower and tub make the master bath a spacious room for relaxation.

Graceful arches contrast with high gables for a stunning exterior on this Craftsman home. Windows with decorative transoms and several French doors flood the open floor plan with natural light.

Above: A tray ceiling adds vertical volume and a French door allows additional sunlight to flood through the master bedroom.

Tray ceilings in the dining room and master bedroom as well as cathedral ceilings in the bedroom/study, great room, kitchen and breakfast area create architectural interest, along with visual space. Built-ins in the great room and additional room in the garage add convenient storage. While a screened porch allows for comfortable outdoor entertaining, a bonus room lies near two additional bedrooms and offers flexibility.

Right: Honey-colored cabinetry combines with granite countertops to showcase stainless steel appliances.

Donald A. Gardner Architects, Inc.

Above: Wainscoting and crown molding adorn the formal dining room, creating an elegant place for meals.

Above: The screened porch off the breakfast and great room brings the outdoors in, serving as an ideal location for summer meals.

Positioned for privacy, the master suite features access to the screened porch, dual walk-in closets and a well-appointed bath, including a private privy, garden tub, double vanity and spacious shower.

Above: Built-ins and custom molding around the fireplace add an elegant touch to the great room.

Donald A. Gardner Architects, Inc.

Satchwell

SCREEN PORCH
25-10 x 9-4

BRKFST.
11-8 x 8-10
(cathedral ceiling)

fireplace

KIT.
11-8 x 12-4

bath

BED RM.
11-0 x 12-0

MASTER BED RM.
16-2 x 13-8

GREAT RM.
19-0 x 15-8
(cathedral ceiling)

cl

cl

walk-in closet

walk-in closet

master bath

bath

FOYER
cl 6-0 x 11-0

DINING
11-0 x 13-0

UTIL.
6-0 x 10-4
w
d

up

BED RM.
11-8 x 11-8

BED RM./ STUDY
11-4 x 12-10
(cathedral ceiling)

cl

PORCH

GARAGE
21-8 x 21-0

STORAGE

First Floor

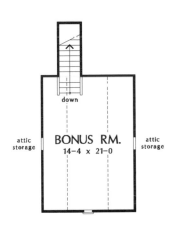

down

attic storage

BONUS RM.
14-4 x 21-0

attic storage

up

Rear Elevation

UDHDG01-967 — 1-866-525-9374

Total Living	First Floor	Second Floor	Bonus	Bed	Bath	Width	Depth	Foundation	Price Category
2097 sq ft	2097 sq ft	N/A	352 sq ft	4	3	64' 10"	59' 6"	Crawl Space*	E

*Other options available. See page 513.

Tasteful Living

Ballard

- UDHFB01-3633
- 1-866-525-9374

Right: Chair-rail molding, an arched entryway and two decorative columns add sophistication to the formal dining room.

Abundant and transitional, the curb appeal of *Ballard* fully reflects its family with a tasteful representation of Traditional and Craftsman accents. Keystone arches draw attention to numerous windows, while confident gables contrast with the hipped roof.

The front porch's covered roof correlates with underscoring from the home's highest gable and also connects the cedar shake from the side elevations. But the wrapping front porch provides more than a welcoming element upon arrival, it is one of the home's greatest relaxation destinations.

Once inside, the two-story foyer foreshadows the openness to come. Showcasing the design flexibility, the two-story family room was modified to create additional square footage upstairs. However, it's the natural traffic flow that makes this home accommodating.

The fireplace showcases stunning architectural detail, while the arched entrance provides an elegant entry into the keeping room.

Built-in cabinetry and television cabinet over the striking fireplace enhances the keeping room.

Adjacent to the keeping room and breakfast nook, the kitchen proves it's the heart of the home with an angled center island. A walk-in pantry is located next to a built-in desk, allowing grocery lists and menus to be made with ease. Also, the desk creates a great homework or computer station, so parents can always be close by – even during meal preparation. A first-floor bedroom is complete with a walk-in closet and bath access for older loved ones and guests.

Above: A tray ceiling draws the eye upward in the master bedroom, and several windows usher natural light throughout the suite.

Upstairs, a secondary bedroom includes a private bath and walk-in closet, while the optional bonus room provides room for a possible fifth bedroom, home gym or other special-function room. Creating a homeowner's retreat, the master suite features a stylish tray ceiling, dual vanities, private toilet, separate shower and a tub. The huge walk-in closet, accessible only from the bath, assures undisturbed rest for those who want to sleep in.

Add the versatile basement and *Ballard* proves to be a home that will meet today's needs as well as those in the future, and overall, a great home to create a past.

Right: The honey-colored hardwood floors are mimicked in the color of the cabinetry, creating a warm, inviting kitchen.

Frank Betz Associates, Inc.

Ballard

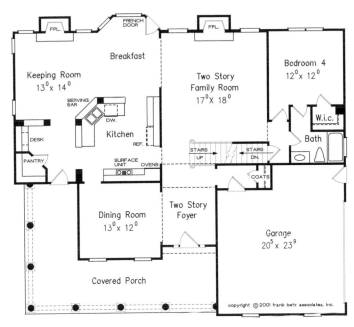

First Floor

Keeping Room 13⁰ x 14⁰
Breakfast
Two Story Family Room 17⁰ X 18⁰
Bedroom 4 12⁰ x 12⁰
Kitchen
Dining Room 13⁰ x 12⁰
Two Story Foyer
Garage 20⁵ x 23⁹
Covered Porch

copyright © 2001 frank betz associates, inc.

Second Floor

Master Suite 13⁰ x 17⁰
Family Room Below
Bedroom 3 12⁰ x 12⁰
Vaulted Bedroom 2 13⁰ x 11³
Foyer Below
Opt. Bonus 12⁵ x 15⁹

Rear Elevation

UDHFB01-3633 — 1-866-525-9374

Total Living	First Floor	Second Floor	Opt. Bonus	Bed	Bath	Width	Depth	Foundation	Price Category
2759 sq ft	1565 sq ft	1194 sq ft	280 sq ft	4	4	53' 0"	48' 6"	Basement, Crawl Space or Slab	H

Frank Betz Associates, Inc.

© The Sater Design Collection, Inc.

Peaceful Retreat

Turnberry Lane

- UDHDS01-6602
- 1-866-525-9374

Right: The formal living room is a "white on white" work of art. Double doors, opening to the veranda, bring the space both natural light and a touch of simple elegance.

Contemporary and classic design elements are combined with superb results in this gracious resort home. Decorative columns, circle-head windows and a double-arched entryway evoke a sense of Mediterranean heritage and Old-World influence, while contemporary lines and sun-drenched stucco give the home a modern feel and a bright, sunny disposition. "Bright and sunny" describes much of the interior of the home as well. Inside the foyer, a mitered glass window provides an open feel and wide garden views.

Right: A unique buffet server acts as a buffer between the formal dining and living rooms, defining the two spaces as separate and, at the same time, keeping them open airy.

The formal living and dining rooms are straight ahead, emanating a captivating first impression while natural lights streams through a unique bow window in the study. Every home has a personality–this one just loves a tropical setting, as you can tell.

Left: The common area consisting of leisure room, kitchen and breakfast nook are open and inviting.

Above: Natural light streams in through a unique bay window in the study, creating an inviting warmth and comfort.

Right: Here, a charming fireplace, book-ended by built-ins, warms the common area consisting of leisure room, kitchen and breakfast nook.

The Sater Design Collection, Inc.

Turnberry Lane

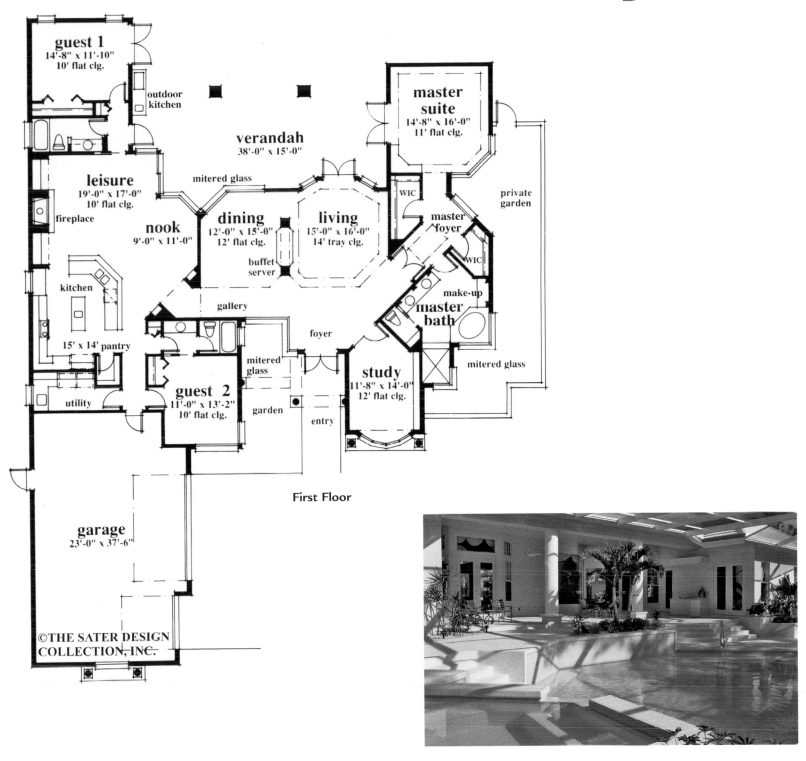

guest 1
14'-8" x 11'-10"
10' flat clg.

outdoor kitchen

verandah
38'-0" x 15'-0"

master suite
14'-8" x 16'-0"
11' flat clg.

mitered glass

leisure
19'-0" x 17'-0"
10' flat clg.

WIC

private garden

fireplace

nook
9'-0" x 11'-0"

dining
12'-0" x 15'-0"
12' flat clg.

living
15'-0" x 16'-0"
14' tray clg.

master foyer

WIC

buffet server

make-up

kitchen

gallery

master bath

15' x 14' pantry

mitered glass

foyer

study
11'-8" x 14'-0"
12' flat clg.

utility

guest 2
11'-0" x 13'-2"
10' flat clg.

garden

mitered glass

entry

First Floor

garage
23'-0" x 37'-6"

©THE SATER DESIGN COLLECTION, INC.

Home photographed may differ from actual construction documents.

Total Living	First Floor	Second Floor	Bonus	Bed	Bath	Width	Depth	Foundation	Price Category
2794 sq ft	2794 sq ft	N/A	N/A	3	3	70' 0"	98' 0"	Slab	H

The Sater Design Collection, Inc.

www.ultimatehomeplans.net

Farmhouse Flair

Arbordale

- UDHDG01-452
- 1-866-525-9374

Right: The door leading to the rear porch enables sunlight to brighten and seasonal breezes to cool the master bedroom.

This beautiful farmhouse with prominent twin gables and bays adds just the right amount of country style to modern family life. The master suite is quietly tucked away downstairs with no bedrooms directly above, and the cook of the family will love the spacious U-shaped kitchen with ample cabinets and pantry.

Accented by striking columns, the living room ushers natural sunlight through the French doors and bay window.

Above: Resting in a bay window, the living room uses French doors to bathe the room in sunlight, while columns punctuate the entrance and enhance the open layout.

The bonus room is easily accessible from the back stairs or second floor, where three large bedrooms share two full baths. Storage space abounds with walk-ins, hall shelves, and a linen closet upstairs. A curved balcony borders a versatile loft/study that overlooks the stunning two-story great room.

Right: The loft creates the ultimate relaxing space for reading on a sleepy Sunday afternoon.

Donald A. Gardner Architects, Inc.

Arbordale

First Floor

PORCH

MASTER
BD. RM.
15-6 x 14-0

FAMILY RM.
18-8 x 23-2

(two story ceiling)

fireplace

balcony above

BRKFST.
13-4 x 13-8

storage

walk-in closet

lin.

master bath

walk-in closet

LIVING RM.
13-4 x 13-6

FOYER
8-8 x 10-2

cl

KIT.
13-4 x 12-0

DINING
13-4 x 13-6

pd. rm.

cl

UTIL.
6-10 x 10-0

pan.

up

GARAGE
21-8 x 28-4

© 1996 DONALD A. GARDNER
All rights reserved

PORCH

Second Floor

family room below

railing

LOFT/
STUDY
9-0 x 14-1

BED RM.
13-4 x 11-10

attic storage

cl cl

lin.

skylights

walk-in closet

bath

down

shelves

walk-in closet

bath

down

down

BONUS RM.
21-8 x 16-5

BED RM.
13-4 x 12-2

railing

balcony

BED RM.
13-4 x 13-6

Rear Elevation

UDHDG01-452 — 1-866-525-9374

Total Living	First Floor	Second Floor	Bonus	Bed	Bath	Width	Depth	Foundation	Price Category
3163 sq ft	2086 sq ft	1077 sq ft	403 sq ft	4	3-1/2	82' 10"	51' 8"	Crawl Space*	G

*Other options available. See page 513.

Donald A. Gardner Architects, Inc.

Instant Attraction

Summerfield

- UDHFB01-3550
- 1-866-525-9374

Right: Truly relaxing, the master bath features a radius window and vaulted ceiling that draw the eye upwards in a luxurious fashion.

Good design should be the basis of any home, and that also means incorporating the wishes and needs of families. It's little wonder that *Summerfield* can gracefully showcase an exterior of board and batten siding and brick that so eloquently pays tribute to the traditional style. It's also the board and batten siding that accentuates the gables, which gives this home remarkable curb appeal.

Above: The vaulted keeping room includes a second fireplace and built-in shelves and cabinetry for showcasing knick-knacks and family photos.

Top Right: A tray ceiling tops the master bedroom, showcasing architectural detail, while the vaulted sitting area increases the room's depth.

Right: The great room features a centrally located fireplace and vibrant wall color to create the ultimate entertaining space.

With subtle arches that add architectural interest to the porch's clean-lined roof and columns, this home is an attention-grabber. At first it might not be obvious that one of the arches perfectly frames the dining room window's curved transom – and that the location of that arch allows a little more light into the house – but once realized, it reaffirms the principle of good design.

Right: Columns and an arched entryway provide the entrance to the elegant dining room.

Far Right: The two-story foyer features transoms that frame the front door and an overhead Palladian window for added illumination.

The floor plan keeps its openness, yet it follows a more Traditional form, using carefully positioned walls to define space. The master suite is located in the private zone, while common rooms are clustered together with those deemed to see the most action – the kitchen and keeping room – furthest away from the master suite.

Creating a dramatic statement, the impressive two-story foyer leads eyes to the vaulted great room, and as the focal point of the great room, the fireplace is flanked by windows that welcome daylight inside the home. Columns are utilized as accents throughout the first floor, and a plant shelf provides a perfect spot for collectibles in the vaulted keeping room.

It isn't just the versatile bonus room that makes the second floor accommodating. Each bedroom has a vanity, and the large attic allows plenty of room for storage – something every family needs and appreciates.

Whether it's the optional basement, pampering master suite, the large laundry room or chef-inspired kitchen, *Summerfield* embodies good design and a whole lot more.

Left: The serving bar creates extra seating in the kitchen, while black appliances nicely compliment the hardwood floors and cabinetry.

Frank Betz Associates, Inc.

Summerfield

First Floor

Second Floor

Rear Elevation

UDHFB01-3550 — 1-866-525-9374

Total Living	First Floor	Second Floor	Opt. Bonus	Bed	Bath	Width	Depth	Foundation	Price Category
2680 sq ft	2087 sq ft	593 sq ft	249 sq ft	3	2-1/2	58' 4"	55' 2"	Basement or Crawl	G

Donald A. Gardner Architects, Inc.

Natural Beauty

Ryecroft

- UDHDG01-824-D
- 1-866-525-9374

Right: Multiple transoms and French doors raise the eye to a striking clerestory window accented by vaulted ceilings.

Arched windows and arches in the covered front porch complement the gable peaks on the façade of this stylish Craftsman home. With a stone and siding exterior and partial finished walkout basement, the *Ryecroft* is an exciting home both inside and out.

Left: Matching wooden cabinetry and appliances turn this kitchen into an instant gathering spot.

Bottom : The sitting area in the master bedroom is hugged by a bay window, granting panoramic views.

Designed for sloping lots, this floor plan positions its common living areas and master suite on the first floor, and a generous recreation room and two family bedrooms on the lower level. The *Ryecroft's* layout proves perfect for those families who love to entertain. The island kitchen is open to multiple rooms, and the breakfast area features a nearby walk-in pantry. A grand fireplace, built-ins and stunning windows create an elegant yet cozy gathering area in the great room. An exciting cathedral ceiling expands the foyer and great room, while the dining room, master bedroom and bath enjoy elegant tray ceilings.

Above: Built-in shelves and stylish transoms become elegant extras in the great room.

With a bay window and back-porch access, the master suite boasts dual walk-in closets and a luxurious bath. Downstairs, the basement features two bedrooms, each with full baths that flank the open rec room. With a wet bar, fireplace, built-in shelves and patio access, this room mirrors the elegance of the great room above it.

Perfect for lots with views, those who enjoy outdoor entertaining, or the added space a finished basement provides, the *Ryecroft* beautifully captures the essence of modern living in a stunning environment.

Donald A. Gardner Architects, Inc.

Ryecroft

DINING
12-0 x 15-0

PORCH

PORCH

MASTER
BED RM.
14-0 x 18-0

fireplace

GREAT RM.
22-0 x 18-6
(cathedral ceiling)

KITCHEN
12-0 x 15-0

BRKFST.
9-8 x 10-0

walk-in
closet

walk-in
closet

UTIL.
5-8 x
6-8
d w

pantry

storage

pd.
rm.

cl FOYER
6-8 x
10-0

railing

down

master
bath

seat

PORCH

GARAGE
21-8 x 23-4

storage

First Floor

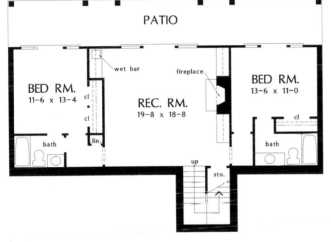

PATIO

BED RM.
11-6 x 13-4

wet bar

fireplace

BED RM.
13-6 x 11-0

cl

cl

REC. RM.
19-8 x 18-8

cl

bath

lin.

bath

up

sto.

Second Floor

Rear Elevation

UDHDG01-824-D — 1-866-525-9374

Total Living	First Floor	Basement	Bonus	Bed	Bath	Width	Depth	Foundation	Price Category
2815 sq ft	1725 sq ft	1090 sq ft	N/A	3	3-1/2	59' 0"	59' 4"	Hillside Walkout	F

Entertainer's Delight

Bainbridge

- UDHDS01-7051
- 1-866-525-9374

Right: The kitchen combines subtle color to distinguish the island counter with rubbed maple cabinetry. The laundry and dining room are located just through the archway.

This welcoming Country home is beautifully designed both inside and out, with a splendid floor plan that provides spacious and transitional spaces to suit any lifestyle. Set back from the street with a cobblestone driveway, an open, airy front porch with an abundance of windows reflects natural light by day and radiates a golden glow at night.

Adorned in warm, vibrant colors, the foyer opens to the great room, which is centered by a high-coffered ceiling and a brick fireplace with white wood mantel. Arranged to provide cozy places to entertain, this open living area can easily host an intimate evening for two or an elaborate party with friends and family. Arches define the casual living spaces and accent an open counter shared by the main kitchen. Suited for entertaining, a wall of French doors opens outside to a covered porch, where guests can move freely and comfortably.

Above: The great room has recessed lighting that frames the soaring coffered ceiling along with extra special touches that make the house a home.

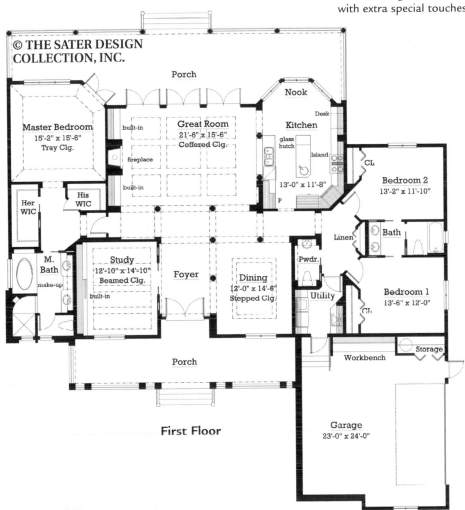

© THE SATER DESIGN COLLECTION, INC.

Porch

Master Bedroom
15'-2" x 15'-6"
Tray Clg.

Great Room
21'-6" x 15'-6"
Coffered Clg.

built-in

fireplace

built-in

Her WIC

His WIC

Nook

Kitchen

Desk

glass hutch

Island

13'-0" x 11'-8"

CL

Bedroom 2
13'-2" x 11'-10"

Linen

Bath

M. Bath

make-up

built-in

Study
12'-10" x 14'-10"
Beamed Clg.

built-in

Foyer

Dining
12'-0" x 14'-6"
Stepped Clg.

Pwdr.

Utility

Bedroom 1
13'-6" x 12'-0"

CL

Porch

Workbench

Storage

Garage
23'-0" x 24'-0"

First Floor

Rear View

UDHDS01-7051 — 1-866-525-9374

Home photographed may differ from actual construction documents.

Total Living	First Floor	Second Floor	Bonus	Bed	Bath	Width	Depth	Foundation	Price Category
2555 sq ft	2555 sq ft	N/A	N/A	3	2-1/2	70' 6"	76' 6"	Crawlspace	G

Donald A. Gardner Architects, Inc.

Refined Residence

Milford

- UDHDG01-331
- 1-866-525-9374

Sometimes with a larger floor plan, the feeling of an intimate, cozy home often gets lost in translation. The *Milford* fulfills the need for a bigger home yet includes a layout designed to unite families. The great room is strategically located in the middle of the house, assuring a central locale for family gatherings. The cathe-dral ceiling, fireplace and rear-porch access grant striking details to the room, while custom molding and built-in bookshelves enhance its uniqueness.

Designed to promote a natural traffic flow, the kitchen uses angled countertops to create a partition between the great and breakfast rooms. Throughout the rest of the home, large, open entryways enable the rooms to spill out into one another, eliminating the need for doors.

The master suite is positioned for privacy and designed with elegance in mind. A tray ceiling crowns the bedroom, while a generous walk-in closet and pampering bath complete the suite.

For formal entertaining, the dining room includes a tray ceiling, while two columns give the room definition.

Nothing says style like a gorgeous brick finish. Dual columns create a dramatic portico, while brick keystones top curved transoms displaying even more detail. With an exterior that matches the panache of the interior, the *Milford* exudes sophistication and elegance.

First Floor

Above: Custom molding around the fireplace and ceiling creates a dramatic look in the great room.

Rear Elevation

UDHDG01-331 — 1-866-525-9374

Total Living	First Floor	Second Floor	Bonus	Bed	Bath	Width	Depth	Foundation	Price Category
2625 sq ft	2625 sq ft	N/A	447 sq ft	4	2-1/2	63' 1"	82' 7"	Crawl Space*	F

*Other options available. See page 513.

Donald A. Gardner Architects, Inc.

Donald A. Gardner Architects, Inc.

Tolliver — UDHDG01-859 — 1-866-525-9374

Total Living	First Floor	Bonus	Bed	Bath	Width	Depth	Foundation	Price Category
1228 sq ft	1228 sq ft	444 sq ft	3	2	47' 0"	40' 4"	Crawl Space*	C

Design Features

- Gables, twin dormers and an elegant arched window strike the perfect balance on this bungalow.

- Easy traffic patterns make all the rooms in this modest home convenient to one another.

- Cathedral ceilings create spaciousness in the great room and master bedroom.

- The kitchen stays connected to the great room by way of a pass-thru.

- An expansive bonus room is located over the garage, offering storage solutions.

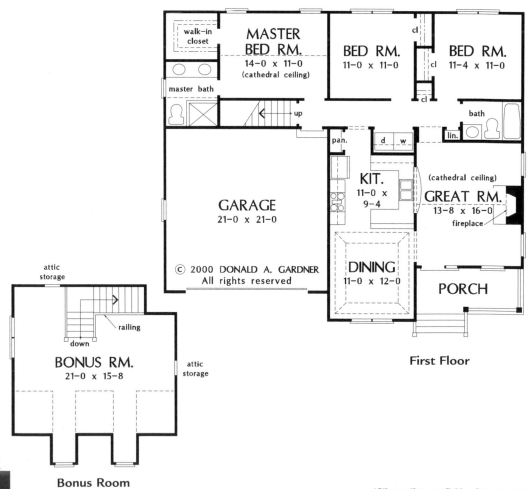

First Floor

Rear Elevation

BONUS RM.
21-0 x 15-8

Bonus Room

*Other options available. See page 513.

© 1997 Frank Betz Associates, Inc.

Moultrie — UDHFB01-1090 — 1-866-525-9374

Total Living	First Floor	Bonus	Bed	Bath	Width	Depth	Foundation	Price Category
1232 sq ft	1232 sq ft	N/A	3	2	46' 0"	44' 4"	Basement, Crawl Space or Slab	E

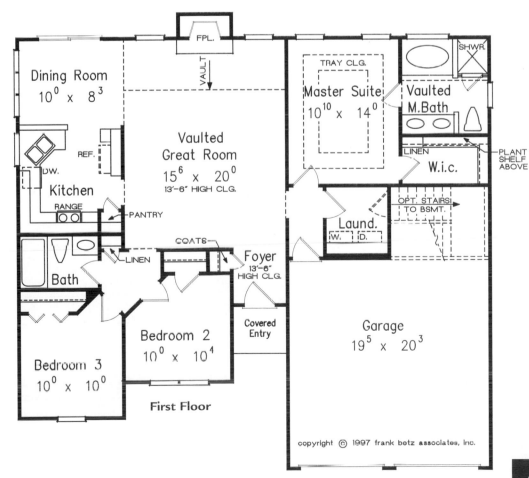

First Floor

copyright © 1997 frank betz associates, inc.

Design Features

■ The vaulted great room acts as a central gathering place between the master suite and secondary bedrooms.

■ Perfect affordable starter home.

■ Floor plan maximizes the most of its square footage.

■ Split-bedroom design allows the homeowners privacy.

Rear Elevation

Ryley — UDHDG01-503 — 1-866-525-9374

Total Living	First Floor	Bonus	Bed	Bath	Width	Depth	Foundation	Price Category
1246 sq ft	1246 sq ft	N/A	3	2	60' 0"	48' 0"	Crawl Space*	C

Design Features

- The front porch wraps slightly, giving the illusion of a larger home on the outside.

- Inside, a cathedral ceiling maximizes space in the open great room and dining room.

- The kitchen features a center skylight, breakfast bar and access to the garage via a screened porch.

- Two bedrooms share a bath up front, while the master suite maintains privacy in back.

Rear Elevation

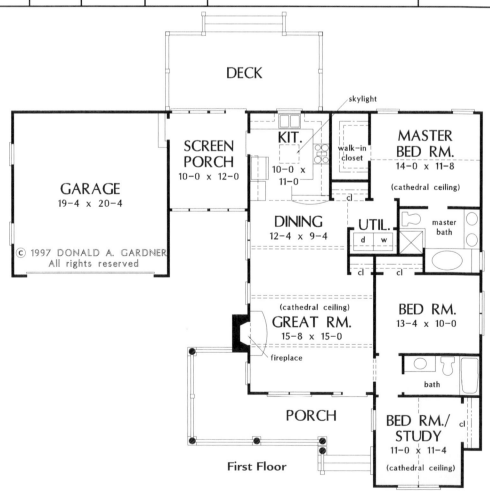

DECK

SCREEN PORCH
10-0 x 12-0

GARAGE
19-4 x 20-4

skylight

KIT.
10-0 x 11-0

walk-in closet

MASTER BED RM.
14-0 x 11-8
(cathedral ceiling)

DINING
12-4 x 9-4

UTIL.
d w

master bath

GREAT RM.
15-8 x 15-0

fireplace

BED RM.
13-4 x 10-0

PORCH

bath

BED RM./
STUDY
11-0 x 11-4
(cathedral ceiling)

First Floor

*Other options available. See page 513.

© The Sater Design Collection, Inc.

Ardenno — UDHDS01-6500 — 1-866-525-9374

Total Living	First Floor	Bonus	Bed	Bath	Width	Depth	Foundation	Price Category
1281 sq ft	1281 sq ft	N/A	2 + Study	2	40' 0"	63' 4"	Slab	E

Veranda
24'-0" x 9'-6"
10'-0" Clg.

Master Suite
14'-4" x 11'-2"
10'-0" Clg.

Dining Room
9'-6" x 11'-2"
11'-0" Clg.

Great Room
15'-0" x 17'-0"
11'-0" Clg.

Master Bath

W.I.C.

Bath

Walk-In Shower

Kitchen
9'-6" x 16'-2"
10'-0" Clg.

Foyer
10'-0" Clg.

Study
9'-7" x 11'-0"
10'-0" Clg.

Bedroom
10'-2" x 11'-10"
10'-0" Clg.

Nook
10'-0" Clg.

Entry
10'-0" Clg.

First Floor

Garage
20'-2" x 23'-6"
8' 0" Clg.

© THE SATER DESIGN COLLECTION, INC.

Design Features

- Grand portico features Doric columns and elegant corbels.

- The master bedroom, great room and dining room have veranda access.

- The kitchen feaures a breakfast nook, ample storage space and a serving bar to the dining room.

- Arched windows add luxury-home details.

Rear Elevation

Not available for construction in Myrtle Beach, South Carolina.

Mallory Square — UDHDS01-6691 — 1-866-525-9374

© The Sater Design Collection, Inc.

Total Living	First Floor	Bonus	Bed	Bath	Width	Depth	Foundation	Price Category
1288 sq ft	1288 sq ft	N/A	2	2	32' 4"	60' 0"	Crawl Space	D

Design Features

- An arched covered entry and transom windows enhance the front exterior.
- The great room opens to backyard views.
- A galley-style kitchen has a pass-thru with views.
- French doors open the master suite, great room and dining room to the covered porch.
- Asymmetrical roof lines blend with front and rear gables.

Rear Elevation

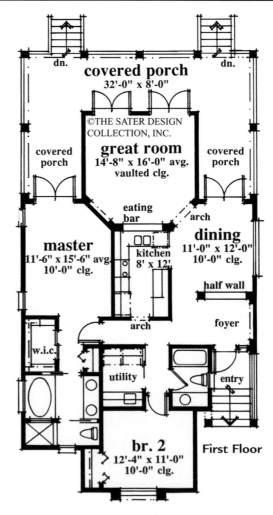

© The Sater Design Collection, Inc.

Bellizza — UDHDS01-6508 — 1-866-525-9374

Total Living	First Floor	Bonus	Bed	Bath	Width	Depth	Foundation	Price Category
1404 sq ft	1404 sq ft	N/A	2 + Study	2	42' 8"	63' 4"	Slab	E

First Floor

Design Features

- A turreted breakfast nook sits along the side of the entryway.

- Covered arch entryway, decorative wrought-iron inserts and gable roof add grandeur to the front elevation.

- Sliding-glass doors offer access to the verandah from the master suite, great room and dining room.

- A pass-thru bar makes the kitchen efficient.

- The master suite has a pampering bath with dual vanities.

Rear Elevation

Sacramento — UDHFB01-1047 — 1-866-525-9374

© 1997 Frank Betz Associates, Inc.

Total Living	First Floor	Opt. Bonus	Bed	Bath	Width	Depth	Foundation	Price Category
1432 sq ft	1432 sq ft	N/A	3	2	49' 0"	52' 4"	Basement, Crawl Space or Slab	E

Design Features

- This home has the charm and amenities of larger homes.

- A bay window sits at the rear of the house, letting warm sunlight flood into the breakfast room and kitchen.

- Situated near the entry is an elegant dining room with columns and an arched opening.

- Split-bedroom design allows residents their privacy.

Rear Elevation

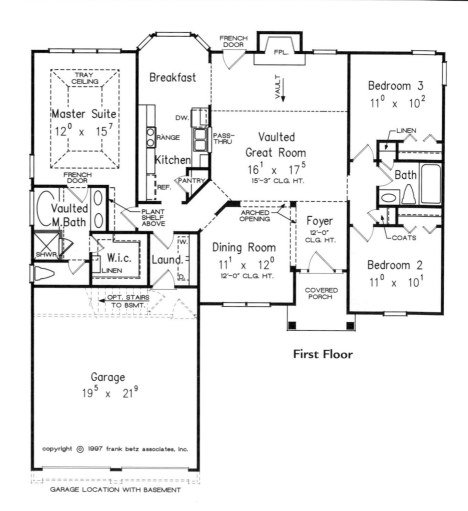

© 1998 Frank Betz Associates, Inc.

Brewster — UDHFB01-1175 — 1-866-525-9374

Total Living	First Floor	Second Floor	Opt. Bonus	Bed	Bath	Width	Depth	Foundation	Price Category
1467 sq ft	1001 sq ft	466 sq ft	292 sq ft	3	2-1/2	42' 0"	42' 0"	Basement, Crawl Space or Slab	F

First Floor

Second Floor

Opt. Loft or Bedroom

Design Features

■ An optional bonus room upstairs makes the perfect playroom or exercise area.

■ The impressive dining room has a rare two-story ceiling, however an optional loft or fourth bedroom can be easily incorporated.

■ Vaulted ceilings and a decorative plant shelf make the main floor of this design interesting and dimensional.

■ The laundry room and a handy coat closet are strategically placed just off the garage.

Rear Elevation

Oakway — UDHDG01-968 — 1-866-525-9374

Total Living	First Floor	Bonus	Bed	Bath	Width	Depth	Foundation	Price Category
1457 sq ft	1457 sq ft	341 sq ft	3	2	50' 4"	46' 4"	Crawl Space*	C

Design Features

- Poised and cozy, this home features a split-bedroom plan.

- The convenient front-entry garage has a versatile bonus room above for expansion purposes.

- Economical and builder-friendly, the floor plan is family-efficient and has a variety of custom-styled touches.

- The master suite is complete with a walk-in closet and master bath.

- Additional bedrooms are located on the opposite side of the house and are separated by a full bath.

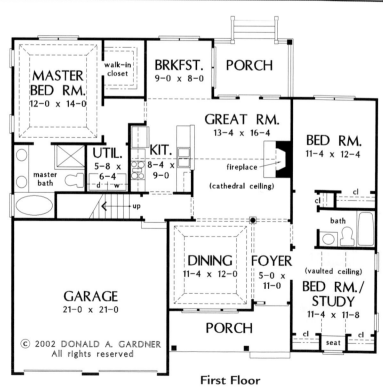

First Floor

Rear Elevation

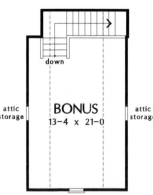

Bonus Room

*Other options available. See page 513.

© The Sater Design Collection, Inc.

Pine Valley Court — UDHDS01-6612 — 1-866-525-9374

Total Living	First Floor	Bonus	Bed	Bath	Width	Depth	Foundation	Price Category
1487 sq ft	1487 sq ft	N/A	3	2	58' 0"	58' 0"	Slab	D

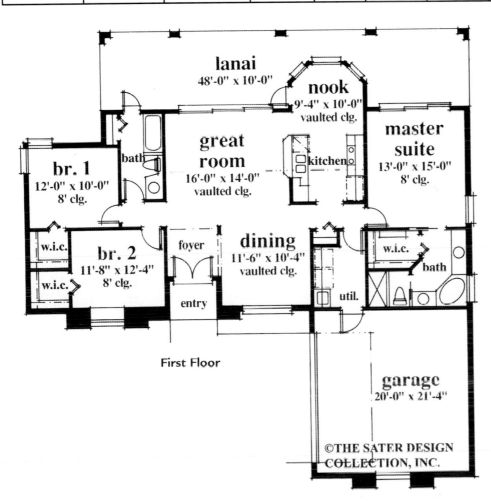

First Floor

©THE SATER DESIGN COLLECTION, INC.

Design Features

- The great room and nook have vaulted ceilings and open to the lanai.
- The kitchen features a bay-windowed breakfast nook.
- Two secondary bedrooms are split from the master.
- The master suite has access to the lanai through sliders.
- The plan includes two elevation concepts.
- With rear access the guest bath doubles as a pool bath.

Rear Elevation

Sargent — UDHDS01-7053 — 1-866-525-9374

© The Sater Design Collection, Inc.

Total Living	First Floor	Bonus	Bed	Bath	Width	Depth	Foundation	Price Category
1487 sq ft	1487 sq ft	N/A	3	2	52' 6"	66' 0"	Crawl Space	D

Design Features

- Slump arches border the elevated entry porch.
- A well-lit floor plan offers wide, open spaces.
- Triple sliding-glass doors connect the great room and outdoors.
- Great room opens to kitchen, nook and dining room.
- Utility room provides easy access to oversized garage.
- Gables featuring casement windows, decorative vents and shutters enhance the front elevation.

Rear Elevation

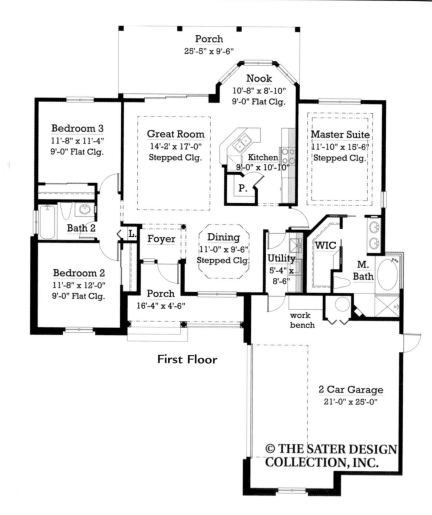

First Floor

Porch
25'-5" x 9'-6"

Nook
10'-8" x 8'-10"
9'-0" Flat Clg.

Bedroom 3
11'-8" x 11'-4"
9'-0" Flat Clg.

Great Room
14'-2" x 17'-0"
Stepped Clg.

Kitchen
9'-0" x 10'-10"

Master Suite
11'-10" x 15'-6"
Stepped Clg.

P.

Bath 2

L.

Foyer

Dining
11'-0" x 9'-6"
Stepped Clg.

WIC

Utility
5'-4" x 8'-6"

M. Bath

Bedroom 2
11'-8" x 12'-0"
9'-0" Flat Clg.

Porch
16'-4" x 4'-6"

work bench

2 Car Garage
21'-0" x 25'-0"

© THE SATER DESIGN COLLECTION, INC.

Griffin — UDHDG01-535 — 1-866-525-9374

Total Living	First Floor	Bonus	Bed	Bath	Width	Depth	Foundation	Price Category
1517 sq ft	1517 sq ft	287 sq ft	3	2	61' 4"	48' 6"	Crawl Space*	D

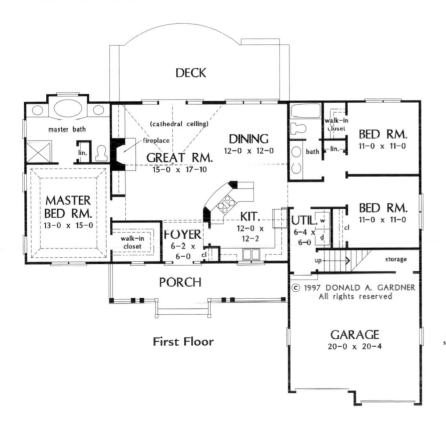

First Floor

© 1997 DONALD A. GARDNER
All rights reserved

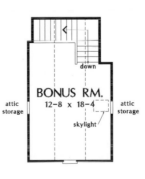

Bonus Room

Design Features

- This compact country home is stylish, with architectural accents such as gables and arched windows.

- Open to one another, the great room, dining room and kitchen are combined under a cathedral ceiling.

- Built-ins flank the fireplace, making decorating easy.

- The master suite is located on one side of the house, with an elegant tray ceiling and walk-in closet.

Rear Elevation

Hilligan — UDHDG01-1015 — 1-866-525-9374

Total Living	First Floor	Bonus	Bed	Bath	Width	Depth	Foundation	Price Category
1535 sq ft	1535 sq ft	355 sq ft	3	2	59' 8"	47' 4"	Crawl Space*	D

Design Features

- With a low-maintenance exterior and front-entry garage, this charmer promotes easy living.

- The family-efficient floor plan is designed as a step-saver and allows a natural traffic flow.

- A bonus room and bedroom/study provide flexibility.

- An angled cooktop counter and columns define spaces.

- The master suite is complete with a walk-in closet and master bath with a double vanity.

Rear Elevation

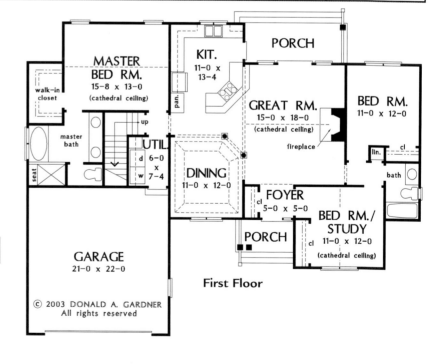

First Floor

Bonus Room

*Other options available. See page 513.

Rosewood — UDHDG01-1092 — 1-866-525-9374

Total Living	First Floor	Bonus	Bed	Bath	Width	Depth	Foundation	Price Category
1536 sq ft	1536 sq ft	346 sq ft	3	2	55' 4"	51' 0"	Crawl Space*	D

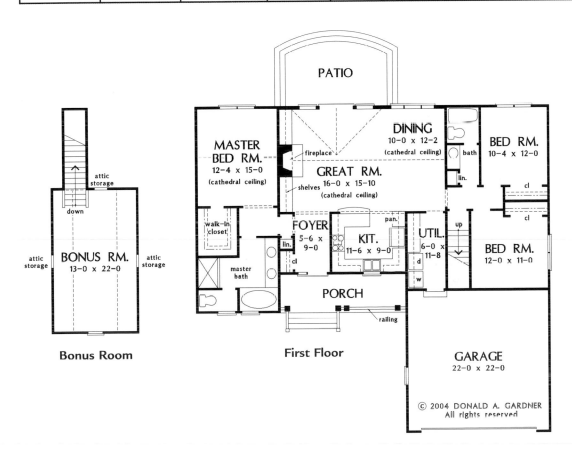

Bonus Room

First Floor

Design Features

- Twin dormers mirror a double-arched entryway in this convenient floor plan.

- Flanked by two gables, the front porch creates an inviting exterior.

- A low-maintenance façade and front-entry garage provide ultimate convenience.

- French doors accent the great room, while a cathedral ceiling expands vertical volume.

- An optional bonus room becomes a perfect space for a child's play-room or media center.

Rear Elevation

Iverson — UDHDG01-1023 — 1-866-525-9374

Total Living	First Floor	Bonus	Bed	Bath	Width	Depth	Foundation	Price Category
1547 sq ft	1547 sq ft	391 sq ft	3	2	51' 8"	59' 0"	Crawl Space*	D

Design Features

- Custom-styled ceiling treatments crown the dining room, master bedroom and great room.

- The kitchen features a smart angled counter, walk-in pantry and a view of the great room's fireplace.

- Two secondary bedrooms share a full bath, and the master suite is located in the quiet zone.

- The master bath is complete with a double vanity, separate shower and garden tub.

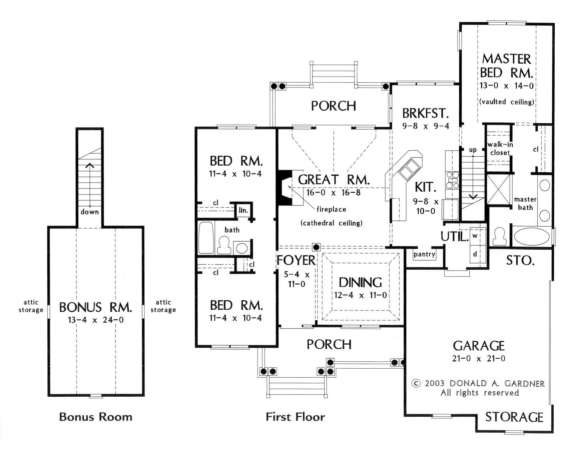

Bonus Room

First Floor

Rear Elevation

*Other options available. See page 513.

Donald A. Gardner Architects, Inc.

Schuyler — UDHDG01-766 — 1-866-525-9374

Total Living	First Floor	Bonus	Bed	Bath	Width	Depth	Foundation	Price Category
1559 sq ft	1559 sq ft	N/A	3	2	54' 4"	52' 0"	Crawl Space*	D

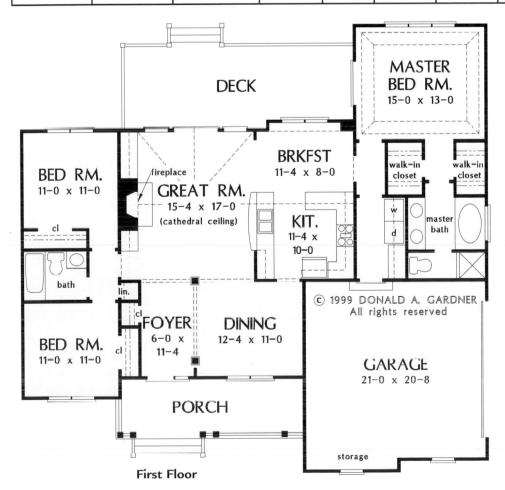

First Floor

Design Features

- Country charm gives this home sensational appeal inside and out.

- The foyer, dining room, kitchen, breakfast and great room are open for a comfortable feel.

- A dramatic cathedral ceiling amplifies the great room and kitchen.

- The master suite is secluded at the back of the home and features deck access.

Rear Elevation

*Other options available. See page 513.

Redding — UDHDG01-385 — 1-866-525-9374

© 1995 Donald A. Gardner Architects, Inc.

Total Living	First Floor	Bonus	Bed	Bath	Width	Depth	Foundation	Price Category
1561 sq ft	1561 sq ft	N/A	3	2	60' 10"	51' 6"	Crawl Space*	D

Design Features

- This home offers an elegant exterior with arched windows, dormers and a charming front porch.
- The openness is continued in the central great room, which features a cathedral ceiling.
- A clerestory window splashes the great room with natural light.
- The master suite with cathedral ceiling features a bath with whirlpool tub and double vanity.
- Two additional bedrooms share a bath, while a garage with storage completes the plan.

Rear Elevation

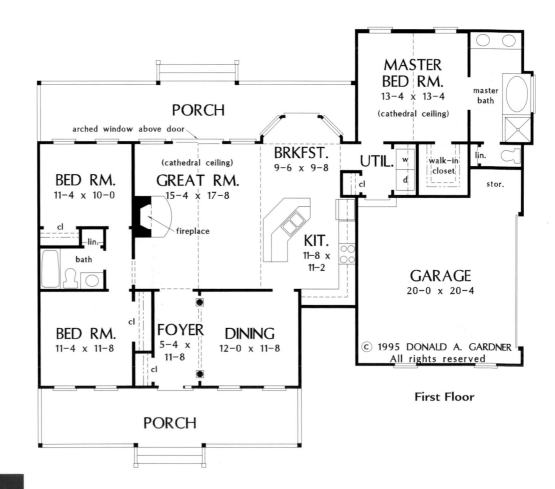

MASTER BED RM.
13-4 x 13-4
(cathedral ceiling)

master bath

PORCH

arched window above door

BRKFST.
9-6 x 9-8

UTIL.

walk-in closet

lin.

stor.

BED RM.
11-4 x 10-0

(cathedral ceiling)

GREAT RM.
15-4 x 17-8

KIT.
11-8 x 11-2

fireplace

GARAGE
20-0 x 20-4

BED RM.
11-4 x 11-8

FOYER
5-4 x 11-8

DINING
12-0 x 11-8

© 1995 DONALD A. GARDNER
All rights reserved

bath

PORCH

First Floor

*Other options available. See page 513.

Graham — UDHDG01-323 — 1-866-525-9374

Total Living	First Floor	Bonus	Bed	Bath	Width	Depth	Foundation	Price Category
1575 sq ft	1575 sq ft	N/A	3	2	60' 6"	47' 3"	Crawl Space*	D

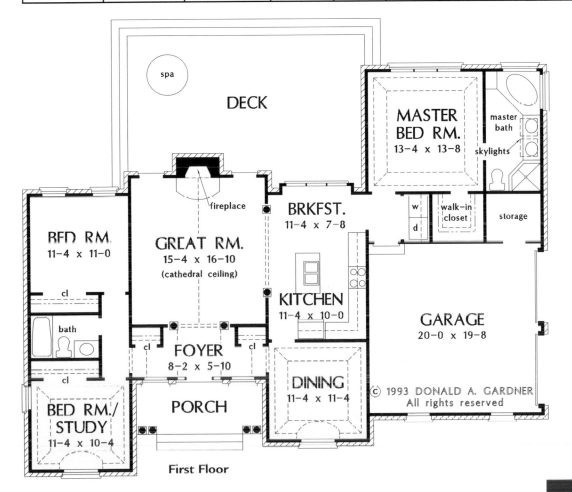

First Floor

Design Features

- Clerestory dormers above the covered porch light the foyer, which leads to the great room with fireplace.

- The great room opens to the island kitchen and accesses a large deck with optional spa.

- Tray ceilings lift the master bedroom, dining room and bedroom/study out of the ordinary.

- The luxurious master bath features double vanity, separate shower and whirlpool tub.

Rear Elevation

Irby — UDHDG01-993 — 1-866-525-9374

© 2002 Donald A. Gardner, Inc.

Total Living	First Floor	Bonus	Bed	Bath	Width	Depth	Foundation	Price Category
1580 sq ft	1580 sq ft	367 sq ft	3	2	55' 6"	46' 0"	Crawl Space*	D

Design Features

- This cottage combines stone and siding for a striking façade.

- A box-bay window is capped with a metal roof, while the front-entry garage adds convenience.

- Sidelights and a transom allow natural light to brighten the foyer.

- The master suite features a large walk-in closet and bath, complete with a shower seat.

- All of the bedrooms are conveniently located near the utility room.

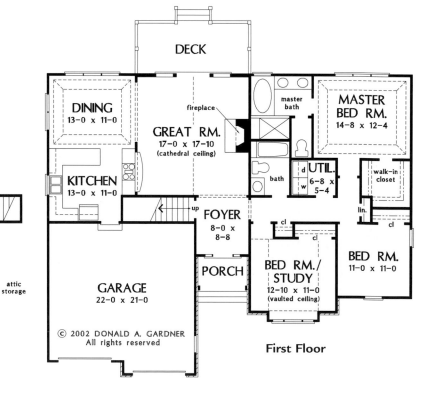

DECK

DINING
13-0 x 11-0

GREAT RM.
17-0 x 17-10
(cathedral ceiling)

fireplace

master bath

MASTER BED RM.
14-8 x 12-4

KITCHEN
13-0 x 11-0

bath

UTIL.
6-8 x 5-4

walk-in closet

lin.

FOYER
8-0 x 8-8

up

cl

cl

BED RM.
11-0 x 11-0

GARAGE
22-0 x 21-0

PORCH

BED RM./ STUDY
12-10 x 11-0
(vaulted ceiling)

© 2002 DONALD A. GARDNER
All rights reserved

First Floor

attic storage

BONUS RM.
14-6 x 21-0

attic storage

down

Bonus Room

Rear Elevation

*Other options available. See page 513.

Currier — UDHDG01-1025 — 1-866-525-9374

Total Living	First Floor	Bonus	Bed	Bath	Width	Depth	Foundation	Price Category
1583 sq ft	1583 sq ft	N/A	3	2	34' 0"	77' 2"	Crawl Space*	D

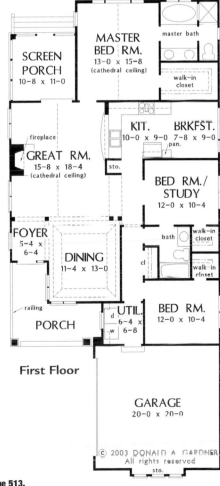

First Floor

SCREEN PORCH 10-8 x 11-0

MASTER BED RM. 13-0 x 15-8 (cathedral ceiling)

master bath

walk-in closet

fireplace

GREAT RM. 15-8 x 18-4 (cathedral ceiling)

KIT. 10-0 x 9-0

BRKFST. 7-8 x 9-0

pan.

sto.

BED RM./ STUDY 12-0 x 10-4

FOYER 5-4 x 6-4

bath

walk-in closet

cl

DINING 11-4 x 13-0

walk-in closet

railing

UTIL. 6-4 x 6-8

BED RM. 12-0 x 10-4

d

w

PORCH

GARAGE 20-0 x 20-0

sto.

Design Features

- Perfect for narrow, long lots, this home evokes images of quaint seaside villages.

- A bedroom/study offers flexibility for changing needs, while each bedroom is positioned for privacy.

- The fireplace can be seen from every common room, and a screened porch creates an outdoor haven.

- The master suite features a cathedral ceiling, a spacious walk-in closet and well-appointed master bath.

Rear Elevation

*Other options available. See page 513.

Aberdeen Place — UDHFB01-3809 — 1-866-525-9374

© 2003 Frank Betz Associates, Inc.

Total Living	First Floor	Second Floor	Opt. Bonus	Bed	Bath	Width	Depth	Foundation	Price Category
1593 sq ft	1118 sq ft	475 sq ft	223 sq ft	3	2-1/2	41' 0"	45' 0"	Basement, Crawl Space or Slab	G

Design Features

- From the *Southern Living®️ Design Collection*

- The *Aberdeen Place* has that cozy cottage appeal with its board and batten exterior and stone accents. Its conservative square footage is rich in style and functional design.

- The breakfast room is bordered by windows that allow natural light to pour in.

- A generously sized master bedroom includes a tray ceiling and views to the back yard.

- An optional bonus area provides the extra space that each homeowner can personalize.

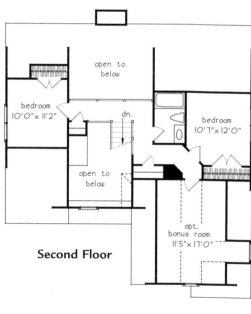

Second Floor

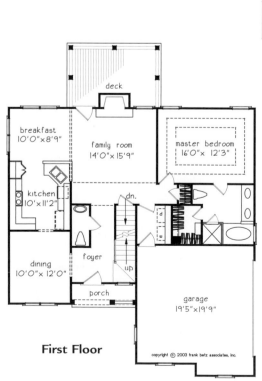

First Floor

Rear Elevation

Jasmine — UDHFB01-1036 — 1-866-525-9374

Total Living	First Floor	Opt. Second Floor	Bed	Bath	Width	Depth	Foundation	Price Category
1604 sq ft	1604 sq ft	288 sq ft	3	2	53' 6"	55' 10"	Basement, Crawl Space or Slab	F

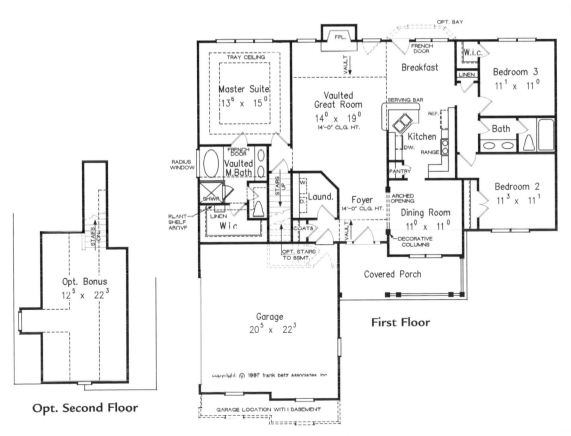

First Floor

Opt. Second Floor

Design Features

- The *Jasmine* has a friendly, cottage-like appeal with its calm combination of natural stone and siding.

- Dormers accent the covered front porch that invites you in to see more.

- The dining room and kitchen have direct access to each other, making entertaining a breeze.

- Careful placement of the guest bath between the secondary bedrooms creates a comfortable separation for added privacy.

Rear Elevation

Donald A. Gardner Architects, Inc.

Kilpatrick — UDHDG01-833 — 1-866-525-9374

Total Living	First Floor	Bonus	Bed	Bath	Width	Depth	Foundation	Price Category
1608 sq ft	1608 sq ft	437 sq ft	3	2	40' 8"	62' 8"	Crawl Space*	D

Please note: Home photographed may differ from blueprint.

Design Features

- This three-bedroom Craftsman home packs a lot of style into its slim façade.

- A tray ceiling tops the formal dining room, while the kitchen features an efficient design.

- The master suite enjoys a space-enhancing cathedral ceiling, back-porch access and dual walk-in closets.

- The utility room is conveniently located in close proximity to the home's three bedrooms.

Rear Elevation

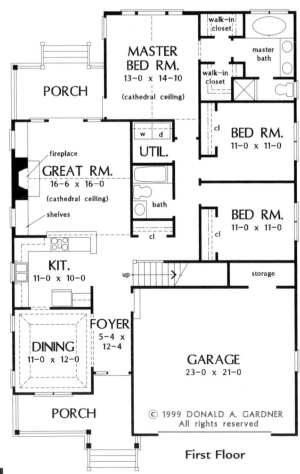

First Floor

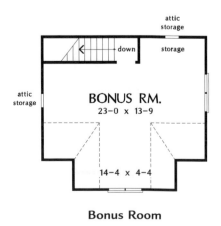

Bonus Room

*Other options available. See page 513.

Pinebluff — UDHDG01-1036 — 1-866-525-9374

Total Living	First Floor	Bonus	Bed	Bath	Width	Depth	Foundation	Price Category
1614 sq ft	1614 sq ft	410 sq ft	3	2	52' 11"	54' 2"	Crawl Space*	D

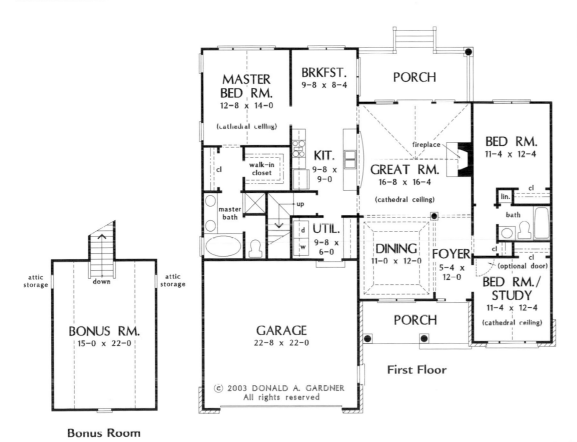

Bonus Room

First Floor

Design Features

- Gables and columns set the stage for a low-maintenance traditional home that's big on living.

- A tray ceiling and column highlight the dining room, and a cathedral ceiling crowns the great room.

- Front and rear porches provide outdoor living space, and a bonus room offers versatility.

- Designed to pamper homeowners, the master suite is complete with modern amenities.

Rear Elevation

Brentwood — UDHFB01-3711 — 1-866-525-9374

© 2002 Frank Betz Associates, Inc.

Total Living	First Floor	Second Floor	Opt. Bonus	Bed	Bath	Width	Depth	Foundation	Price Category
1634 sq ft	1177 sq ft	457 sq ft	249 sq ft	3	2-1/2	41' 0"	48' 4"	Basement or Crawl Space	F

Design Features

- Brick and stone, set off by multi-pane windows, highlight the street presence of this classic home.

- A sheltered entry leads to a two-story foyer and wide interior vistas that extend to the back property. Rooms in the public zone are open, allowing the spaces to flex for planned events as well as family gatherings.

- At the heart of the home, the vaulted family room frames a fireplace with tall windows that bring in natural light.

- The main-level master suite boasts a tray ceiling, while two upper-level bedrooms are connected by a balcony bridge that overlooks the foyer and family room.

Rear Elevation

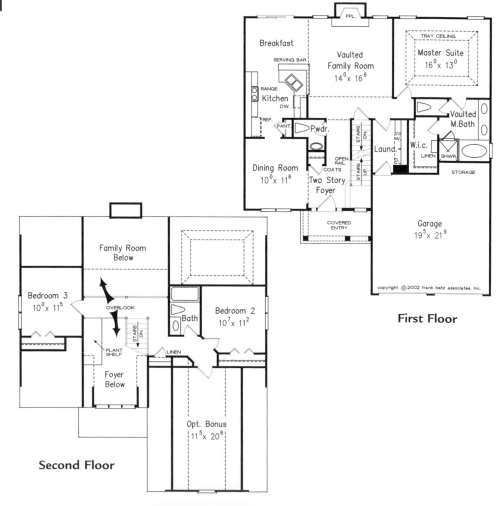

First Floor

Second Floor

Jewell — UDHDG01-1079 — 1-866-525-9374

Total Living	First Floor	Bonus	Bed	Bath	Width	Depth	Foundation	Price Category
1640 sq ft	1640 sq ft	379 sq ft	3	2	55' 10"	55' 6"	Crawl Space*	D

Design Features

- A cathedral ceiling adds flair, while a striking fireplace enhances the great room.

- The master bedroom features a soaring cathedral ceiling and large walk-in closet.

- With a double vanity and garden tub, the master bath is ready to spoil homeowners.

- The bonus room lies just off the master bedroom and could make a great home gym.

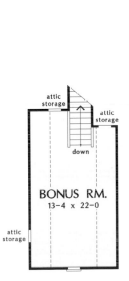

Bonus Room

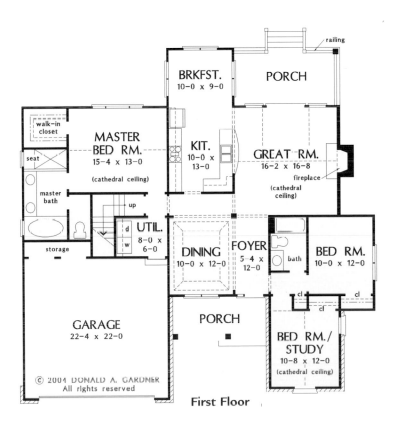

First Floor

Rear Elevation

*Other options available. See page 513.

Anniston — UDHDG01-540 — 1-866-525-9374

Total Living	First Floor	Second Floor	Bonus	Bed	Bath	Width	Depth	Foundation	Price Category
1652 sq ft	1652 sq ft	N/A	367 sq ft	3	2	64' 4"	51' 0"	Crawl Space*	D

Design Features

- A classic country exterior enriches the appearance of this economical home.

- The front porch and two skylit back porches encourage weekend relaxation.

- Interior columns define entry to the formal dining room with an elegant tray ceiling.

- The great room features a cathedral ceiling and fireplace with adjacent built-in.

- Designed for efficiency, the kitchen is open to the breakfast and great room.

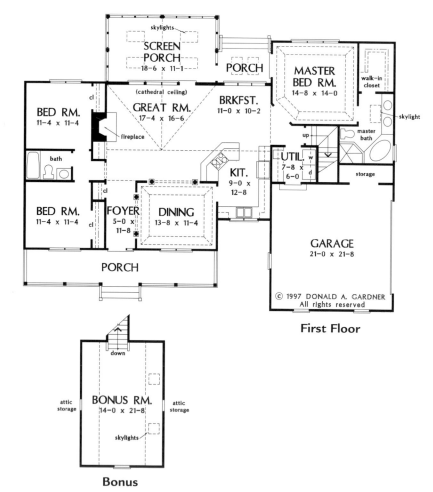

First Floor

Rear Elevation

Bonus

*Other options available. See page 513.

Armond — UDHDG01-989 — 1-866-525-9374

Total Living	First Floor	Bonus	Bed	Bath	Width	Depth	Foundation	Price Category
1654 sq ft	1654 sq ft	356 sq ft	3	2	60' 4"	47' 10"	Crawl Space*	D

Design Features

- Affordable and easy-to-build, this traditional home offers a low-maintenance exterior.

- Custom-styled features include a tray ceiling in the dining room and cathedral ceiling in the great room.

- French doors lead to the rear porch and also complement the study, which could be used as a bedroom.

- The kitchen includes a convenient pass-thru that services the great room.

Bonus Room

BONUS RM.
13-8 x 21-0

attic storage

down

First Floor

DINING
13-0 x 11-8

PORCH

MASTER BED RM.
14-0 x 14-0
(vaulted ceiling)

shelves

GREAT RM.
18-0 x 18-0

KIT.
13-0 x 9-8

fireplace

(cathedral ceiling)

shelves

walk-in closet

cl

master bath

storage

up

lin.

FOYER
6-8 x 8-8

UTIL.

w
d

cl

cl

bath

GARAGE
21-0 x 21-0

BED RM./ STUDY
11-0 x 12-0

PORCH

desk

cl

BED RM.
11-8 x 11-4
(cathedral ceiling)

cl

Rear Elevation

River Hill — UDHFB01-3915 — 1-866-525-9374

© 2004 Frank Betz Associates, Inc.

Total Living	First Floor	Opt. Second Floor	Bed	Bath	Width	Depth	Foundation	Price Category
1656 sq ft	1656 sq ft	717 sq ft	4	3	54' 0"	54' 0"	Basement, Crawl Space or Slab	F

Design Features

- A vaulted family room is the focal point from the foyer, with a cozy fireplace as its backdrop.

- The master suite is secluded from the other bedrooms giving home-owners privacy.

- A serving bar in the kitchen caters to the breakfast area and family room — convenient for entertaining.

- An optional second floor adds a bedroom and bath, as well as a bonus room that can be used as the homeowner's wish.

Rear Elevation

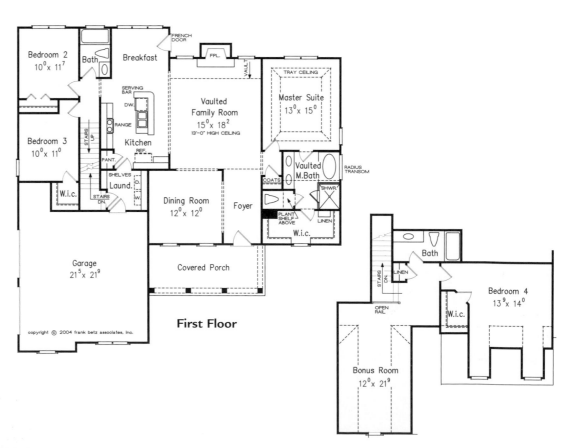

First Floor

Opt. Second Floor

Violet — UDHDG01-1016 — 1-866-525-9374

Total Living	First Floor	Bonus	Bed	Bath	Width	Depth	Foundation	Price Category
1660 sq ft	1660 sq ft	374 sq ft	3	2	65' 4"	48' 8"	Crawl Space*	D

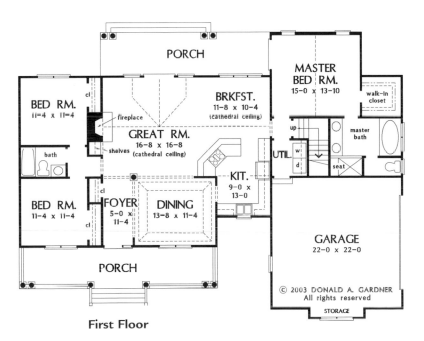

First Floor

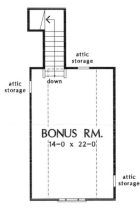

Bonus Room

Design Features

- A welcoming front porch with bold columns creates tremendous curb appeal.

- A sidelight and elliptical transom usher natural light into the foyer.

- A single column and tray ceiling distinguish the dining room without enclosing space.

- A built-in cabinet is positioned next to the fireplace and may conveniently hold media equipment.

- With access to the rear porch, the master suite also features a walk-in closet and private bath.

Rear Elevation

Donald A. Gardner Architects, Inc.

Thackery — UDHDG01-283 — 1-866-525-9374

Total Living	First Floor	Second Floor	Bonus	Bed	Bath	Width	Depth	Foundation	Price Category
1663 sq ft	1145 sq ft	518 sq ft	380 sq ft	3	2-1/2	59' 4"	56' 6"	Crawl Space*	D

Design Features

- A covered porch wraps around this classic farmhouse with multiple dormers.

- A clerestory window bathes the two-story foyer in natural light.

- The large great room with fireplace opens to the dining/breakfast/kitchen space.

- A first-level master bedroom offers privacy and luxury with a separate shower and garden tub.

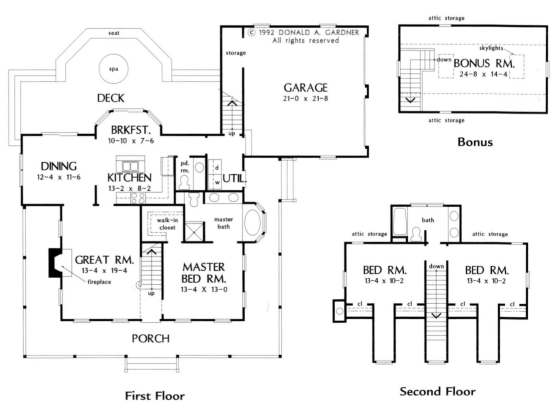

First Floor

Bonus

Second Floor

Rear Elevation

*Other options available. See page 513.

© 2002 Donald A. Gardner, Inc.

Zimmerman — UDHDG01-987 — 1-866-525-9374

Total Living	First Floor	Second Floor	Bonus	Bed	Bath	Width	Depth	Foundation	Price Category
2259 sq ft	2259 sq ft	N/A	352 sq ft	4	3	64' 10"	59' 6"	Crawl Space*	E

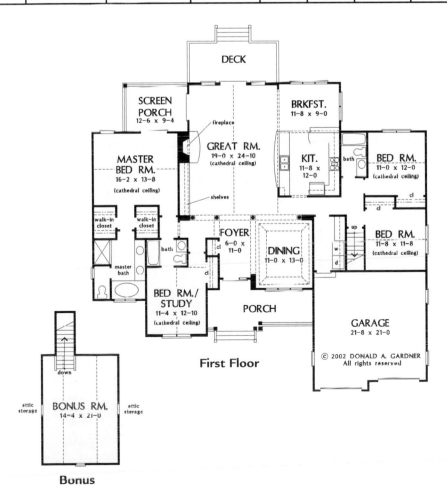

First Floor

© 2002 DONALD A. GARDNER
All rights reserved

Bonus

Design Features

- This classic cottage features a convenient front-entry garage and low-maintenance exterior.

- Arched windows soften high gables to add Craftsman appeal.

- The front porch is accented with columns and decorative railing.

- The dining room is distinguished by columns and a tray ceiling.

- Versatility is offered in a bedroom/study and bonus room above the garage.

Rear Elevation

Hudson — UDHDG01-512 — 1-866-525-9374

Total Living	First Floor	Second Floor	Bonus	Bed	Bath	Width	Depth	Foundation	Price Category
1669 sq ft	1219 sq ft	450 sq ft	406 sq ft	3	2-1/2	50' 4"	49' 2"	Crawl Space*	D

Design Features

- This narrow-lot home offers some of the extras usually reserved for larger homes.

- Columns and a bay window add distinction to the dining room.

- The kitchen is designed for efficiency and offers access to the side porch.

- The master suite is located on the first floor, while two secondary bedrooms are upstairs.

- For growing families, the bonus room can be turned into a fourth bedroom with bath.

Rear Elevation

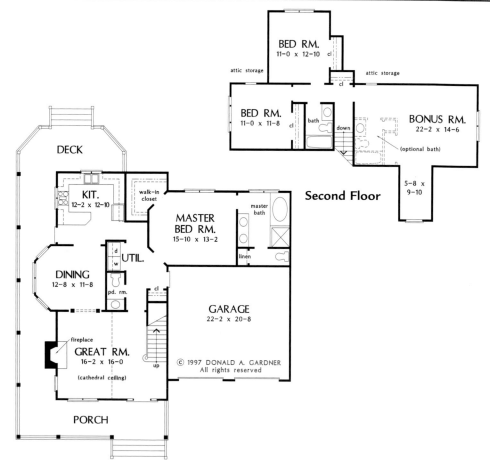

Second Floor

First Floor

*Other options available. See page 513.

Lochmere — UDHDG01-773 — 1-866-525-9374

Total Living	First Floor	Bonus	Bed	Bath	Width	Depth	Foundation	Price Category
1674 sq ft	1674 sq ft	321 sq ft	3	2	50' 0"	63' 8"	Crawl Space*	D

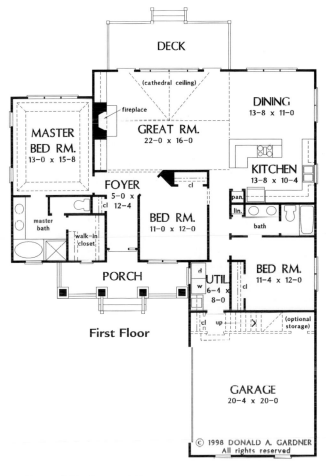

First Floor

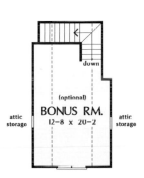

Bonus Room

Design Features

- Stucco, stone and cedar shake create an interesting exterior for this attractive bungalow.

- The dining room and kitchen are open to one another for casual, relaxed living.

- The master suite features an elegant tray ceiling and private bath with walk-in closet.

- A bonus room over the garage allows for ample storage and future expansion.

Rear Elevation

*Other options available. See page 513.

Dewfield — UDHDG01-1030 — 1-866-525-9374

© 2003 Donald A. Gardner, Inc.

Total Living	First Floor	Bonus	Bed	Bath	Width	Depth	Foundation	Price Category
1676 sq ft	1676 sq ft	376 sq ft	3	2	56' 8"	48' 4"	Crawl Space*	D

Design Features

- The curve of a Palladian window softens the strong stone wall and gable.

- The common rooms and the master bedroom are positioned to take advantage of rear views.

- A cathedral ceiling and fireplace highlight the great room.

- The bedrooms are grouped together to form a quiet zone.

- The master bedroom features a large walk-in closet and bath.

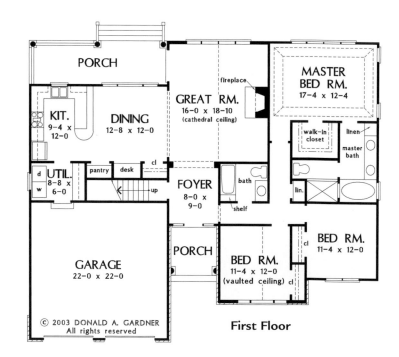

First Floor

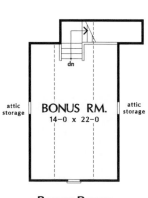

Bonus Room

Rear Elevation

*Other options available. See page 513.

Knoxville — UDHDG01-1035 — 1-866-525-9374

Total Living	First Floor	Bonus	Bed	Bath	Width	Depth	Foundation	Price Category
1677 sq ft	1677 sq ft	355 sq ft	3	2	64' 4"	49' 10"	Crawl Space*	D

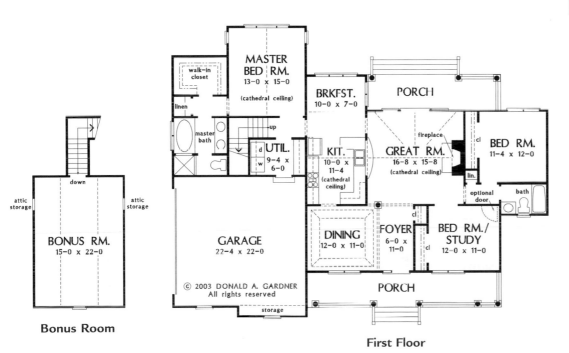

Bonus Room

First Floor

Design Features

- For its modest size, this home lives large and possesses lots of curb appeal.

- Columns frame a welcoming front porch topped by a prominent gable with clerestory window.

- A rear porch creates a perfect spot for outdoor relaxation.

- Other custom touches include a striking fireplace, breakfast counter and French doors.

Rear Elevation

Shadow Lane — UDHDS01-6686 — 1-866-525-9374

© The Sater Design Collection, Inc.

Total Living	First Floor	Second Floor	Bonus	Bed	Bath	Width	Depth	Foundation	Price Category
1684 sq ft	1046 sq ft	638 sq ft	N/A	3	3	25' 0"	72' 2"	Post/Pier	E

Design Features

- Built-ins and a media niche frame the fireplace in the great room.

- The formal dining room opens to the wraparound covered porch.

- The gourmet kitchen shares an eating bar with the great room.

- The second-level master suite includes a private observation deck.

- A vestibule leads to a viewing-loft stair, where a built-in window seat offers quiet relaxation.

Rear Elevation

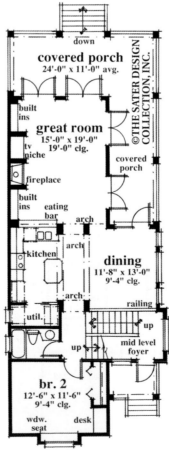

First Floor

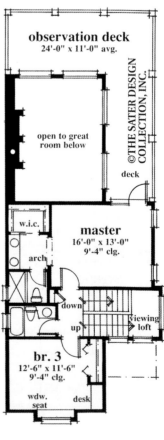

Second Floor

Henderson — UDHDG01-439 — 1-866-525-9374

Total Living	First Floor	Bonus	Bed	Bath	Width	Depth	Foundation	Price Category
1685 sq ft	1685 sq ft	331 sq ft	3	2	62' 4"	57' 4"	Crawl Space*	D

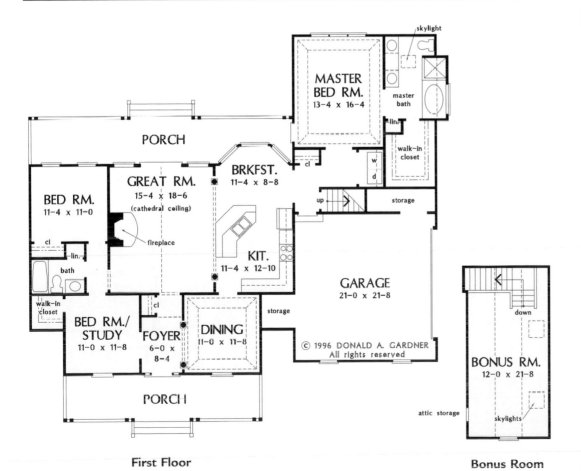

First Floor

Bonus Room

Rear Elevation

Design Features

- This popular country design is enlarged by adding a sky-lit bonus room over the garage.

- An open kitchen and great room with cathedral ceiling and fireplace provide the perfect gathering spot for family and friends.

- The master suite has a tray ceiling, back-porch access and private sky-lit bath.

- Outside, full front and back porches expand living spaces.

*Other options available. See page 513.

Urbandale — UDHDG01-1088 — 1-866-525-9374

Total Living	First Floor	Bonus	Bed	Bath	Width	Depth	Foundation	Price Category
1685 sq ft	1685 sq ft	N/A	3	2	36' 4"	88' 8"	Crawl Space*	D

Design Features

- Perfect for long, narrow lots, this plan combines everyday needs with exciting extras.

- The porte-cochere, defined by decorative columns, becomes quick, covered parking for vehicles.

- Wraparound countertops expand areas for meal preparation in the kitchen.

- The master suite features his-and-hers sinks, a garden tub and a generous walk-in closet.

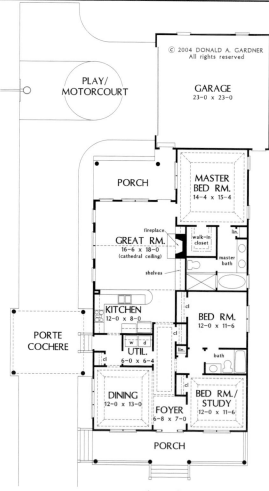

First Floor

Rear Elevation

*Other options available. See page 513.

© 2004 Frank Betz Associates, Inc.

Greystone — UDHFB01-3875 — 1-866-525-9374

Total Living	First Floor	Opt. Second Floor	Bed	Bath	Width	Depth	Foundation	Price Category
1694 sq ft	1694 sq ft	588 sq ft	4	3	54' 0"	52' 0"	Basement or Crawl Space	F

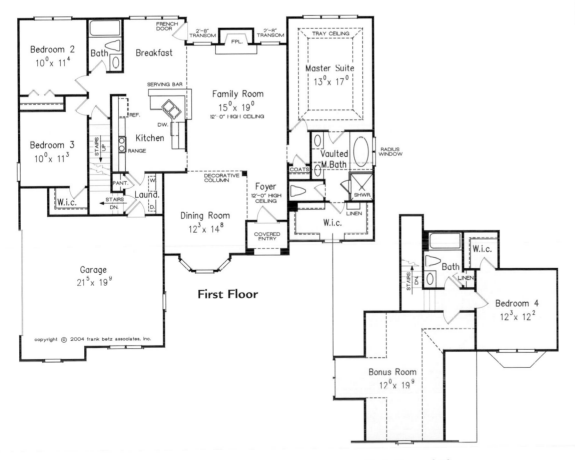

First Floor

copyright © 2004 frank betz associates, inc.

Opt. Second Floor

Design Features

- A decorative column creates an unobtrusive border that defines the dining room, making the entrance of the home feel open and spacious.

- Transom windows in the family room invite plenty of sunshine into the room, keeping this space bright and cheery.

- An optional second floor has been made available for those who may need room to grow.

Rear Elevation

Meredith — UDHDG01-355 — 1-866-525-9374

Total Living	First Floor	Second Floor	Bonus	Bed	Bath	Width	Depth	Walls/Foundation	Price Category
1694 sq ft	1100 sq ft	594 sq ft	N/A	3	2	36' 8"	45' 0"	Crawl Space*	D

Design Features

- This rustic home invites casual, comfortable living in impressive indoor spaces.

- The clever kitchen features an island cooktop with counter, which is ideal for entertaining.

- The second-floor master suite pampers owners with a whirlpool tub and a walk-in closet.

- Extra storage space is available in the attic.

Second Floor

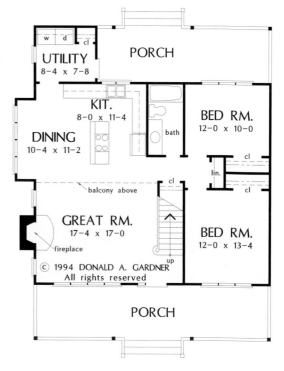

First Floor

Rear Elevation

*Other options available. See page 513.

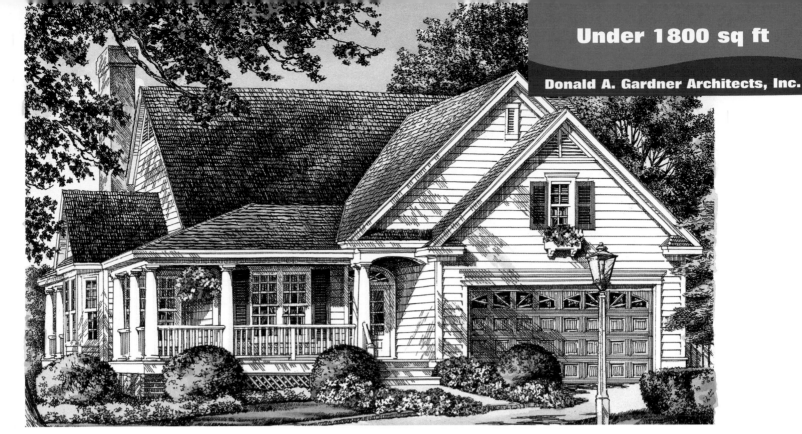

Donald A. Gardner Architects, Inc.

© 2002 Donald A. Gardner, Inc.

Jonesboro — UDHDG01-983 — 1-866-525-9374

Total Living	First Floor	Bonus	Bed	Bath	Width	Depth	Foundation	Price Category
1700 sq ft	1700 sq ft	333 sq ft	3	2	49' 0"	65' 4"	Crawl Space*	D

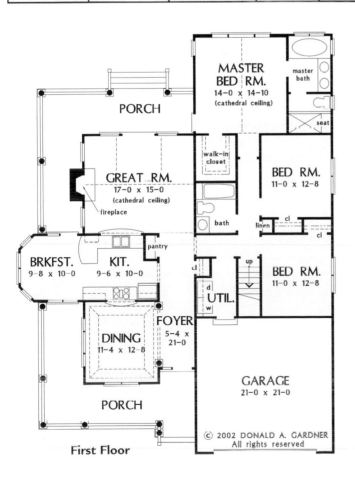

First Floor

© 2002 DONALD A. GARDNER
All rights reserved

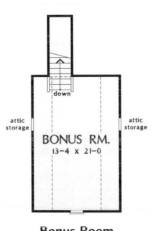

Bonus Room

Design Features

- An abundance of windows invites the natural surroundings inside.

- The kitchen is complete with two handy pass-thrus that service both the great room and dining room.

- The bonus room is conveniently located near the bedroom wing and can be converted to a playroom.

- Closets that act as noise barriers separate the additional bedrooms.

Rear Elevation

*Other options available. See page 513.

Southland Hills — UDHFB01-3747 — 1-866-525-9374

© 2002 Frank Betz Associates, Inc.

Total Living	First Floor	Opt. Second Floor	Bed	Bath	Width	Depth	Foundation	Price Category
1725 sq ft	1725 sq ft	256 sq ft	3	3	58' 0"	54' 6"	Basement, Crawl Space or Slab	F

Design Features

- Cheery dormers grace the exterior of the home and invite you in to see more.

- Each bedroom is buffered from the others, providing personal space for each resident.

- The master suite is designed as its own retreat, tucked away off the breakfast area, creating a private haven for the homeowner.

- Additional bedrooms are separated by a bath and a laundry room.

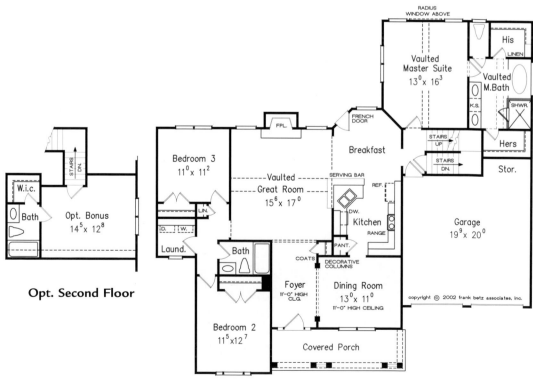

Opt. Second Floor

First Floor

Rear Elevation

© The Sater Design Collection, Inc.

Florianne — UDHDS01-6514 — 1-866-525-9374

Total Living	First Floor	Bonus	Bed	Bath	Width	Depth	Foundation	Price Category
1727 sq ft	1727 sq ft	N/A	2 + Study	2	47' 0"	74' 0"	Slab	F

First Floor

Master Suite
12'-4" x 14'-6"
11'-0" Clg.
Tray Clg.

W.I.C. | W.I.C.

Outdoor Grille

Solana
30' 0" x 12' 10"
10'-0" Clg

Outdoor Fireplace

Whirlpool | Master Bath

Great Room
16'-4" x 19'-0"
10'-8" Clg.
Stepped Clg.

Dining
13'-4" x 9'-4"
10'-8" Clg.
Stepped Clg.

Walk-In Shower

Linen

Kitchen
13'-4" x 11'-10"
10'-8" Clg.

Bath

Bedroom
11'-10" x 11'-2"
10'-0" Clg.

Foyer
10'-0" Clg.

Study/ Guest
11'-2" x 12'-10"
10'-0" Clg.

Utility

Entry
10'-0" Clg.

Garage
20'-2" x 21'-4"
10'-0" Clg.

© THE SATER DESIGN COLLECTION, INC.

Design Features

- The solana features an outdoor grill and fireplace and is easily accessible from the master suite, great room and dining room.

- The great room features disappearing glass walls to the solana, a stepped ceiling and open access to the dining room.

- Decorative wrought-iron inserts, a covered arch entryway and transom window add allure to the front of the home.

- The master suite boasts two walk-in closets, a tray ceiling and privacy from the other rooms in the house.

Rear Elevation

Not available for construction in Myrtle Beach, South Carolina.

Sterling — UDHDG01-1073 — 1-866-525-9374

Total Living	First Floor	Bonus	Bed	Bath	Width	Depth	Foundation	Price Category
1729 sq ft	1729 sq ft	404 sq ft	3	2	47' 4"	61' 6"	Crawl Space*	D

Design Features

- Shutters and arches with keystones frame half-circle transoms on this traditional home.
- The foyer's tray ceiling creates an elegant entrance, which leads to the stunning great room.
- Storage space fills every nook: under the stairs, in the utility room and near every bedroom.
- A fireplace, cathedral ceiling and French doors highlight the great room.

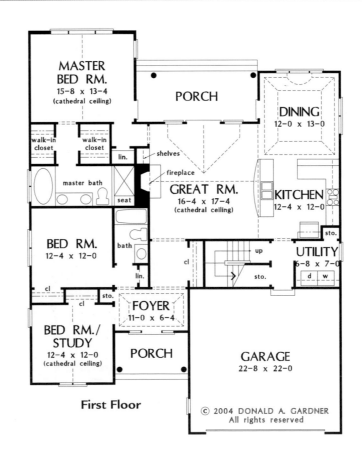

First Floor

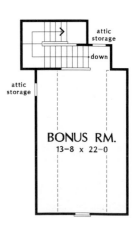

Bonus Room

Rear Elevation

*Other options available. See page 513.

Jarrell — UDHDG01-1017 — 1-866-525-9374

Total Living	First Floor	Bonus	Bed	Bath	Width	Depth	Foundation	Price Category
1727 sq ft	1727 sq ft	346 sq ft	3	2	46' 0"	66' 4"	Crawl Space*	D

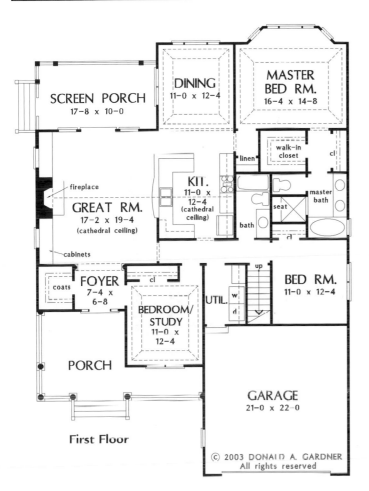

First Floor

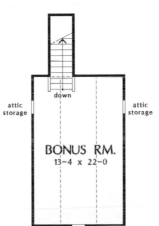

Bonus Room

Design Features

- This home offers room-definition, yet the floor plan remains open.

- A bay window and French doors invite light inside, while a screened porch takes living outdoors.

- With a breakfast counter, the kitchen is the heart of the home.

- A fireplace, flanked by high windows, enhances the great room.

- The bonus room is perfectly positioned to create an additional bedroom or home gym.

Rear Elevation

Queensfield — UDHDG01-1037 — 1-866-525-9374

Total Living	First Floor	Second Floor	Bonus	Bed	Bath	Width	Depth	Foundation	Price Category
1737 sq ft	1737 sq ft	N/A	299 sq ft	3	2	54' 4"	54' 10"	Crawl Space*	D

Design Features

- Arched transoms soften gable peaks while adding curb appeal to this modest home.

- Three sets of columns create a dramatic front entry.

- Decorative ceiling treatments and a breakfast bar keep the common rooms open.

- A barrel-vault crowns a Palladian window in the master bedroom.

- A double vanity, separate shower, garden tub and private privy complete the master bath.

Rear Elevation

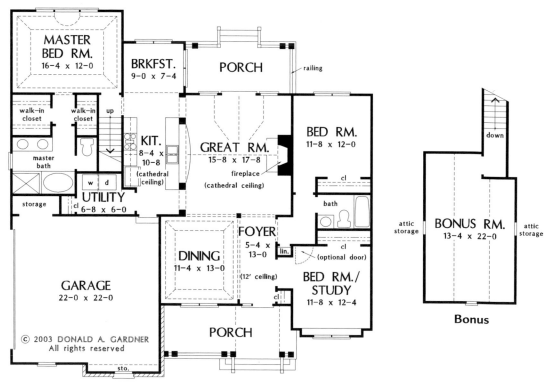

First Floor

Bonus

*Other options available. See page 513.

© The Sater Design Collection, Inc.

Tamarron — UDHDS01-6760 — 1-866-525-9374

Total Living	First Floor	Bonus	Bed	Bath	Width	Depth	Foundation	Price Category
1746 sq ft	1746 sq ft	N/A	3 + Study	2	58' 0"	59' 4"	Slab	E

First Floor

Bedroom 2
11'-10" x 11'-6"
8'-0" Clg.

Bath 1

Cl

Bedroom 1
11'-10" x 10'-4"
8'-0" Clg.

WIC

WIC

Study
12'-2" x 10'-2"
8'-0" Clg.

Foyer

Entry

Lanai
Vaulted Clg.

Nook
9'-2" x 7'-0"
Vaulted Clg.

Great Room
16'-0" x 11' 10"
Vaulted Clg.

Kitchen
9'-4" x 10'-8"
Vaulted Clg.

Master
Suite
13'-2" x 15'-0"
8'-0" Clg.

Dining
Room
11'-6" x 10'-6"
Vaulted Clg.

Cl

Util.
6'-8" x 7'-10"
8'-0" Clg.

WIC   M. Bath
8'-0" Clg.

Walk-In
Shower

Whirlpool

Garage
20'-4" x 21'-6"
8'-0" Clg.

© THE SATER DESIGN
COLLECTION, INC.

Design Features

- Vaulted ceilings add dramatic flare to the great room, kitchen, nook and dining room.

- Pocketing doors in the great room and master suite open to the lanai.

- The kitchen area opens into the great room creating a welcoming living space.

- Spare bedrooms are located away from the master suite ensuring privacy.

Rear Elevation

Brennan — UDHDG01-350 — 1-866-525-9374

Total Living	First Floor	Bonus	Bed	Bath	Width	Depth	Foundation	Price Category
1737 sq ft	1737 sq ft	N/A	3	2	65' 10"	59' 8"	Crawl Space*	D

Design Features

- Clever use of interior space gives this home a feeling much larger than its 1737 square feet.
- The breakfast bay is open to the kitchen with island, pantry and back-porch access.
- The master bedroom with tray ceiling is privately situated with a luxurious bath.
- The front bedroom with its cathedral ceiling and large circle-top window doubles as a study.
- Wrapping front and back porches invite quiet relaxation.

Rear Elevation

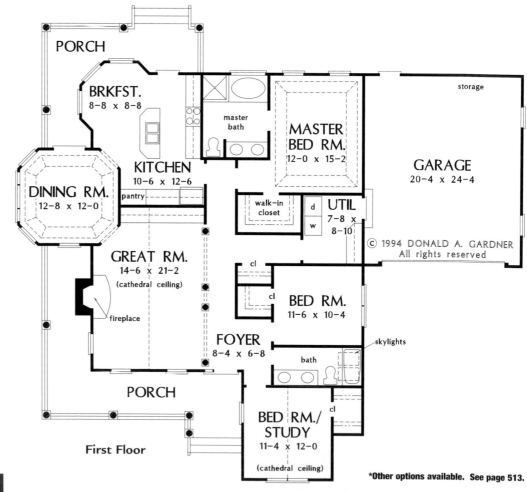

First Floor

*Other options available. See page 513.

Please note: Home photographed may differ from blueprint.

Sunderland — UDHDG01-545 — 1-866-525-9374

Total Living	First Floor	Second Floor	Bonus	Bed	Bath	Width	Depth	Foundation	Price Category
1761 sq ft	1271 sq ft	490 sq ft	N/A	3	2-1/2	77' 8"	50' 0"	Crawl Space*	D

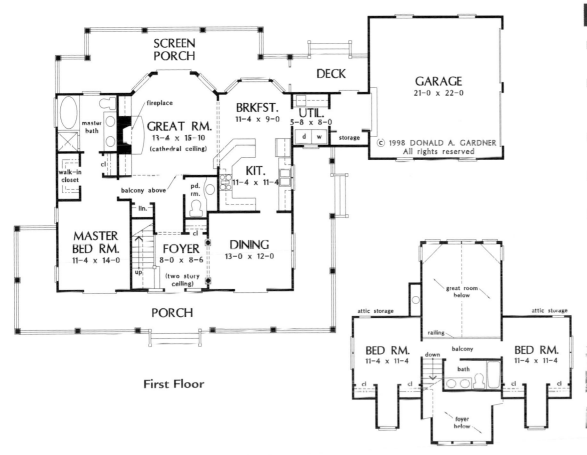

First Floor

Second Floor

Design Features

- This country farmhouse looks and lives bigger than its square footage indicates.

- The large center dormer directs light through clerestory windows into the two-story foyer.

- Interior columns mark entrance to the formal dining room.

- The heart of the home is the central great room with fireplace and built-ins.

- Upstairs bedrooms sport dormer alcoves and are separated by a balcony.

Rear Elevation

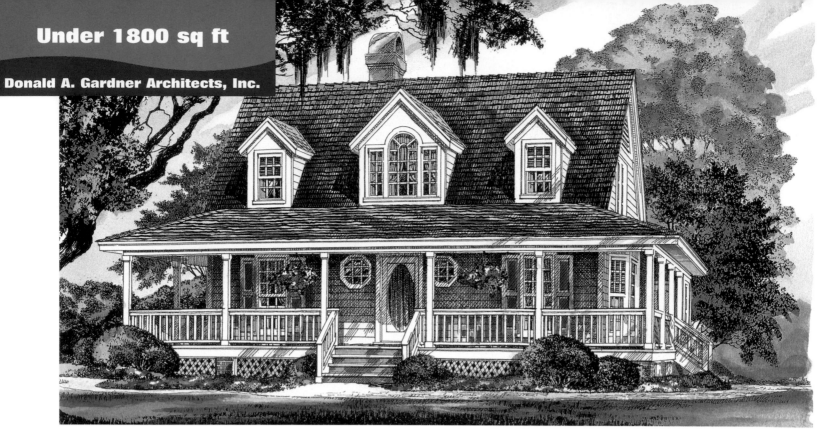

Morninglory — UDHDG01-236 — 1-866-525-9374

© 1991 Donald A. Gardner Architects, Inc.

Total Living	First Floor	Second Floor	Bonus	Bed	Bath	Width	Depth	Foundation	Price Category
1778 sq ft	1325 sq ft	453 sq ft	N/A	3	2-1/2	48' 4"	40' 4"	Crawl Space*	D

Design Features

- Custom-style windows dress up the exterior of this charming home.

- The U-shaped kitchen includes a pass-thru to the vaulted great room.

- The private, first-level master suite opens to a rear deck.

- The master bath pampers with double lavs, garden tub and shower.

Rear Elevation

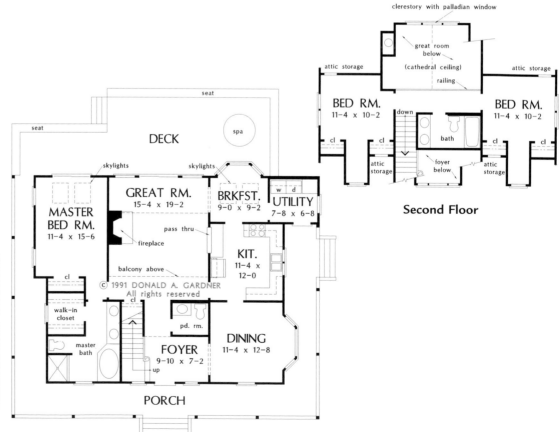

Second Floor

First Floor

*Other options available. See page 513.

Swansboro — UDHDG01-853 — 1-866-525-9374

Total Living	First Floor	Second Floor	Bonus	Bed	Bath	Width	Depth	Foundation	Price Category
1787 sq ft	964 sq ft	823 sq ft	331 sq ft	3	2-1/2	57' 2"	42' 8"	Crawl Space*	D

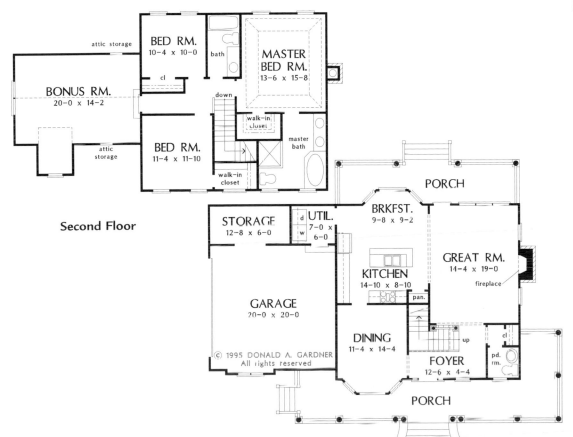

Second Floor

First Floor

Design Features

- A trio of dormers and a wrapping front porch with gable entry create a genteel façade.

- The great room is generously proportioned and open to the kitchen and breakfast area.

- Another bay window expands the dining room.

- Front and back porches provide ample outdoor living space.

- A tray ceiling tops the master bedroom, which features a walk-in closet and private bath.

Rear Elevation

Priceville — UDHFB01-1179 — 1-866-525-9374

© 1998 Frank Betz Associates, Inc.

Total Living	First Floor	Opt. Second Floor	Bed	Bath	Width	Depth	Foundation	Price Category
1795 sq ft	1795 sq ft	254 sq ft	3	2	54' 0"	53' 0"	Basement, Crawl Space or Slab	E

Design Features

- Brick and siding with cheery dormers and copper accents join to make a front elevation that is casual yet elegant.

- Simple changes can easily convert the formal living room into a sitting room for the master suite. French doors lead to the master bath, where highlights include a seated shower and his-and-her closets.

- Plant shelves, radius windows and decorative columns are tastefully placed throughout the home.

- Coat closets have been thoughtfully placed just inside each entrance.

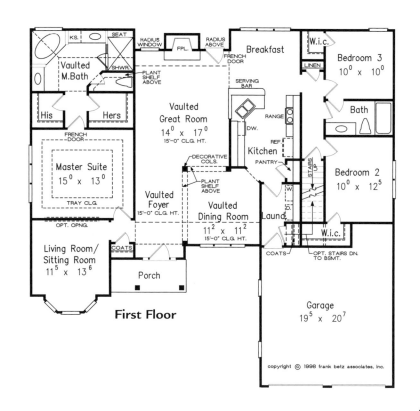

First Floor

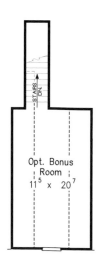

Opt. Second Floor

Rear Elevation

Luxembourg — UDHDG01-979 — 1-866-525-9374

Total Living	First Floor	Second Floor	Bonus	Bed	Bath	Width	Depth	Foundation	Price Category
1797 sq ft	1345 sq ft	452 sq ft	349 sq ft	3	2-1/2	63' 0"	40' 0"	Crawl Space*	D

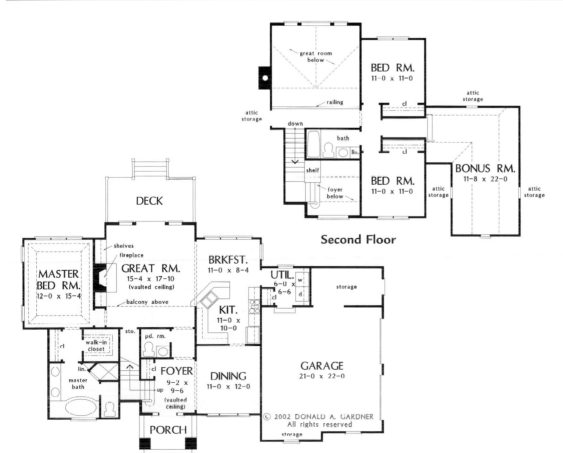

Second Floor

First Floor

Design Features

- Incorporating Old-World style, this house combines stone and stucco in its façade.

- The grand portico leads to an open floor plan, which is equally impressive.

- Built-in cabinetry, French doors and a fireplace enhance the great room.

- The first-floor master suite is located in the quiet zone with no rooms above it.

- Upstairs, the bonus room features convenient second-floor access.

Rear Elevation

Cheraw — UDHDG01-1060 — 1-866-525-9374

© 2004 Donald A. Gardner, Inc.

Total Living	First Floor	Bonus	Bed	Bath	Width	Depth	Foundation	Price Category
1795 sq ft	1795 sq ft	444 sq ft	3	2	57' 6"	56' 6"	Crawl Space*	D

Design Features

- With a brick and siding facade, this home features a front-entry garage for convenience.
- Gables direct eyes upward, while circle-top transoms soften exterior lines and angles.
- Front and rear porches take living outdoors, creating areas for entertaining and relaxing.
- The open, family-efficient floor plan allows a natural traffic flow.

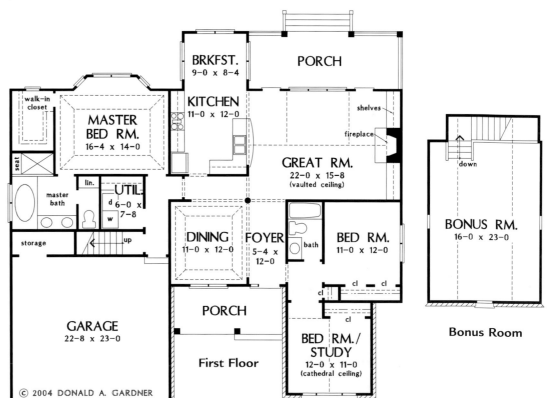

First Floor

Bonus Room

Rear Elevation

*Other options available. See page 513.

© 1998 Frank Betz Associates, Inc.

Gershwin — UDHFB01-1122 — 1-866-525-9374

Total Living	First Floor	Second Floor	Opt. Bonus	Bed	Bath	Width	Depth	Foundation	Price Category
1811 sq ft	916 sq ft	895 sq ft	262 sq ft	3	2-1/2	44' 0"	38' 0"	Basement, Crawl Space or Slab	G

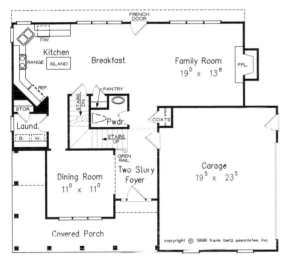

First Floor

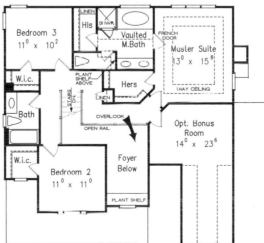

Second Floor

Design Features

- Front porches are once again popular among today's homeowners, so we situated a cozy wraparound porch on this home.

- The plan maintains an open feeling inside as the family room, kitchen and breakfast area enjoy common space.

- The master suite features a tray ceiling, double vanities and his-and-her closets.

Rear Elevation

Bookworth — UDHDG01-1027 — 1-866-525-9374

Total Living	First Floor	Bonus	Bed	Bath	Width	Depth	Foundation	Price Category
1820 sq ft	1820 sq ft	N/A	3	2	61' 10"	62' 6"	Crawl Space*	D

Design Features

- This cottage showcases a beautiful mixture of stone and siding.
- Coat closets and columns flank the entrance to the great room with its cathedral ceiling and French doors.
- A linen closet faces the secondary bedrooms, while the master suite is positioned for privacy.
- A side porch creates a service entrance into the utility room.

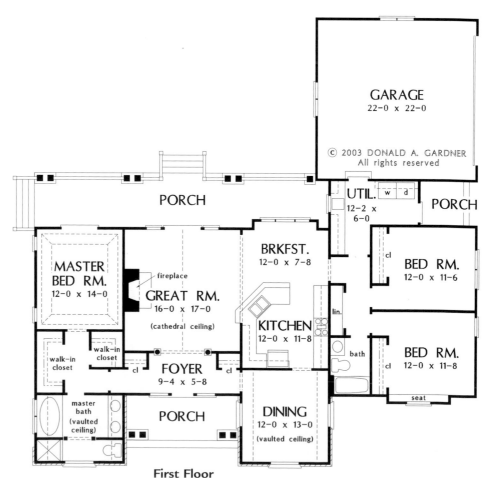

First Floor

Rear Elevation

*Other options available. See page 513.

Gibson — UDHDG01-821 — 1-866-525-9374

Total Living	First Floor	Second Floor	Bonus	Bed	Bath	Width	Depth	Foundation	Price Category
1821 sq ft	1293 sq ft	528 sq ft	355 sq ft	3	2-1/2	48' 8"	50' 0"	Crawl Space*	D

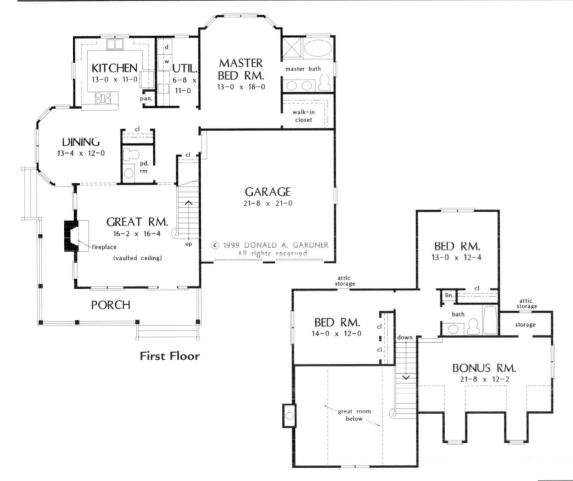

First Floor

Second Floor

Design Features

- A charming gable and a wrapping front porch enhance this bungalow.

- The kitchen features a practical design and includes a handy pantry.

- A nearby utility room boasts a sink, additional cabinets and countertop space.

- The downstairs master suite enjoys a private bath and walk-in closet.

Rear Elevation

Ravencroft — UDHDG01-1062 — 1-866-525-9374

Total Living	First Floor	Bonus	Bed	Bath	Width	Depth	Foundation	Price Category
1821 sq ft	1821 sq ft	345 sq ft	3	2	54' 4"	61' 4"	Crawl Space*	D

Design Features

- A hipped roof combines with stucco and stone to create an elegant exterior with Old-World flair.
- By using columns and a minimum of walls to designate rooms, the floor plan is remarkably open.
- Ceiling treatments in the great room and dining room add sophistication and visual space.
- A French door leads from the master bedroom to the rear porch.

Rear Elevation

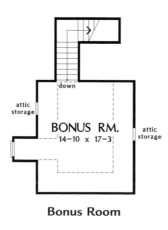

Bonus Room

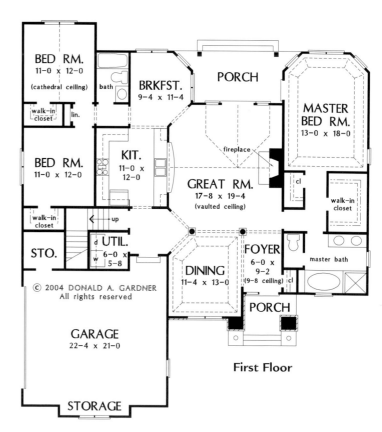

First Floor

*Other options available. See page 513.

© The Sater Design Collection, Inc.

Chantel — UDHDS01-7011 — 1-866-525-9374

Total Living	First Floor	Bonus	Bed	Bath	Width	Depth	Foundation	Price Category
1822 sq ft	1822 sq ft	N/A	3 + Study	2	58' 0"	67' 2"	Finished Basement	E

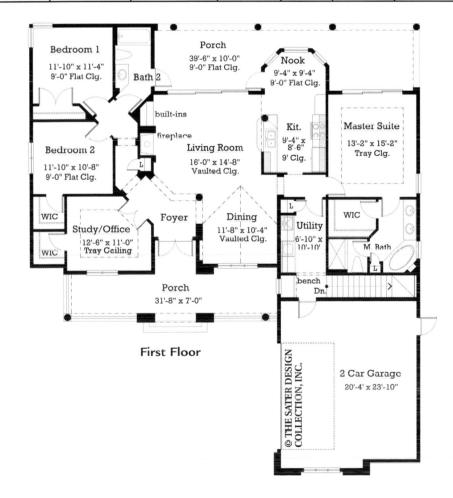

Bedroom 1
11'-10" x 11'-4"
9'-0" Flat Clg.

Bath 2

built-ins

fireplace

Bedroom 2
11'-10" x 10'-8"
9'-0" Flat Clg.

WIC

WIC

Study/Office
12'-6" x 11'-0"
Tray Ceiling

Foyer

Porch
39'-6" x 10'-0"
9'-0" Flat Clg.

Nook
9'-4" x 9'-4"
9'-0" Flat Clg.

Kit.
9'-4" x
8'-6"
9' Clg.

Master Suite
13'-2" x 15'-2"
Tray Clg.

Living Room
16'-0" x 14'-8"
Vaulted Clg.

Dining
11'-8" x 10'-4"
Vaulted Clg.

Utility
6'-10" x
10'-10'

WIC

M. Bath

bench

Dn.

Porch
31'-8" x 7'-0"

© THE SATER DESIGN COLLECTION, INC.

2 Car Garage
20'-4" x 23'-10"

First Floor

Design Features

- The living and dining rooms have vaulted ceilings.

- The living and master open to the rear porch.

- A U-shaped kitchen has a convenient pass-thru.

- Louvered shutters accentuate the office window.

- A Palladian window is the home's focal point.

Rear Elevation

Wallace — UDHFB01-3629 — 1-866-525-9374

© 2001 Frank Betz Associates, Inc.

Total Living	First Floor	Opt. Second Floor	Bed	Bath	Width	Depth	Foundation	Price Category
1823 sq ft	1823 sq ft	576 sq ft	4	3-1/2	55' 0"	57' 0"	Basement, Crawl Space or Slab	G

Design Features

- Roomy dimensions give the *Wallace* a spacious, unrestricted feeling inside.

- Large radius windows in the dining and grand rooms allow the natural light to pour into these main living areas.

- The secondary bedrooms are generously proportioned, and one features a walk-in closet.

- An optional second floor provides the opportunity to expand, adding an additional bedroom, bath and bonus area.

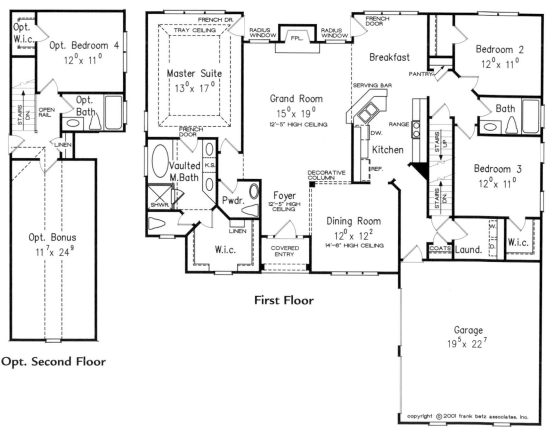

First Floor

Opt. Second Floor

Rear Elevation

Gentry — UDHDG01-977 — 1-866-525-9374

Total Living	First Floor	Bonus	Bed	Bath	Width	Depth	Foundation	Price Category
1827 sq ft	1827 sq ft	384 sq ft	3	2	61' 8"	62' 8"	Crawl Space*	D

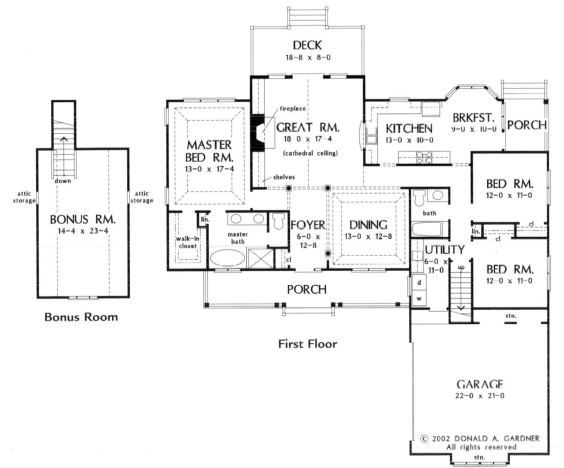

Bonus Room

First Floor

Design Features

- This quaint farmhouse lacks nothing, and even has a bonus room to accommodate expansion needs.

- With its welcoming front porch and Palladian windows, this home adds curb appeal to any streetscape.

- A breakfast room off the kitchen is the perfect place to enjoy early-morning coffee.

- The utility room is complete with a sink.

Rear Elevation

Oglethorpe — UDHDG01-518 — 1-866-525-9374

© 1997 Donald A. Gardner, Inc.

Total Living	First Floor	Bonus	Bed	Bath	Width	Depth	Foundation	Price Category
1829 sq ft	1829 sq ft	424 sq ft	3	2	54' 11"	58' 7"	Crawl Space*	D

Design Features

- A grand hipped roof and four front-facing gables create a dignified façade for this brick traditional.
- The single front dormer lights the foyer, while two rear dormers bring plenty of light into the great room.
- A cathedral ceiling expands the great room, which features built-in bookshelves flanking the fireplace.
- The master suite pampers homeowners with his-and-her walk-in closets and a spectacular bayed bath.

First Floor

Bonus Room

Rear Elevation

*Other options available. See page 513.

© 2004 Donald A. Gardner, Inc.

Gresham — UDHDG01-1084 — 1-866-525-9374

Total Living	First Floor	Bonus	Bed	Bath	Width	Depth	Foundation	Price Category
1830 sq ft	1830 sq ft	354 sq ft	3	2	54' 4"	61' 4"	Crawl Space*	D

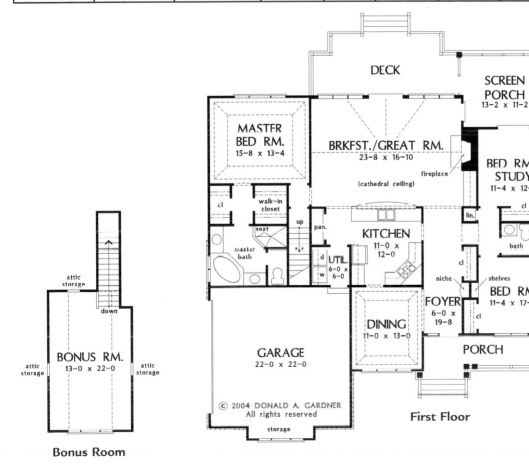

First Floor

Bonus Room

Design Features

- Gables and decorative dormers accentuate the hipped roof, while a box-bay window de-emphasizes the garage.

- The screened porch can be accessed from the versatile bedroom/study and great room.

- Other special features include a bonus room, reach-in pantry and built-in cabinetry.

- An art niche and spacious closet enhance the foyer, and the master bath is quite the retreat.

Rear Elevation

*Other options available. See page 513.

Periwinkle — UDHDG01-731 — 1-866-525-9374

© 1998 Donald A. Gardner, Inc.

Total Living	First Floor	Bonus	Bed	Bath	Width	Depth	Foundation	Price Category
1792 sq ft	1792 sq ft	351 sq ft	3	3	66' 4"	62' 4"	Crawl Space*	D

Design Features

- This home's stucco exterior is complemented by gables with cedar shake and a stone foundation.

- Porches and windows take maximum advantage of views from the rear of this custom-style home.

- Both master suites enjoy their own baths, walk-in closets and private porches.

- A bonus room over the garage offers flexibility and options for expansion.

Rear Elevation

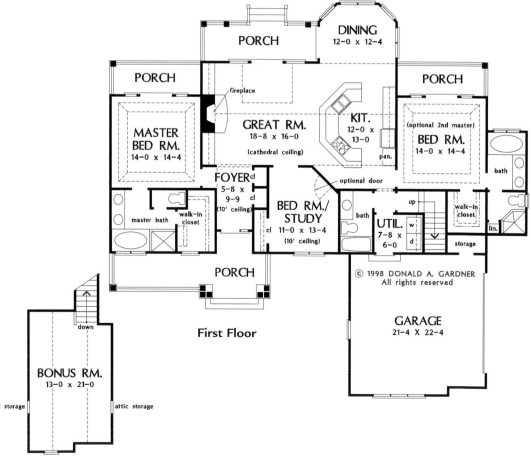

First Floor

Bonus Room

© 1998 DONALD A. GARDNER
All rights reserved

*Other options available. See page 513.

Glenwood — UDHDG01-224 — 1-866-525-9374

Total Living	First Floor	Second Floor	Bonus	Bed	Bath	Width	Depth	Foundation	Price Category
1831 sq ft	1289 sq ft	542 sq ft	393 sq ft	3	2-1/2	66' 4"	40' 4"	Crawl Space*	D

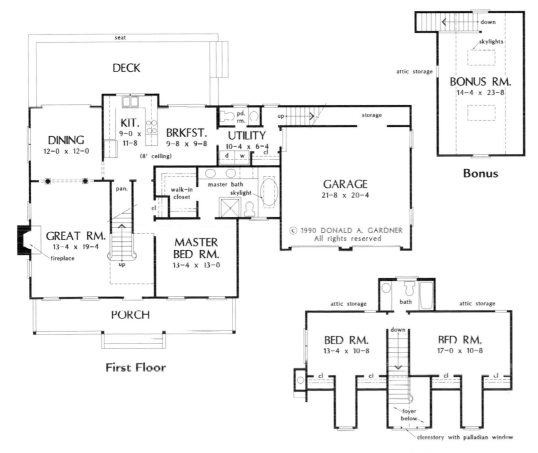

First Floor

Second Floor

Bonus

Design Features

- An unfinished bonus room and an optional basement offer flexibility.

- An elegant Palladian window in a clerestory dormer washes the two-story foyer in natural light.

- Columns between the great and dining rooms add drama and accent nine-foot ceilings.

- A luxurious first-level master suite makes a great parent get-away.

- The master bath features a cheery skylight above the whirlpool tub.

Rear Elevation

*Other options available. See page 513.

Photographed home may have been modified from original construction documents.

Vittorio Terrace — UDHDS01-6866 — 1-866-525-9374

© The Sater Design Collection, Inc.

Total Living	First Floor	Second Floor	Lower Level	Bed	Bath	Width	Depth	Foundation	Price Category
1886 sq ft	1342 sq ft	511 sq ft	33 sq ft	3	2-1/2	44' 0"	40' 0"	Island Basement	E

Design Features

- Bold forms, keystone arches, detailed fretwork and exposed brackets enhance the front façade.

- The foyer provides interior vistas that extend through the great room and an open arrangement of the dining room and kitchen.

- The master suite enjoys access to a private porch, a walk-in closet and spacious bath.

- The upper level features a computer loft with plenty of space for books, and an overlook to the great room.

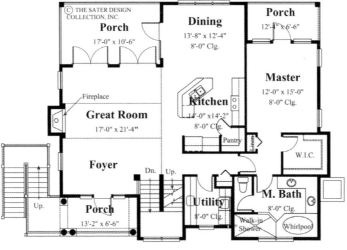

First Floor

Second Floor

Rear Elevation

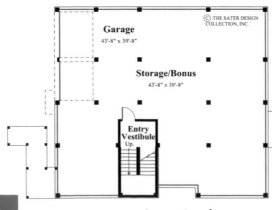

Lower Level

© The Sater Design Collection, Inc.

Nassau Cove — UDHDS01-6654 — 1-866-525-9374

Total Living	First Floor	Second Floor	Bonus	Bed	Bath	Width	Depth	Foundation	Price Category
1853 sq ft	1342 sq ft	511 sq ft	N/A	3	2	44' 0"	40' 0"	Post/Pier	E

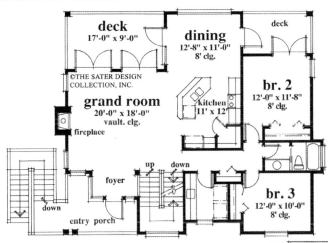

First Floor

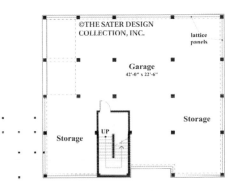

Lower Level

Second Floor

Design Features

- Double French doors lead to the deck from the grand room.

- Both sides of the dining room open to decks.

- The well-appointed kitchen over looks the living area.

- Upstairs, a hall with balcony over-look leads to the master's retreat.

- The master bath boasts a windowed whirlpool tub and a morning kitchen.

Rear Elevation

Hampton — UDHDG01-390 — 1-866-525-9374

© 1995 Donald A. Gardner Architects, Inc.

Total Living	First Floor	Bonus	Bed	Bath	Width	Depth	Foundation	Price Category
1879 sq ft	1879 sq ft	360 sq ft	3	2	66' 4"	55' 2"	Crawl Space*	D

Design Features

- Dormers cast light and interest into the foyer that sets the tone in a home full of today's amenities.

- The great room, defined by columns, is conveniently located adjacent to the breakfast room and kitchen.

- Tray ceilings and picture windows with circle tops accent the front bedroom and dining room.

- A secluded master suite includes a bath with skylight, garden tub, separate shower and spacious walk-in closet.

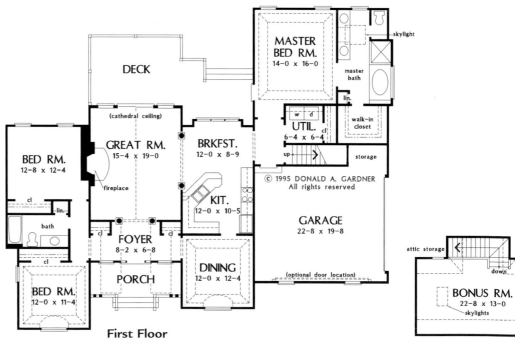

First Floor

Bonus Room

Rear Elevation

*Other options available. See page 513.

Photographed home may have been modified from original construction documents.

Courtney — UDHDG01-706 — 1-866-525-9374

Total Living	First Floor	Second Floor	Bonus	Bed	Bath	Width	Depth	Foundation	Price Category
1859 sq ft	1336 sq ft	523 sq ft	225 sq ft	3	2-1/2	45' 0"	53' 0"	Crawl Space*	D

Second Floor

First Floor

Design Features

- This classic cottage offers maximum comfort for its economic design and narrow-lot width.
- The foyer features a generous coat closet and a niche for displaying collectibles.
- Two clerestory dormers and a balcony overlooking the second floor grant drama to the great room.
- The kitchen services both dining room and great room with ease.

Rear Elevation

*Other options available. See page 513.

Barclay — UDHDG01-248 — 1-866-525-9374

Total Living	First Floor	Second Floor	Bonus	Bed	Bath	Width	Depth	Foundation	Price Category
1861 sq ft	1416 sq ft	445 sq ft	284 sq ft	3	2-1/2	58' 3"	53' 5"	Crawl Space*	D

Design Features

- Interior columns add elegance while visually dividing the foyer from the dining room.
- A box-bay window adds space to the formal dining room.
- The master suite boasts his-and-her walk-in closets and garden tub with skylight.
- Two bedrooms upstairs share another skylit bath.

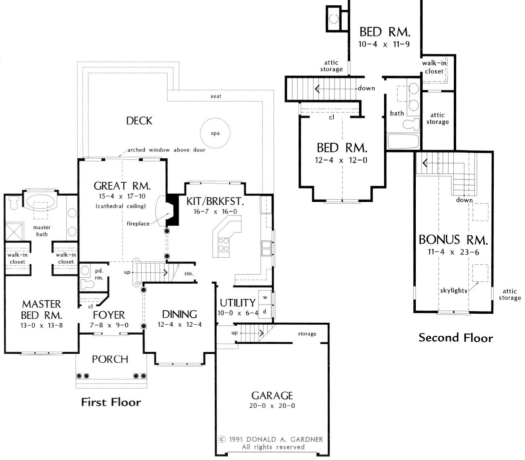

First Floor

Second Floor

Rear Elevation

*Other options available. See page 513.

Photographed home may have been modified from original construction documents.

Donald A. Gardner Architects, Inc.

© 1993 Donald A. Gardner Architects, Inc.

Pennyhill — UDHDG01-294 — 1-866-525-9374

Total Living	First Floor	Bonus	Bed	Bath	Width	Depth	Foundation	Price Category
1867 sq ft	1867 sq ft	422 sq ft	3	2-1/2	71' 0"	56' 4"	Crawl Space*	D

Design Features

- This country home surprises with an open floor plan featuring a great room with cathedral ceiling.
- The kitchen with an angled counter opens to the breakfast area and great room for easy entertaining.
- The secluded master bedroom has a cathedral ceiling and nearby access to the deck with optional spa.
- Skylights over the tub accent the luxurious master bath.
- A bonus room over the garage makes expansion easy.

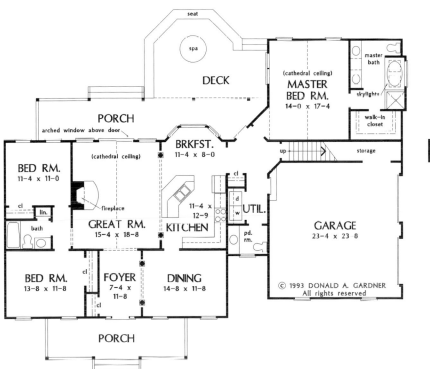

First Floor

Bonus Room

Rear Elevation

Rivermeade — UDHFB01-3668 — 1-866-525-9374

© 2002 Frank Betz Associates, Inc.

Total Living	First Floor	Second Floor	Opt. Bonus	Bed	Bath	Width	Depth	Foundation	Price Category
1879 sq ft	1359 sq ft	520 sq ft	320 sq ft	3	2-1/2	45' 0"	52' 4"	Basement or Crawl Space	G

Design Features

- Volume makes this home feel larger than it is, with vaulted, tray and two-story ceilings throughout the main level.

- The laundry area can also be a mudroom with direct access off the garage.

- A handy pass-thru from the kitchen to the great room makes entertaining easier.

- A large covered porch adds interest to the front façade.

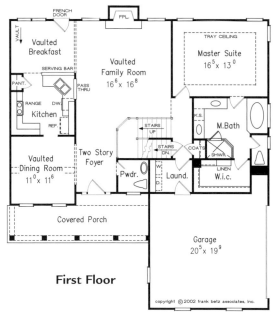

First Floor

copyright © 2002 frank betz associates, inc.

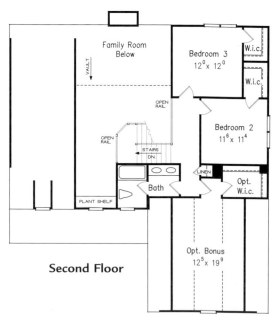

Second Floor

Rear Elevation

Cartwright — UDHDG01-801 — 1-866-525-9374

Total Living	First Floor	Bonus	Bed	Bath	Width	Depth	Foundation	Price Category
1882 sq ft	1882 sq ft	359 sq ft	3	2-1/2	61' 4"	55' 0"	Crawl Space*	D

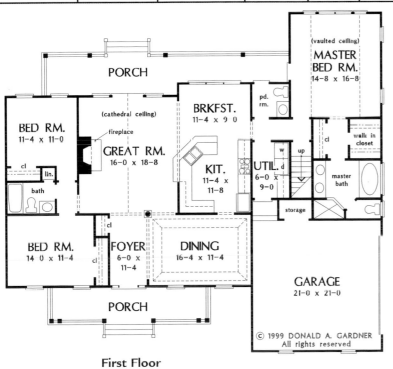

First Floor

BONUS RM.
14-0 x 21-0

attic storage   attic storage

Bonus Room

Design Features

- An arched window in a center, front-facing gable lends style and beauty to the façade.

- A breakfast area separates the master suite from the great room for optimal privacy.

- The master suite is expanded by a dramatic vaulted ceiling and includes access to the back porch.

- The spacious dining room offers a tray ceiling and convenient kitchen access.

Rear Elevation

Liberty Hill — UDHDG01-414 — 1-866-525-9374

© 1995 Donald A. Gardner Architects, Inc.

Total Living	First Floor	Second Floor	Bonus	Bed	Bath	Width	Depth	Foundation	Price Category
1883 sq ft	1803 sq ft	80 sq ft	918 sq ft	3	2	63' 8"	57' 4"	Crawl Space*	D

Design Features

- Growing families will adore this farmhouse with plenty of versatile unfinished bonus space.

- Living and entertaining space expands to the deck.

- A tray ceiling adds interest and volume to the master bedroom.

- The master suite includes a walk-in closet and skylit bath with a garden tub.

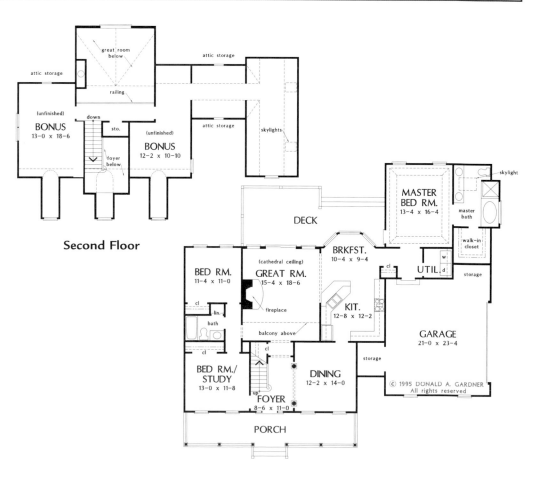

Second Floor

First Floor

Rear Elevation

*Other options available. See page 513.

© The Sater Design Collection, Inc.

Aruba Bay — UDHDS01-6840 — 1-866-525-9374

Total Living	First Floor	Second Floor	Lower Level	Bed	Bath	Width	Depth	Foundation	Price Category
1886 sq ft	1342 sq ft	511 sq ft	33 sq ft	3	2-1/2	44' 0"	40' 0"	Island Basement	G

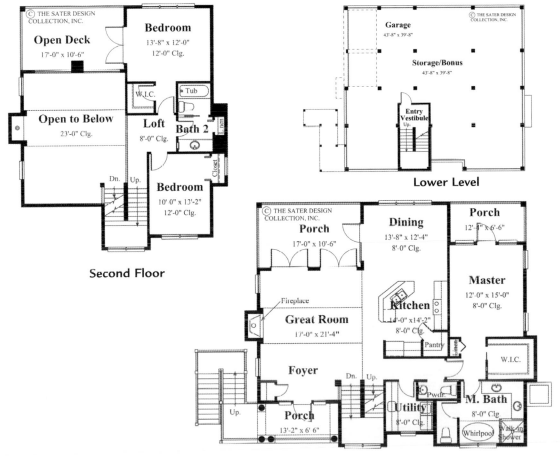

Second Floor

Lower Level

First Floor

Design Features

- An elevated balcony entryway, multiple porches, varied rooflines and a widow's peak garner attention from those who pass-by.

- A smart great room/dining room/kitchen design creates an inviting atmosphere.

- The great room features a fireplace and arched transom windows that heighten views.

- The kitchen offers ample storage and serving space with its deep, curved counter and a long wall of cabinetry culminating in a corner pantry.

Rear Elevation

Bagwell — UDHFB01-797 — 1-866-525-9374

© 1994 Frank Betz Associates, Inc.

Total Living	First Floor	Opt. Second Floor	Bed	Bath	Width	Depth	Foundation	Price Category
1891 sq ft	1891 sq ft	354 sq ft	3	3-1/2	56' 0"	60' 0"	Basement, Crawl Space or Slab	G

Design Features

- The *Bagwell's* floor plan is fresh and innovative with plenty of details to keep even the most discriminating homeowner happy.

- Vaulted ceilings and an open layout among the common rooms make the center of this home feel roomy and spacious.

- A built-in command center in the kitchen provides a designated spot for mail and paperwork. The serving bar in the kitchen provides additional seating for holiday gatherings and entertaining.

Rear Elevation

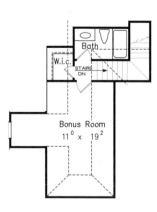

Opt. Second Floor

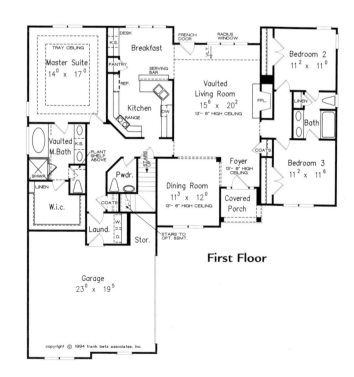

First Floor

Saluda — UDHDG01-795 — 1-866-525-9374

Total Living	First Floor	Second Floor	Bonus	Bed	Bath	Width	Depth	Foundation	Price Category
1891 sq ft	1309 sq ft	582 sq ft	570 sq ft	3	2-1/2	65' 8"	39' 4"	Crawl Space*	D

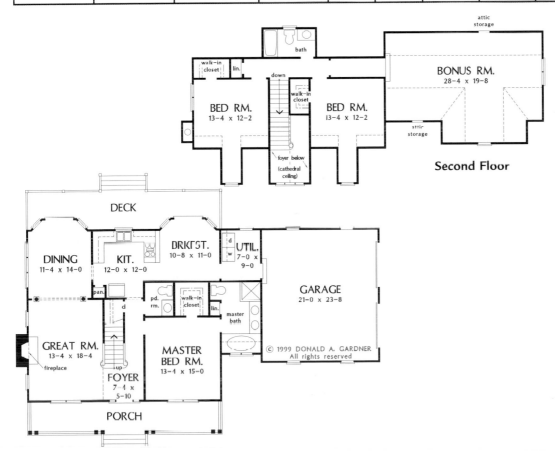

Second Floor

First Floor

Design Features

- This one-and-a-half-story home features a relaxing front porch and a generous great room.

- Like the master suite, both upstairs bedrooms include walk-in closets.

- Dormer alcoves add interest and illumination to the second-floor family bedrooms.

- An oversized bonus room offers an abundance of space for storage or future expansion.

Rear Elevation

Merrifield — UDHDG01-235 — 1-866-525-9374

Total Living	First Floor	Second Floor	Bonus	Bed	Bath	Width	Depth	Foundation	Price Category
1898 sq ft	1356 sq ft	542 sq ft	378 sq ft	3	2-1/2	59' 0"	64' 4"	Crawl Space*	D

Design Features

- A Palladian window in the clerestory dormer bathes the two-story foyer in natural light.

- Nine-foot ceilings throughout the first level add drama.

- The first-floor master suite has a whirlpool tub, shower, double lavs and walk-in closet.

- Upstairs, two bedrooms with dormers and attic-storage access share a full bath.

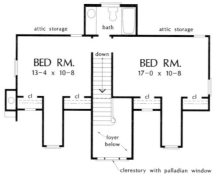

Second Floor

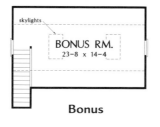

Bonus

First Floor

Rear Elevation

*Other options available. See page 513.

Photographed home may have been modified from original construction documents.

Mayfield — UDHDG01-537 — 1-866-525-9374

Total Living	First Floor	Bonus	Bed	Bath	Width	Depth	Foundation	Price Category
1899 sq ft	1899 sq ft	315 sq ft	3	2	58' 0"	66' 10"	Crawl Space*	D

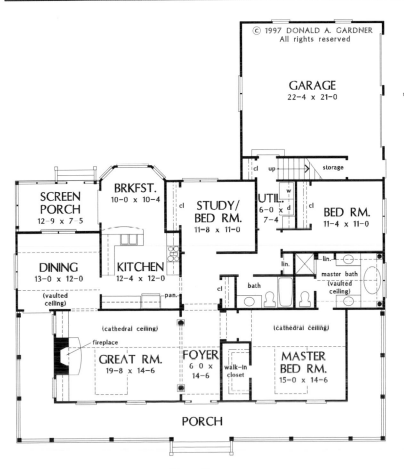

First Floor

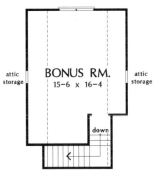

Bonus Room

Design Features

- An inviting wraparound porch surrounds the welcoming façade of this three-dormered, one-story farmhouse.

- A cathedral ceiling enhances the great room where a clerestory dormer bathes the room in natural light.

- The dining room features front-porch access, while the screened porch is off the breakfast bay.

- A utility room separates the flexible bedroom/study from the third bedroom.

Rear Elevation

Tradewind Court — UDHDS01-6617 — 1-866-525-9374

© The Sater Design Collection, Inc.

Total Living	First Floor	Second Floor	Bonus	Bed	Bath	Width	Depth	Foundation	Price Category
1904 sq ft	1302 sq ft	602 sq ft	N/A	3	2-1/2	46' 0"	45' 0"	Piling	F

Design Features

■ Two sets of French doors open the great room and dining room to the verandah.

■ The great room features a vaulted ceiling, fireplace and easy access to the dining room and kitchen.

■ The master suite boasts a luxurious bath and private access to a secluded area of the verandah.

■ Upstairs, a secondary bedroom shares a full bath with a cozy loft or third bedroom.

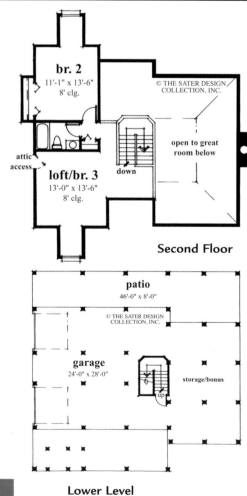

Second Floor

First Floor

Lower Level

Rear Elevation

© The Sater Design Collection, Inc.

Georgetown Cove — UDHDS01-6690 — 1-866-525-9374

Total Living	First Floor	Second Floor	Bonus	Bed	Bath	Width	Depth	Foundation	Price Category
1910 sq ft	873 sq ft	1037 sq ft	N/A	3	2-1/2	27' 6"	64' 0"	Piling/Garage on Slab	E

Design Features

■ The quaint front balcony has a glass-paneled entry to the foyer.

■ The great room has French doors to the outside and a fireplace framed by built-in cabinetry.

■ The formal dining room opens to a private area of the covered porch.

■ Double French doors fill the upper-level master suite with sunlight and open to a sundeck.

■ The study has a walk-in closet and views to the side property.

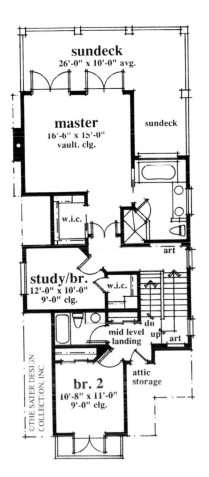

Second Floor

First Floor

Rear Elevation

Tirano — UDHDS01-6509 — 1-866-525-9374

© The Sater Design Collection, Inc.

Total Living	First Floor	Bonus	Bed	Bath	Width	Depth	Foundation	Price Category
1919 sq ft	1919 sq ft	N/A	3 + Study	2	47' 2"	75' 0"	Slab	F

Design Features

- The turreted, covered entry adds elegance to the façade.
- The interior flows around a large central great room.
- The dining room and great room have convenient access to the solana.
- The U-shaped kitchen has a work island.
- An expansive solana gives ample room to an outdoor grille and fireplace.

First Floor

©THE SATER DESIGN COLLECTION, INC.

Rear Elevation

Not available for construction in Myrtle Beach, South Carolina.

Whitley — UDHDG01-863 — 1-866-525-9374

Total Living	First Floor	Second Floor	Bonus	Bed	Bath	Width	Depth	Foundation	Price Category
1921 sq ft	1408 sq ft	513 sq ft	444 sq ft	3	2-1/2	40' 4"	55' 2"	Crawl Space*	D

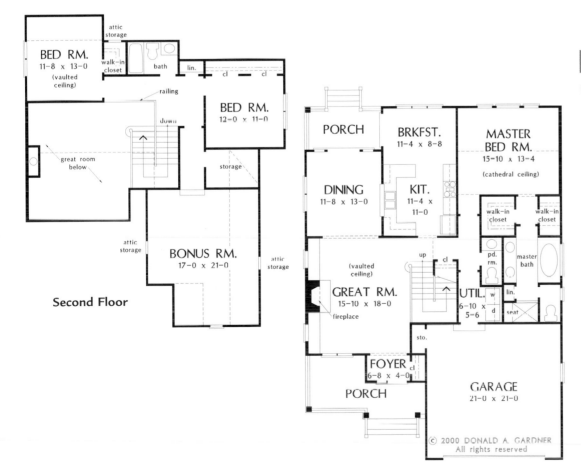

Second Floor

First Floor

Design Features

- Double gables, a cozy front porch, and arched windows create charm.

- A vaulted ceiling expands the great room, overlooked by the second-floor hallway.

- Built-in cabinets topped by small windows flank the fireplace in the great room.

- Two bedrooms with ample closet space are located on the second floor.

Rear Elevation

Bentridge — UDHFB01-3666 — 1-866-525-9374

© 2002 Frank Betz Associates, Inc.

Total Living	First Floor	Second Floor	Bonus	Bed	Bath	Width	Depth	Foundation	Price Category
1928 sq ft	947 sq ft	981 sq ft	N/A	4	2-1/2	41' 0"	39' 4"	Basement, Crawl Space or Slab	G

Design Features

- Simply elegant outside and in, the *Bentridge* is well planned and functional.

- The main floor is dedicated solely to living space, while four bedrooms share the upper level.

- Ornamental columns and knee walls offset the family room, separating it from the breakfast area, yet allowing for easy transition from one spot to the next.

- A handy serving bar provides additional seating or serving space in the kitchen.

- If four bedrooms are not necessary, an alternate design is included with a master sitting room option.

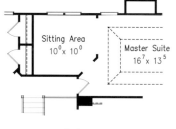

Opt. Sitting Room

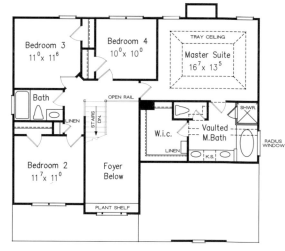

Second Floor

First Floor

Rear Elevation

Edelweiss — UDHDG01-1013 — 1-866-525-9374

Total Living	First Floor	Bonus	Bed	Bath	Width	Depth	Foundation	Price Category
1929 sq ft	1929 sq ft	335 sq ft	3	2	54' 8"	68' 4"	Crawl Space	D

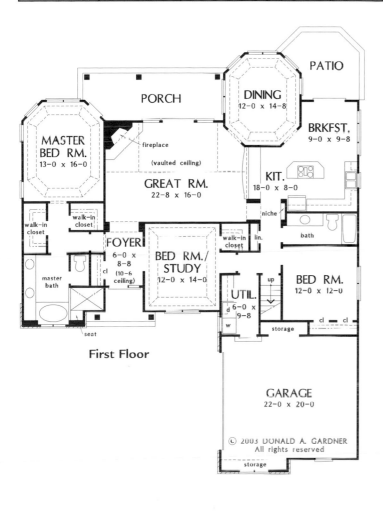

First Floor

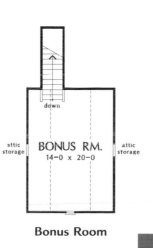

Bonus Room

Design Features

- Stone, siding and a hipped roof create cottage charm.
- Arches contrast with gables to provide architectural interest, and custom transoms usher in natural light.
- A vaulted ceiling tops the great room, which includes French doors and a corner fireplace.
- A cooktop island keeps the kitchen open, and a private patio is adjacent to the breakfast nook.
- Expanded by a bay, the master suite is positioned for privacy.

Rear Elevation

Wilshire — UDHDG01-976 — 1-866-525-9374

© 2002 Donald A. Gardner, Inc.

Total Living	First Floor	Opt. Bonus	Bed	Bath	Width	Depth	Foundation	Price Category
1904 sq ft	1904 sq ft	366 sq ft	3	2	53' 10"	57' 8"	Crawl Space*	D

Design Features

- Blending stone with siding, this cottage has many wonderful architectural features.
- Lush amenities include built-in cabinetry, tray ceilings and a cooktop island.
- A pass-thru connects the great room and kitchen, and adds convenience.
- The master suite includes dual walk-in closets, private toilet, garden tub and separate shower.

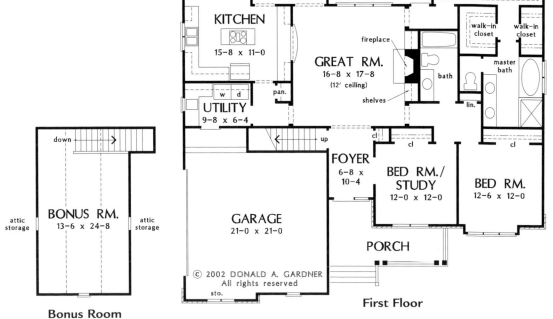

First Floor

Bonus Room

Rear Elevation

*Other options available. See page 513.

© 2002 Frank Betz Associates, Inc.

Guilford — UDHFB01-3689 — 1-866-525-9374

Total Living	First Floor	Opt. Second Floor	Bed	Bath	Width	Depth	Foundation	Price Category
1933 sq ft	1933 sq ft	519 sq ft	4	3-1/2	62' 0"	50' 0"	Basement or Crawl Space	G

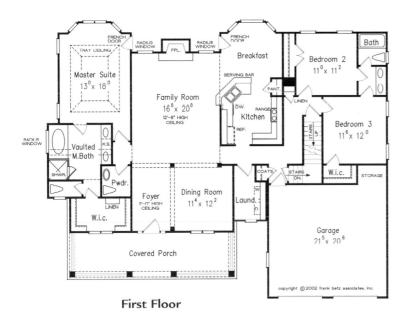

First Floor

Opt. Second Floor

Design Features

- Quaint...Timeless...Classic... all of these so accurately describe the charm that the *Guilford* exudes.
- Inside, the master suite features a wall of windows with views to the backyard. Two additional bedrooms share a divided bath.
- Decorative columns surround the dining room, enhancing the space without impeding it.
- An optional second floor adds 519 square feet to this design, adding an additional bed, bath and bonus area that can have flexible use.

Rear Elevation

Harmony Point — UDHDG01-1080 — 1-866-525-9374

© 2004 Donald A. Gardner, Inc.

Total Living	First Floor	Bonus	Bed	Bath	Width	Depth	Foundation	Price Category
1939 sq ft	1939 sq ft	876 sq ft	3	2	56' 6"	62' 0"	Crawl Space*	D

Design Features

- Metal roofs accentuate the front porch and box bay, while a screened porch creates an outdoor oasis.
- Displaying more traditional room definition, the great room is separated from the other gathering areas.
- The octagonal dining room is almost completely surrounded by windows and crowned with a tray ceiling.
- A cathedral ceiling highlights the great room, while a bonus room allows expansion.

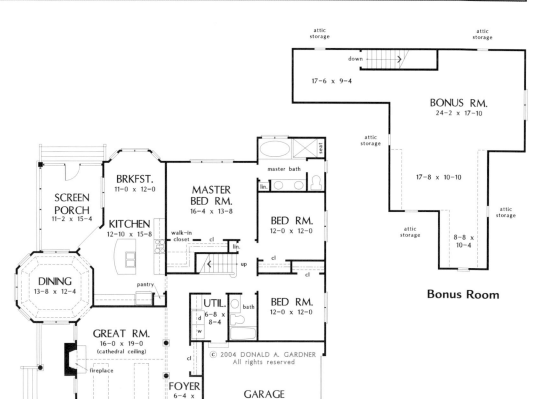

Bonus Room

First Floor

Rear Elevation

*Other options available. See page 513.

© 2005 Frank Betz Associates, Inc.

Bagwell Place — UDHFB01-3930 — 1-866-525-9374

Total Living	First Floor	Opt. Second Floor	Bed	Bath	Width	Depth	Foundation	Price Category
1949 sq ft	1949 sq ft	398 sq ft	3	3-1/2	56' 0"	65' 0"	Basement, Crawl Space or Slab	G

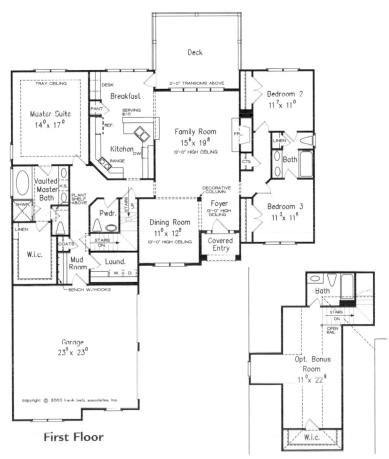

First Floor

Opt. Second Floor

Design Features

- This courtyard entry, traditional brick plan fits into any neighborhood.

- The master bedroom encompasses one side of the home.

- There are two additional bedrooms on the main level, with an optional bonus room on the second floor.

- The family room offers a rear wall of windows to allow in natural light.

Rear Elevation

Applemoor — UDHDG01-970 — 1-866-525-9374

© 2002 Donald A. Gardner, Inc.

Total Living	First Floor	Bonus	Bed	Bath	Width	Depth	Foundation	Price Category
1952 sq ft	1952 sq ft	339 sq ft	4	3	50' 0"	60' 0"	Crawl Space*	D

Design Features

- At home in a development or on an open plain, this design combines country charm with Craftsman appeal.

- A Palladian-style window fills the bedroom/study with light.

- An angled counter separates the kitchen from the great room and breakfast nook.

- With two full additional baths and bonus room, this home has plenty of space for growing families.

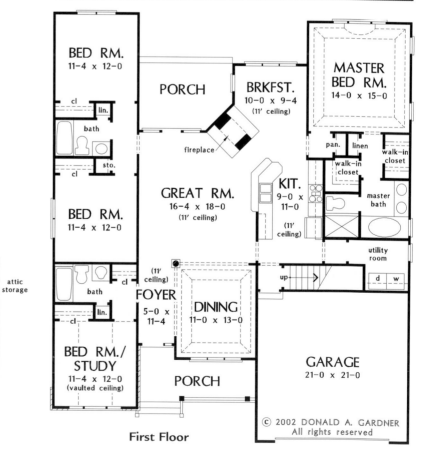

Bonus Room

BONUS RM.
13-4 x 21-0

attic storage — down — attic storage

First Floor

BED RM.
11-4 x 12-0

cl / lin. / bath / sto. / cl

PORCH

BRKFST.
10-0 x 9-4
(11' ceiling)

fireplace

MASTER BED RM.
14-0 x 15-0

pan. / linen / walk-in closet / walk-in closet / master bath

BED RM.
11-4 x 12-0

GREAT RM.
16-4 x 18-0
(11' ceiling)

KIT.
9-0 x 11-0
(11' ceiling)

utility room

bath / cl / lin.

(11' ceiling)

FOYER
5-0 x 11-4

DINING
11-0 x 13-0

up

d / w

BED RM./STUDY
11-4 x 12-0
(vaulted ceiling)

PORCH

GARAGE
21-0 x 21-0

Rear Elevation

*Other options available. See page 513.

Gillespie — UDHDG01-992 — 1-866-525-9374

Total Living	First Floor	Bonus	Bed	Bath	Width	Depth	Foundation	Price Category
1955 sq ft	1955 sq ft	329 sq ft	3	2	56' 0"	58' 4"	Crawl Space*	D

First Floor

Bonus Room

Design Features

- A metal roof tops the box-bay window, and the front porch captures timelessness with columns and arches.
- Decorative windows and shutters complement high gables.
- Two columns and a tray ceiling distinguish the dining room, while a fireplace enhances the great room.
- A barrel-vault arch in the master bedroom's tray ceiling crowns a Palladian window.
- Two additional bedrooms and a bonus room meet the needs of a growing family.

Rear Elevation

Unison Creek — UDHDG01-1055 — 1-866-525-9374

© 2004 Donald A. Gardner, Inc.

Total Living	First Floor	Bonus	Bed	Bath	Width	Depth	Foundation	Price Category
1956 sq ft	1956 sq ft	358 sq ft	3	2	57' 0"	66' 8"	Crawl Space*	D

Design Features

- A stone base, columns and gables create an abundance of curb appeal.
- Siding provides a low-maintenance exterior, so less time will be spent on upkeep.
- A courtyard entrance to the garage helps the house make the most of smaller lots.
- Inside, the gathering rooms are open to each other, providing a natural traffic flow in a circular pattern.

Rear Elevation

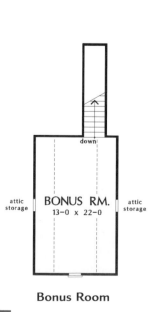

Bonus Room

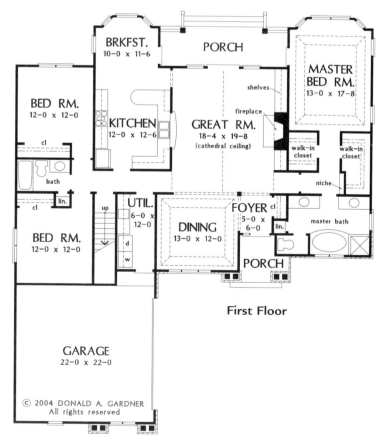

First Floor

*Other options available. See page 513.

© 2002 Frank Betz Associates, Inc.

Stonechase — UDHFB01-3662 — 1-866-525-9374

Total Living	First Floor	Second Floor	Opt. Bonus	Bed	Bath	Width	Depth	Foundation	Price Category
1974 sq ft	1458 sq ft	516 sq ft	168 sq ft	3	2-1/2	50' 0"	46' 0"	Basement or Crawl Space	G

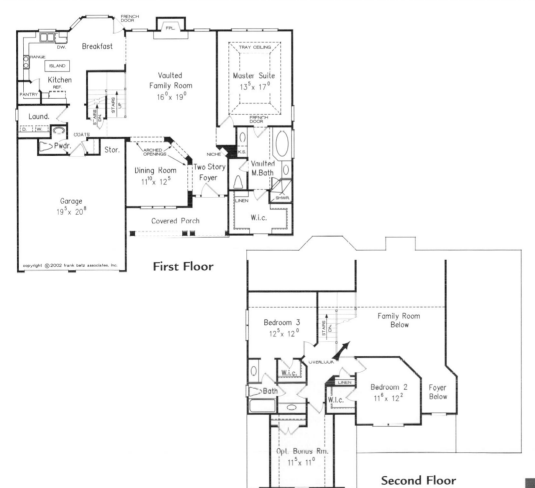

First Floor

Second Floor

Design Features

- Stone accents, carriage doors and board-and-batten shutters come together to create the cottage-like appeal that is so desirable today. The creativity continues inside, where an art niche is positioned as a focal point in the foyer.

- The master suite is secluded from secondary bedrooms, encompassing an entire wing of the main level.

- A powder room and coat closet are strategically placed near the garage entrance, keeping shoes and coats in their place.

- The secondary bedrooms have an overlook to the vaulted family room.

Rear Elevation

Fieldstone — UDHDG01-1047 — 1-866-525-9374

© 2004 Donald A. Gardner, Inc.

Total Living	First Floor	Bonus	Bed	Bath	Width	Depth	Foundation	Price Category
1975 sq ft	1975 sq ft	361 sq ft	4	3	62' 0"	57' 8"	Crawl Space*	D

Design Features

- A front porch and rear deck merge indoor/outdoor living, which enhances the ambience fashioned by the exterior.

- A front-entry garage helps this home make the most of its lot.

- Columns and ceiling treatments define rooms without enclosing space, adding to the open, airy floor plan.

- A bay window expands the breakfast nook, while a pass-thru connects the kitchen to the great room.

Rear Elevation

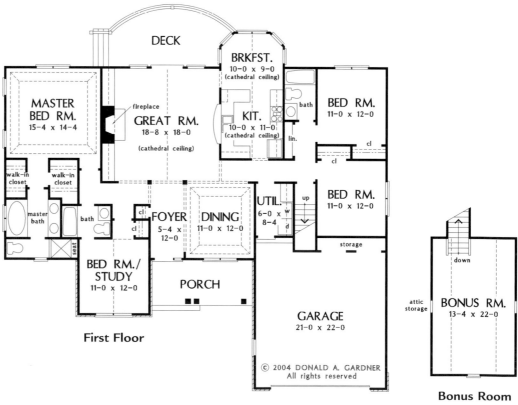

First Floor

Bonus Room

© 2004 DONALD A. GARDNER
All rights reserved

*Other options available. See page 513.

© 2005 Frank Betz Associates, Inc.

Stoneleigh Cottage — UDHFB01-3919 — 1-866-525-9374

Total Living	First Floor	Second Floor	Opt. Bonus	Bed	Bath	Width	Depth	Foundation	Price Category
1975 sq ft	1448 sq ft	527 sq ft	368 sq ft	3	2-1/2	46' 0"	62' 0"	Basement or Crawl Space	G

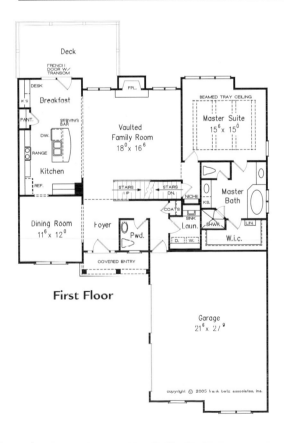

First Floor

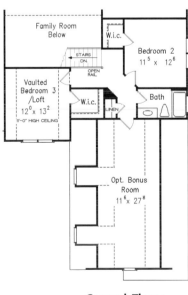

Second Floor

Design Features

- Especially designed for small and corner lots the *Stoneleigh Cottage* offers amenities usually reserved for much larger homes.

- The open floor plan allows for easy flow between rooms.

- Upstairs, there are two additional bedrooms, both with walk-in closets and an optional bonus room.

- The master suite encompasses one wing of the home. This suite has a back wall of windows allowing in both natural light and rear views.

Rear Elevation

Willow Creek — UDHFB01-3539 — 1-866-525-9374

© 2000 Frank Betz Associates, Inc.

Total Living	First Floor	Second Floor	Opt. Bonus	Bed	Bath	Width	Depth	Foundation	Price Category
1975 sq ft	1399 sq ft	576 sq ft	221 sq ft	3	2-1/2	52' 4"	46' 10"	Basement, Crawl Space or Slab	H

Design Features

- From the *Southern Living® Design Collection*

- The *Willow Creek's* inviting exterior combines an attractive combination of stone and siding, graced by a columned front porch.

- The kitchen is conveniently linked to a large laundry room, which is a must-have for growing families.

- The master bath contains all the luxuries including double vanities, a garden tub, separate shower and walk-in closet.

First Floor

Second Floor

Rear Elevation

Ingraham — UDHDG01-332 — 1-866-525-9374

Total Living	First Floor	Bonus	Bed	Bath	Width	Depth	Foundation	Price Category
1977 sq ft	1977 sq ft	430 sq ft	3	2	69' 8"	59' 6"	Crawl Space*	D

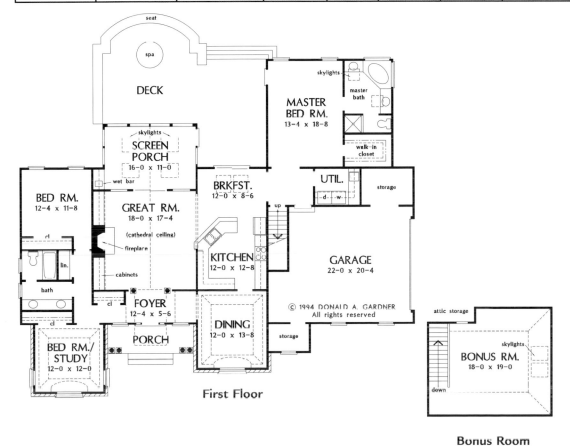

First Floor

Bonus Room

Design Features

- With an elegant exterior, this executive home makes both everyday life and entertaining a breeze.

- A Palladian window floods the foyer with light for a dramatic entrance.

- The screened porch, breakfast area and master suite access the deck with optional spa.

- The large master suite, located in the rear for privacy, features a luxurious skylit bath with separate shower.

Rear Elevation

*Other options available. See page 513.

Buckhurst Lodge — UDHDS01-6807 — 1-866-525-9374

© The Sater Design Collection, Inc.

Total Living	First Floor	Second Floor	Bonus	Bed	Bath	Width	Depth	Foundation	Price Category
1978 sq ft	1383 sq ft	595 sq ft	N/A	3	2	48' 0"	42' 0"	Unfinished Walkout Basement	E

Design Features

- Asymmetrical gables, decorative shutters, multiple decks and covered porches combine with a bold mix of textures to create a refined rustic feel.

- The open floor plan encourages flow between the great room, kitchen, dining room and covered porch.

- Built-ins, a fireplace, and extensive views through a wall of windows add to the appeal of the great room.

- Wrapping counters, an angled double sink and ample storage enhance the kitchen.

Rear Elevation

Second Floor

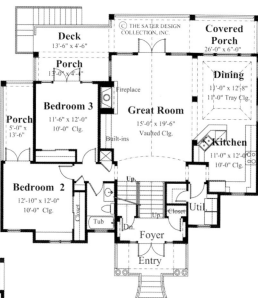

First Floor

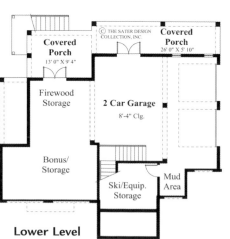

Lower Level

© The Sater Design Collection, Inc.

Santa Rosa — UDHDS01-6808 — 1-866-525-9374

Total Living	First Floor	Second Floor	Bonus	Bed	Bath	Width	Depth	Foundation	Price Category
1978 sq ft	1383 sq ft	595 sq ft	N/A	3	2	48' 0"	42' 0"	Island Basement	F

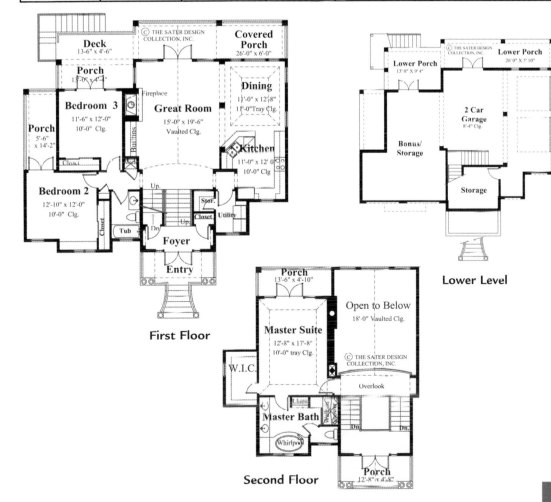

First Floor

Second Floor

Lower Level

Design Features

- The great room is bright with soaring ceilings and a fireplace.

- A chef-friendly kitchen features an angled island.

- Two generous bedrooms enjoy private porches.

- The upper level features a dramatic master suite.

Rear Elevation

Williamston — UDHDG01-391 — 1-866-525-9374

Total Living	First Floor	Second Floor	Bonus	Bed	Bath	Width	Depth	Foundation	Price Category
1991 sq ft	1480 sq ft	511 sq ft	363 sq ft	3	2-1/2	73' 0"	45' 0"	Crawl Space*	D

Design Features

- The kitchen features an angled island peninsula for effortless entertaining.

- Bay windows accent the formal dining room and breakfast bay.

- The secluded master suite accesses the deck and includes a private bath.

- Upstairs, two bedrooms with dormers share a bath from a balcony that overlooks the great room.

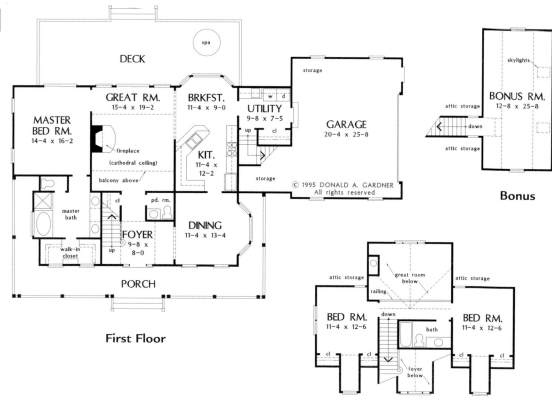

First Floor

Bonus

Second Floor

Rear Elevation

*Other options available. See page 513.

Delaney — UDHFB01-3744 — 1-866-525-9374

Total Living	First Floor	Opt. Second Floor	Bed	Bath	Width	Depth	Foundation	Price Category
1996 sq ft	1996 sq ft	258 sq ft	4	4	60' 0"	47' 6"	Basement or Crawl Space	G

First Floor

Opt. Second Floor

Design Features

- The eye-catching exterior of the *Delaney* draws attention to three graceful arches across the front of the home.
- Traffic flows easily from the kitchen area into the great room, creating functional space for entertaining.
- The study easily converts into a fourth bedroom for larger families or overnight guests.
- The optional second floor gives the homeowners the ability to create a larger home by finishing the bonus room, bath and closet.

Rear Elevation

Hampton Wick — UDHDG01-1077 — 1-866-525-9374

© 2004 Donald A. Gardner, Inc.

Total Living	First Floor	Bonus	Bed	Bath	Width	Depth	Foundation	Price Category
2019 sq ft	2019 sq ft	277 sq ft	3	2	57' 0"	65' 8"	Crawl Space*	E

Design Features

- Stone and siding join a hipped roof and gables to give this home a European ambiance.

- A single dormer highlights the courtyard-entry garage that features columns, an arch and circle-head transom.

- Double-doors lead from the foyer into the bedroom/study, with a second entrance near the bonus-room stairs.

- Built-in cabinetry flanks the fireplace, while columns and a tray ceiling define the dining room.

Rear Elevation

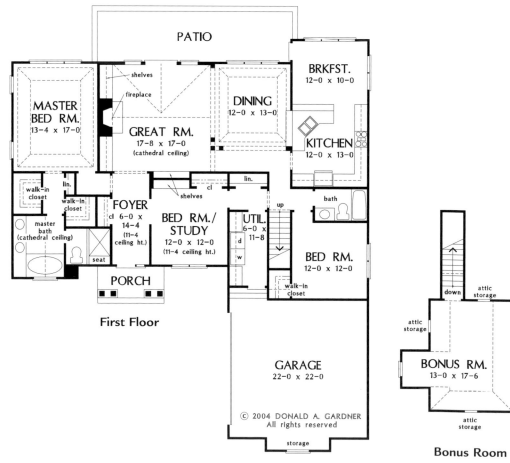

First Floor

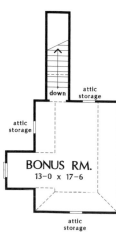

Bonus Room

*Other options available. See page 513.

Donald A. Gardner Architects, Inc.

Hanover — UDHDG01-489 — 1-866-525-9374

Total Living	First Floor	Second Floor	Bonus	Bed	Bath	Width	Depth	Foundation	Price Category
2023 sq ft	1489 sq ft	534 sq ft	393 sq ft	3	2-1/2	59' 4"	58' 7"	Crawl Space*	E

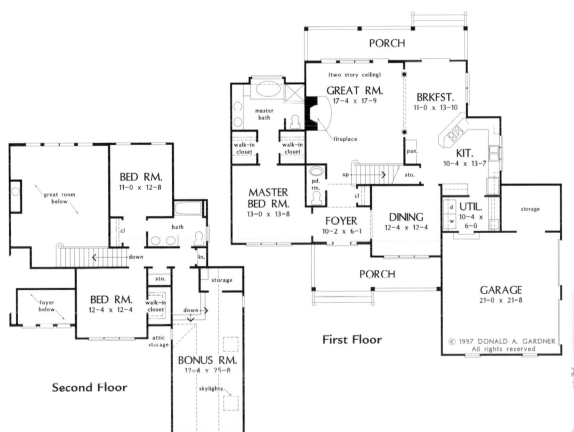

First Floor

Second Floor

Design Features

- A smart exterior and open interior space combine to create this roomy, yet practical, home.
- The two-story foyer leads to a two-story great room and back-porch access.
- Columns divide the great room from breakfast room.
- A handy utility room leads to a two-car garage with ample storage space.
- A split-bedroom plan places the master suite down and additional bedrooms upstairs.

Rear Elevation

McArthur Park — UDHFB01-3837 — 1-866-525-9374

© 2003 Frank Betz Associates, Inc.

Total Living	First Floor	Second Floor	Opt. Bonus	Bed	Bath	Width	Depth	Foundation	Price Category
2024 sq ft	1480 sq ft	544 sq ft	253 sq ft	3	2-1/2	52' 0"	46' 4"	Basement, Crawl Space or Slab	G

Design Features

- It has been said that beauty is often found in simplicity -- and the *McArthur Park* brings truth to that statement. Its understated exterior and uncomplicated roofline make this home both appealing and cost-effective to build.

- The kitchen, breakfast area and keeping room share common space, making an ideal space for entertaining.

- An optional bonus room is available on the upper floor that has endless possibilities. It can be easily finished as a fourth bedroom, playroom, exercise area or craft room.

First Floor

Rear Elevation

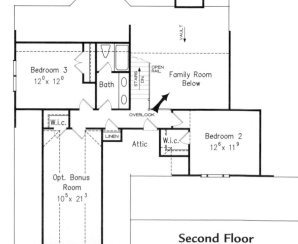

Second Floor

Prynwood — UDHDG01-818 — 1-866-525-9374

Total Living	First Floor	Second Floor	Bonus	Bed	Bath	Width	Depth	Foundation	Price Category
2037 sq ft	1502 sq ft	535 sq ft	275 sq ft	3	2-1/2	43' 0"	57' 6"	Crawl Space*	E

Design Features

- A stunning center dormer with Palladian-style window complements this home's façade.

- A pass-thru from the kitchen to the vaulted great room makes entertaining easy.

- The first-floor master suite enjoys a tray ceiling, back-porch access and a private bath.

- Two upstairs bedrooms are divided by a balcony that overlooks both the foyer and the great room.

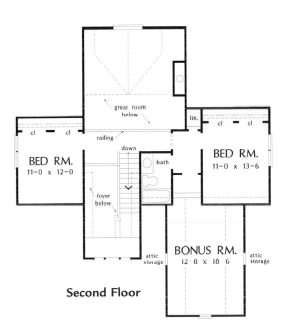

Second Floor

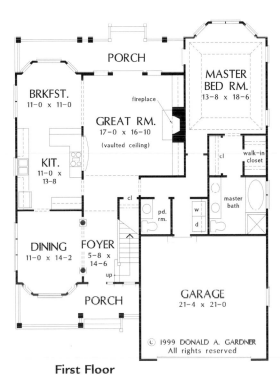

First Floor

Rear Elevation

Gastonia — UDHFB01-3721 — 1-866-525-9374

© 2002 Frank Betz Associates, Inc.

Total Living	First Floor	Second Floor	Opt. Bonus	Bed	Bath	Width	Depth	Foundation	Price Category
2040 sq ft	935 sq ft	1105 sq ft	N/A	4	2-1/2	44' 0"	39' 0"	Basement, Crawl Space or Slab	G

Design Features

- Smaller homes don't have to lack upscale amenities! The *Gastonia* includes many special features often hard to find even in larger homes.

- The master suite has a comfortable sitting room, large enough for lounging furniture. If a fourth bedroom is a higher priority, this space can be easily converted to accommodate it.

- Each secondary bedroom features a walk-in closet.

- An island serves as the center point of the kitchen and helps with meal preparation.

First Floor

Rear Elevation

Second Floor

Donald A. Gardner Architects, Inc.

O'Neale — UDHDG01-1138 — 1-866-525-9374

Total Living	First Floor	Second Floor	Bonus	Bed	Bath	Width	Depth	Foundation	Price Category
2130 sq ft	1653 sq ft	477 sq ft	445 sq ft	4	3	65' 0"	50' 2"	Crawl Space*	E

First Floor

Second Floor

Design Features

- This striking façade incorporates European style and elements in its exterior.

- Built-in cabinetry, French doors and a fireplace enhance the great room.

- The bonus room features convenient second-floor access.

- The master suite and study/bedroom are tucked away for privacy.

Rear Elevation

Cottonwood — UDHDG01-523 — 1-866-525-9374

Total Living	First Floor	Second Floor	Bonus	Bed	Bath	Width	Depth	Foundation	Price Category
2048 sq ft	1471 sq ft	577 sq ft	368 sq ft	3	2-1/2	75' 5"	52' 0"	Crawl Space*	E

Design Features

- Surrounded by porches, this farmhouse boasts front and back clerestory dormers for natural light.
- The unconventional rear staircase is located in the great room for convenience.
- The master suite is privately situated downstairs and features a magnificent bath.
- Both second-story bedrooms boast dormer alcoves and walk-in closets.

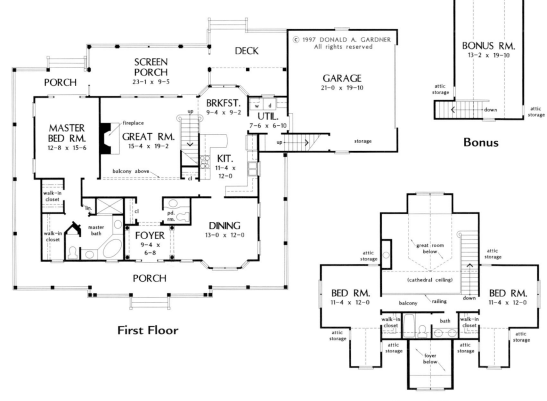

First Floor

Second Floor

Bonus

Rear Elevation

*Other options available. See page 513.

© 2002 Frank Betz Associates, Inc.

Ferdinand — UDHFB01-3727 — 1-866-525-9374

Total Living	First Floor	Opt. Second Floor	Bed	Bath	Width	Depth	Foundation	Price Category
2054 sq ft	2054 sq ft	304 sq ft	4	4	60' 0"	54' 6"	Basement or Crawl Space	G

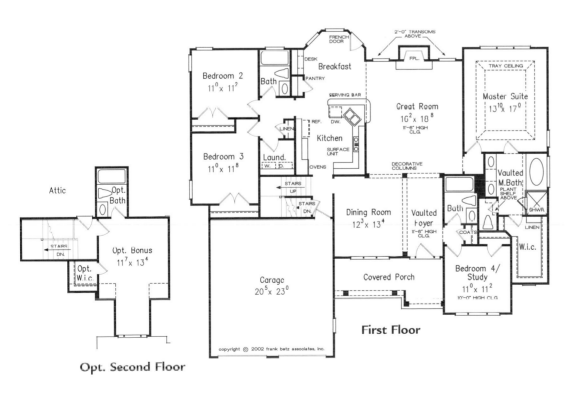

Attic

Opt. Second Floor

First Floor

Design Features

- The extra details — like those in the *Ferdinand* — make all the difference when it comes to convenience for day-to-day living.
- A handy coat closet is tucked away just off the foyer, keeping jackets and shoes in their place.
- A desk is designed into the breakfast area so mail, calendars and schoolwork have their place.
- Transom windows in the family room allow natural light into the space, keeping it bright and airy.
- The fourth bedroom can be converted into a study or home office.

Rear Elevation

Fernley — UDHDG01-980 — 1-866-525-9374

Total Living	First Floor	Bonus	Bed	Bath	Width	Depth	Foundation	Price Category
2037 sq ft	2037 sq ft	361 sq ft	3	2-1/2	62' 4"	61' 8"	Crawl Space	E

Design Features

- This traditional starts with impressive columns that frame two large windows on the front porch.
- Arched transoms top the entryway and windows in the gables, ushering in natural light.
- While generating curb appeal, a box-bay window adds storage space in the garage.
- Inside, an open floor plan creates a natural traffic flow and visual space.

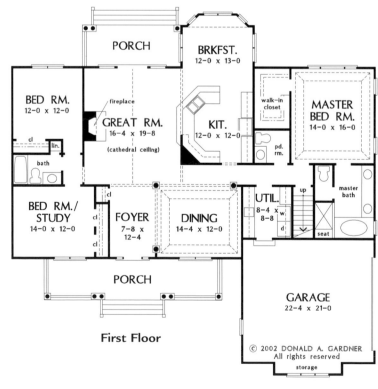

First Floor

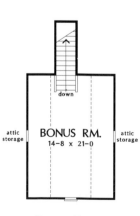

Bonus Room

Rear Elevation

© 1998 Donald A. Gardner, Inc.

Orchard Park — UDHDG01-703 — 1-866-525-9374

Total Living	First Floor	Bonus	Bed	Bath	Width	Depth	Foundation	Price Category
2042 sq ft	2042 sq ft	475 sq ft	3	2-1/2	75' 11"	56' 7"	Crawl Space*	E

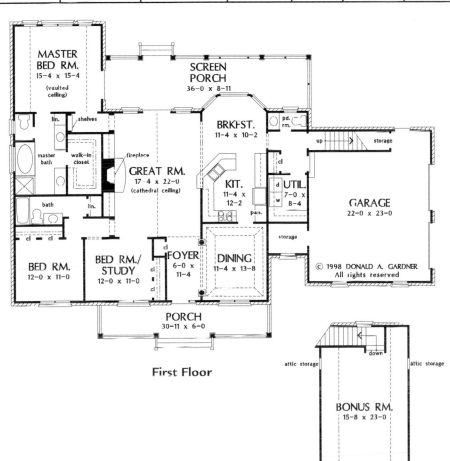

First Floor

Design Features

- Built-ins flank the fireplace in the great room, while a soaring cathedral ceiling expands the room visually.

- More built-in shelves just outside the master suite provide room for books and curios.

- The vaulted master bedroom adjoins a private bath with over-sized walk-in closet.

- The front bedroom and bedroom/study share a roomy hall bath with large linen closet.

Rear Elevation

Bonus Room

Woodsfield — UDHDG01-341 — 1-866-525-9374

Total Living	First Floor	Bonus	Bed	Bath	Width	Depth	Foundation	Price Category
1954 sq ft	1954 sq ft	436 sq ft	3	2-1/2	71' 11"	57' 3"	Crawl Space*	D

Design Features

- This plan offers the best of both worlds for those torn between traditional and country styles.

- Stairs to the skylit bonus room are conveniently located near the kitchen and master suite.

- Growing families will appreciate the extra half bath.

- Cathedral ceilings add volume to the master suite, which is located in the rear for privacy.

- The well-appointed skylit master bath features a whirlpool tub, separate shower and dual vanities.

Rear Elevation

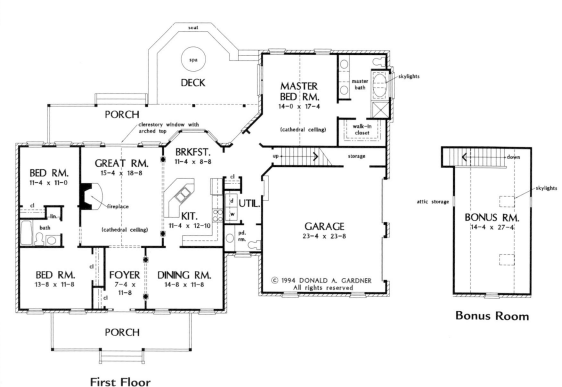

First Floor

Bonus Room

*Other options available. See page 513.

© 2003 Frank Betz Associates, Inc.

Palmdale — UDHFB01-3776 — 1-866-525-9374

Total Living	First Floor	Opt. Second Floor	Bed	Bath	Width	Depth	Foundation	Price Category
2073 sq ft	2073 sq ft	350 sq ft	4	3-1/2	59' 0"	57' 0"	Basement or Crawl Space	G

Opt. Second Floor

First Floor

Design Features

■ Special details and added extras give the *Palmdale* an edge over its one-level competitors.

■ Step inside to find exceptional floor planning and details. A unique niche is incorporated into the foyer, providing the ideal location for that special furniture piece or artwork.

■ Transom windows allow extra light to pour into the family room.

■ A generously sized optional bonus area provides an additional bedroom, a home office or exercise room.

Rear Elevation

Radcliffe — UDHDG01-799 — 1-866-525-9374

Total Living	First Floor	Second Floor	Bonus	Bed	Bath	Width	Depth	Foundation	Price Category
2075 sq ft	1588 sq ft	487 sq ft	363 sq ft	3	2-1/2	60' 1"	50' 11"	Crawl Space*	E

Design Features

- With its hip roof, gables and brick and siding exterior, this home possesses traditional elegance.

- The generous great room with cathedral ceiling and fireplace is centrally located.

- A patio extends living space beyond the great room.

- A cozy back porch expands the breakfast area.

- Two secondary bedrooms and a bonus room share a full bath upstairs.

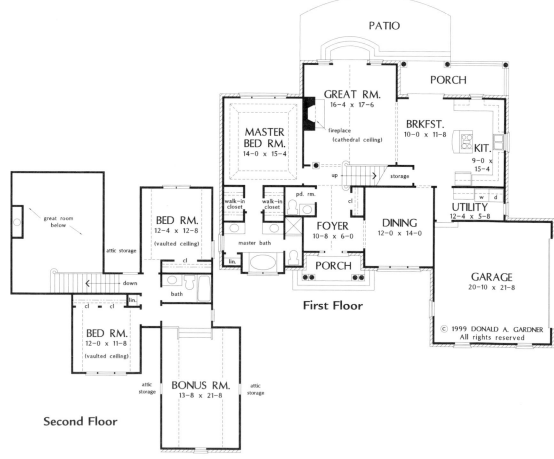

First Floor

Second Floor

Rear Elevation

*Other options available. See page 513.

Northwyke — UDHDG01-759 — 1-866-525-9374

Total Living	First Floor	Bonus	Bed	Bath	Width	Depth	Foundation	Price Category
2078 sq ft	2078 sq ft	339 sq ft	3	2-1/2	62' 2"	47' 8"	Crawl Space*	E

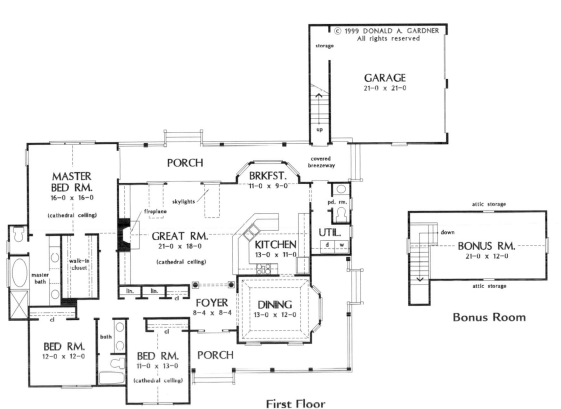

First Floor

Bonus Room

Design Features

- An L-shaped front porch lends charm and grace to this country home with dual dormers and gables.

- The generous great room features a fireplace with built-ins, skylights and access to a back porch.

- A cathedral ceiling enhances the master bedroom, which enjoys a large walk-in closet and luxurious bath.

- Two more bedrooms, one with a cathedral ceiling, share a generous hall bath with dual vanities.

Rear Elevation

*Other options available. See page 513.

Madaridge — UDHDG01-974 — 1-866-525-9374

© 2002 Donald A. Gardner, Inc.

Total Living	First Floor	Second Floor	Bonus	Bed	Bath	Width	Depth	Foundation	Price Category
2111 sq ft	1496 sq ft	615 sq ft	277 sq ft	3	2-1/2	40' 4"	70' 0"	Crawl Space*	E

Design Features

- Craftsman materials on this Traditional design create incredible curb appeal.

- The front-entry garage is ideal for narrow lots.

- The open floor plan features a first-floor master suite and screened porch.

- Upstairs, a loft overlooks the open great room and foyer.

- Note the built-in hutch in the dining room and double vanities in both full baths.

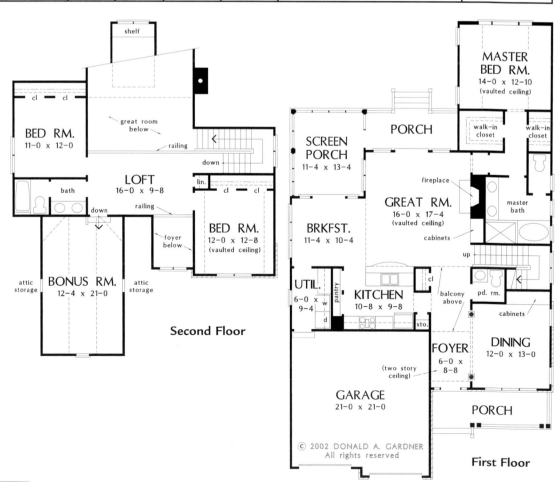

Second Floor

First Floor

Rear Elevation

*Other options available. See page 513.

© The Sater Design Collection, Inc.

Duvall Street — UDHDS01-6701 — 1-866-525-9374

Total Living	First Floor	Second Floor	Bonus	Bed	Bath	Width	Depth	Foundation	Price Category
2123 sq ft	878 sq ft	1245 sq ft	N/A	4	2-1/2	27' 6"	64' 0"	Post/Pier	F

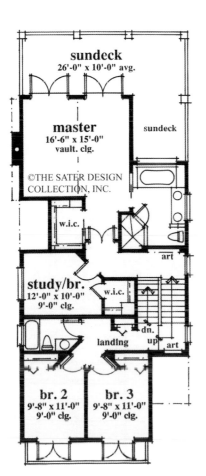

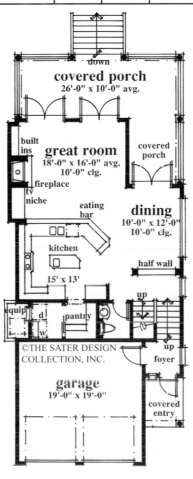

Design Features

- Two sets of French doors open the great room to the porch.

- A gourmet kitchen boasts a prep sink and eating bar.

- The mid-level landing leads to two bedrooms and a bath.

- French doors open the master suite to a sundeck.

- The master bath has a windowed soaking tub.

Rear Elevation

Second Floor

First Floor

Brookhaven — UDHFB01-963 — 1-866-525-9374

© 1996 Frank Betz Associates, Inc.

Total Living	First Floor	Second Floor	Opt. Bonus	Bed	Bath	Width	Depth	Foundation	Price Category
2126 sq ft	1583 sq ft	543 sq ft	251 sq ft	4	3	53' 0"	47' 0"	Basement, Crawl Space or Slab	H

Design Features

- The ageless combination of a covered front porch, brick and classic siding gives the *Brookhaven* curb appeal that is familiar and friendly.

- Careful planning inside is evident with highly functional spaces and growth areas.

- A bedroom on the main level has direct access to a bathing area, making this space an ideal guest room or home office.

- The upstairs bedrooms feature walk-in closets and share a bath with separate private sink areas.

First Floor

Second Floor

Rear Elevation

© 1999 Frank Betz Associates, Inc.

Holly Hill — UDHFB01-1237 — 1-866-525-9374

Total Living	First Floor	Second Floor	Opt. Bonus	Bed	Bath	Width	Depth	Foundation	Price Category
2126 sq ft	1583 sq ft	543 sq ft	251 sq ft	4	3	53' 0"	47' 0"	Basement, Crawl Space or Slab	I

Design Features

- From the *Southern Living®*
  Design Collection

- The *Holly Hill* is an attentive and
  articulate design that has quickly
  become a favorite.

- Set just off the entry is a formal dining
  room set apart by decorative columns.

- Thoughtful planning has made the
  dining room easily accessible from
  the kitchen, ideal for entertaining.

- The kitchen offers ample cabinet space
  and a serving bar for extra seating.

First Floor

Second Floor

Rear Elevation

1800 sq ft—2200 sq ft

Donald A. Gardner Architects, Inc.

Irwin — UDHDG01-297 — 1-866-525-9374

© 1993 Donald A. Gardner Architects, Inc.

Total Living	First Floor	Second Floor	Bonus	Bed	Bath	Width	Depth	Foundation	Price Category
2130 sq ft	1694 sq ft	436 sq ft	345 sq ft	4	3	54' 0"	53' 8"	Crawl Space*	E

Design Features

- A hip roof, brick and arched windows lend an air of refinement to this home.
- The foyer opens to a great room with sloped ceiling and clerestory window.
- Cathedral ceilings and arched windows bathe the dining and breakfast rooms in natural light.
- The private master suite has a cathedral ceiling and sumptuous bath.
- Two more bedrooms and a bonus room upstairs share a third bath.

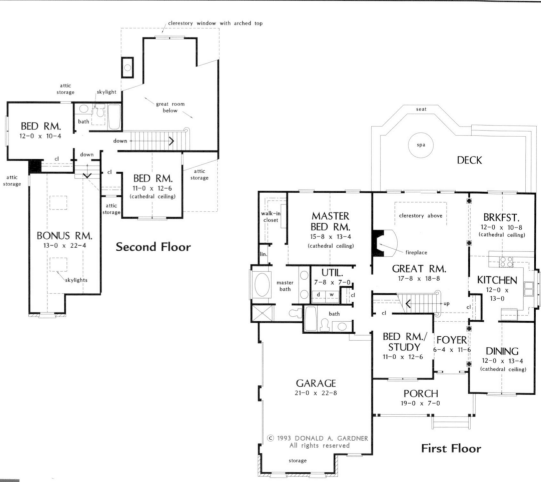

Rear Elevation

© The Sater Design Collection, Inc.

Via Pascoli — UDHDS01-6842 — 1-866-525-9374

Total Living	First Floor	Lower Level	Bonus	Bed	Bath	Width	Depth	Foundation	Price Category
2137 sq ft	2137 sq ft	N/A	N/A	3	2	44' 0"	61' 0"	Island Basement	F

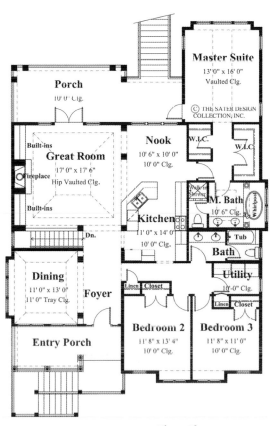

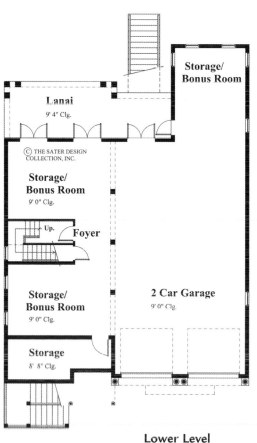

Design Features

- Lovely architecture and brilliant windows adorn this villa.

- A hip vaulted ceiling highlights the great room.

- French doors open the family space to a sheltered porch.

- Lower-level bonus spaces convert to hobby or storage rooms.

- The master suite is secluded and has many views.

First Floor

Lower Level

Rear Elevation

Pasadena — UDHFB01-3756 — 1-866-525-9374

© 2002 Frank Betz Associates, Inc.

Total Living	First Floor	Second Floor	Opt. Bonus	Bed	Bath	Width	Depth	Foundation	Price Category
2139 sq ft	1561 sq ft	578 sq ft	274 sq ft	3	2-1/2	50' 0"	57' 0"	Basement, Crawl Space or Slab	H

Design Features

- Charm and character abound from the façade of the *Pasadena*, with its tapered architectural columns and carriage doors.

- Inside, the master suite is tucked away on the rear of the main level, giving the homeowner a peaceful place to unwind.

- An art niche is situated in the breakfast area, providing the perfect spot for a favorite art piece or floral arrangement.

- The kitchen is complete with a large island, making mealtime easier.

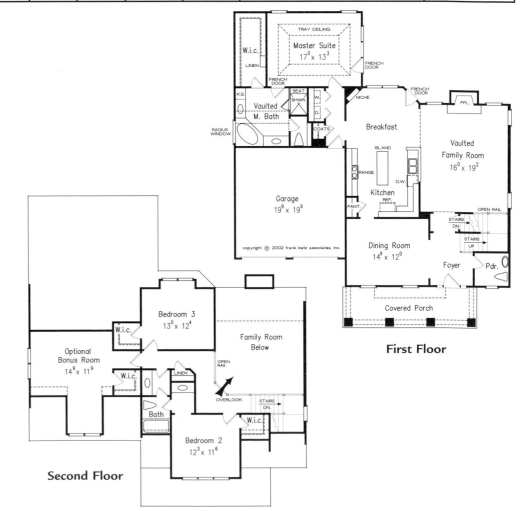

First Floor

Second Floor

Rear Elevation

© 2002 Frank Betz Associates, Inc.

Colonnade — UDHFB01-3699 — 1-866-525-9374

Total Living	First Floor	Second Floor	Opt. Bonus	Bed	Bath	Width	Depth	Foundation	Price Category
2138 sq ft	1589 sq ft	549 sq ft	248 sq ft	4	3	53' 0"	47' 6"	Basement or Crawl Space	H

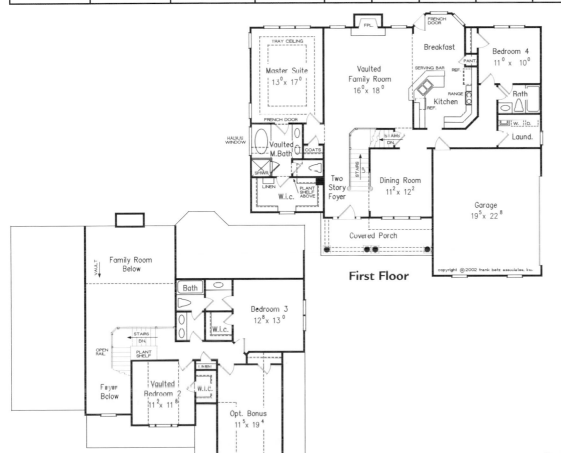

First Floor

Second Floor

Design Features

- Many homeowners today want function with flexibility. The *Colonnade* was created to provide both of these elements.

- The family room, kitchen and breakfast area connect to create the home's center point.

- The size and location of the main-floor bedroom also make it a perfect home office or den.

- Optional bonus space on the upper level of this home gives homeowners the opportunity to add additional living space to their home.

Rear Elevation

Inverness — UDHFB01-1185 — 1-866-525-9374

© 1998 Frank Betz Associates, Inc.

Total Living	First Floor	Second Floor	Opt. Bonus	Bed	Bath	Width	Depth	Foundation	Price Category
2146 sq ft	1142 sq ft	1004 sq ft	156 sq ft	4	3	52' 4"	38' 6"	Basement, Crawl Space or Slab	G

Design Features

- The *Inverness* has an abundance of flexible space that gives the home-owner plenty of options in finalizing the layout of their new home.

- The fourth bedroom can easily convert into a home office.

- Optional bonus space has been carefully designed that would finish into a playroom, craft room or exercise area.

- Still need more space? The living room can easily transform into a study.

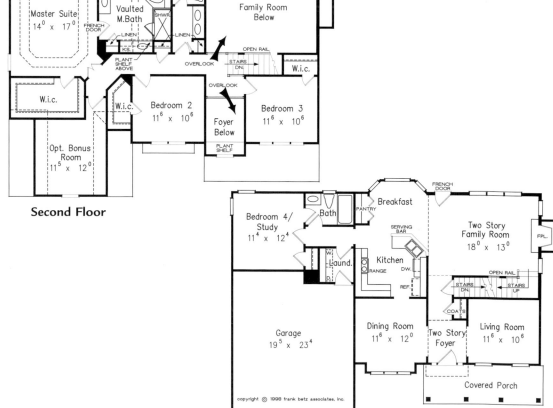

Second Floor

First Floor

Rear Elevation

Serenade — UDHDG01-779 — 1-866-525-9374

Total Living	First Floor	Bonus	Bed	Bath	Width	Depth	Foundation	Price Category
2152 sq ft	2152 sq ft	453 sq ft	3	2-1/2	61' 8"	69' 9"	Crawl Space*	E

Design Features

- Stone, stucco and cedar shakes combine to create an enchanting exterior for this bungalow.
- The spacious kitchen features a useful center island and is open to both breakfast bay and great room.
- The master suite enjoys a bay window, tray ceiling, dual walk-in closets and private bath.
- Two family bedrooms share a hall bath on the opposite side of the home near a versatile bonus room.

First Floor

Bonus Room

Rear Elevation

Huntleigh — UDHFB01-3892 — 1-866-525-9374

© 2004 Frank Betz Associates, Inc.

Total Living	First Floor	Opt. Second Floor	Bed	Bath	Width	Depth	Foundation	Price Category
2158 sq ft	2158 sq ft	366 sq ft	3	3-1/2	69' 6"	59' 0"	Basement, Crawl Space or Slab	H

Design Features

- From the *Southern Living®* *Design Collection*.

- The kitchen, breakfast and family room have subtle borders between them, allowing each space to stream easily into the next — a great feature for entertaining friends and family.

- A deck and screened porch off the back of the home create outdoor living areas that serve as additional dining or recreational spaces to enjoy.

Rear Elevation

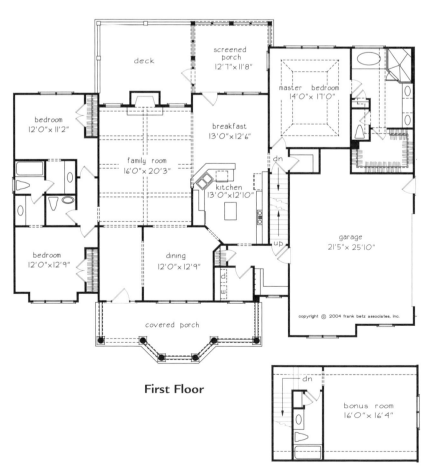

First Floor

Opt. Second Floor

© 1996 Frank Betz Associates, Inc.

Mallory — UDHFB01-992 — 1-866-525-9374

Total Living	First Floor	Second Floor	Opt. Bonus	Bed	Bath	Width	Depth	Foundation	Price Category
2155 sq ft	1628 sq ft	527 sq ft	207 sq ft	3	2-1/2	54' 0"	46' 10"	Basement, Crawl Space or Slab	I

First Floor

Design Features

- Earthy fieldstone and cedar shake accents give the *Mallory* a casual elegance that Old-World style encompasses.

- A vaulted breakfast area and keeping room with fireplace adjoin the kitchen.

- Two secondary bedrooms—each with a walk-in closet—share a divided bathing area on the second floor.

- An optional bonus room is ready to finish into a fourth bedroom, playroom or exercise area.

Second Floor

Rear Elevation

Midland — UDHDG01-371 — 1-866-525-9374

Total Living	First Floor	Second Floor	Bonus	Bed	Bath	Width	Depth	Foundation	Price Category
2164 sq ft	1499 sq ft	665 sq ft	332 sq ft	4	2-1/2	69' 8"	43' 6"	Crawl Space*	E

Design Features

- The great room opens to both the deck and the island kitchen with convenient pantry.

- Nine-foot ceilings on the first level expand volume.

- The master suite welcomes owners with whirlpool tub, dual vanities and deck access.

- The bonus room can be finished at initial construction or at a later time.

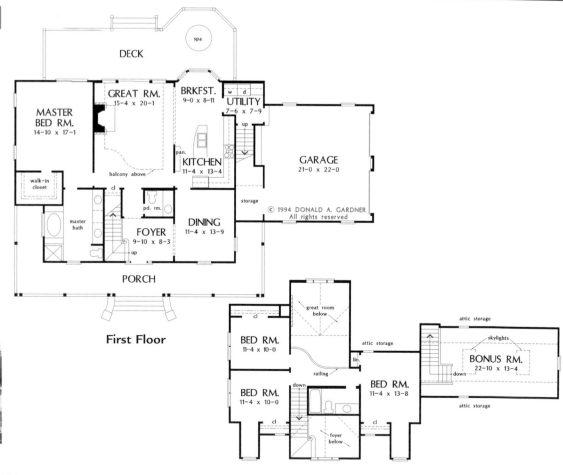

First Floor

Second Floor

Rear Elevation

*Other options available. See page 513.

Wyndham — UDHDG01-793 — 1-866-525-9374

Total Living	First Floor	Second Floor	Bonus	Bed	Bath	Width	Depth	Foundation	Price Category
2163 sq ft	1668 sq ft	495 sq ft	327 sq ft	4	3	52' 7"	50' 11"	Crawl Space*	E

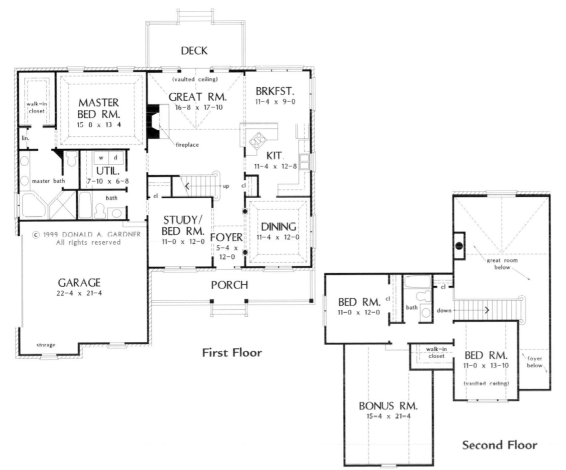

First Floor

Second Floor

Design Features

- A stunning combination of a hip roof and bold, front-facing gables creates curb appeal.

- Tray and vaulted ceilings increase the feeling of spaciousness in key rooms.

- The home's openness and easy flow create a comfortable, casual atmosphere.

- The first-floor study/bedroom is a versatile space with a nearby full bath.

- Upstairs, two bedrooms share a hall bath and access to the large bonus room.

Rear Elevation

Julian — UDHFB01-1262 — 1-866-525-9374

© 1999 Frank Betz Associates, Inc.

Total Living	First Floor	Second Floor	Opt. Bonus	Bed	Bath	Width	Depth	Foundation	Price Category
2167 sq ft	1626 sq ft	541 sq ft	256 sq ft	3	2-1/2	53' 0"	43' 4"	Basement, Crawl Space or Slab	H

Design Features

- Decorative columns separate the kitchen area from the vaulted family room.

- Built-in cabinetry and a fireplace make the family room a comfortable and charming place to spend time with family and friends.

- The master suite has a private sitting area offset from the rest of the room by pedestal columns.

- An optional bonus room is available on the second floor, making space for a playroom, crafting room or exercise area.

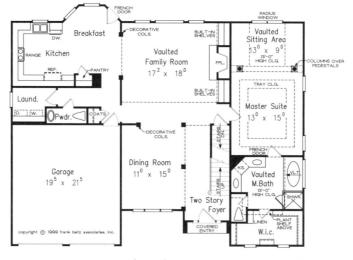

First Floor

Second Floor

Rear Elevation

Xavier — UDHDG01-960 — 1-866-525-9374

Total Living	First Floor	Bonus	Bed	Bath	Width	Depth	Foundation	Price Category
2174 sq ft	2174 sq ft	299 sq ft	4	3	66' 8"	56' 6"	Crawl Space	E

Design Features

- This striking house combines traditional design with Craftsman materials.
- Twin dormers and columns establish a symmetrical frame to the entryway.
- Built-ins, a vaulted ceiling and a fireplace highlight the great room.
- French doors in the master bedroom and great room lead to the rear porch.
- A bedroom/study and bonus room allow for versatility, and the master suite is situated for privacy.

First Floor

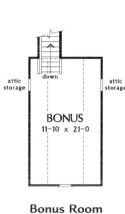

Bonus Room

Rear Elevation

Forsythe — UDHDG01-792 — 1-866-525-9374

Total Living	First Floor	Bonus	Bed	Bath	Width	Depth	Foundation	Price Category
2151 sq ft	2151 sq ft	354 sq ft	4	2-1/2	65' 9"	60' 5"	Crawl Space*	E

Design Features

- Stunning cathedral ceilings enhance the great room, kitchen, breakfast room and bedroom/study.
- A fireplace flanked by built-in shelves and cabinets creates warmth and interest in the great room.
- Boasting access to the screened porch, the master suite features a well-appointed bath and walk-in closet.
- The versatile bedroom/study has a single-door option for enlarging the adjacent powder room into a full bath.

Rear Elevation

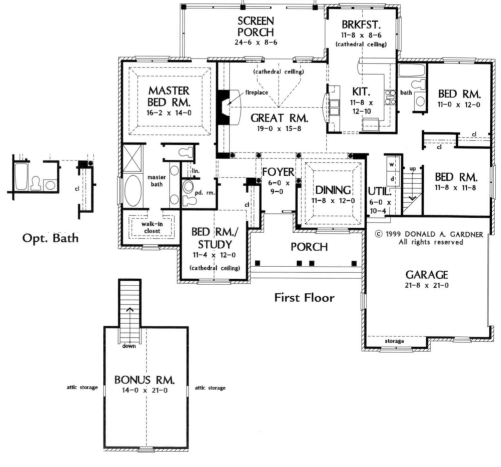

Opt. Bath

First Floor

Bonus Room

*Other options available. See page 513.

Spaulding — UDHDG01-316 — 1-866-525-9374

Total Living	First Floor	Second Floor	Bonus	Bed	Bath	Width	Depth	Foundation	Price Category
2182 sq ft	1346 sq ft	836 sq ft	N/A	4	3-1/2	49' 8"	45' 4"	Crawl Space*	E

*Other options available. See page 513.

Design Features

- Palladian windows flood the two-level foyer and great room with natural light.
- Both the master bedroom and great room access the covered rear porch.
- The master bath features a walk-in closet, twin vanities, separate shower and whirlpool tub.
- One of three upstairs bedrooms enjoys a private bath and walk-in closet.

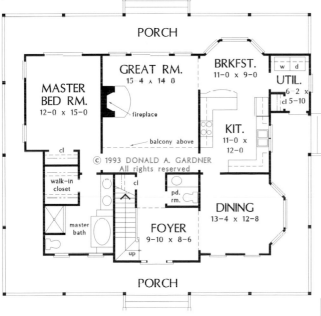

First Floor

PORCH

GREAT RM.
15-4 x 14-0

BRKFST.
11-0 x 9-0

UTIL.
6-2 x
cl 5-10

w d

MASTER BED RM.
12-0 x 15-0

fireplace

balcony above

cl

KIT.
11-0 x 12-0

© 1993 DONALD A. GARDNER
All rights reserved

walk-in closet

master bath

pd. rm.

DINING
13-4 x 12-8

FOYER
9-10 x 8-6

up

PORCH

Second Floor

bath

walk-in closet

cl

great room below

railing

BED RM.
11-0 x 12-0

cl

lin.

walk-in closet

down

bath

BED RM.
11-0 x 17-8

foyer below

BED RM.
11-0 x 12-8

clerestory with palladian window

clerestory with palladian window

Rear Elevation

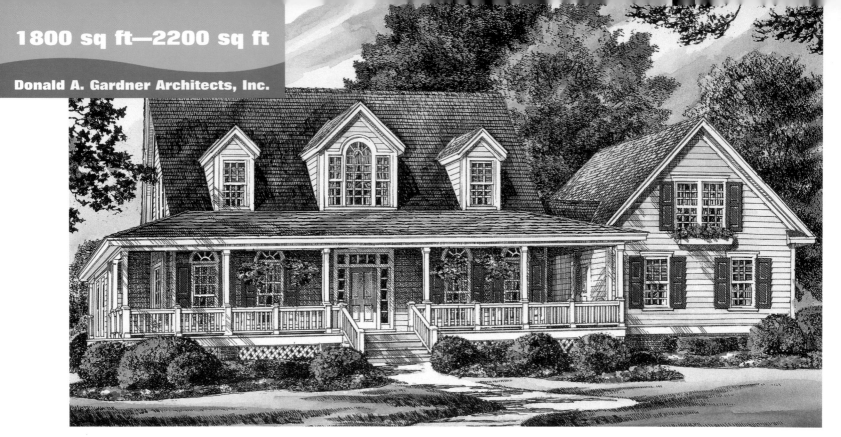

Burgess — UDHDG01-290 — 1-866-525-9374

Total Living	First Floor	Second Floor	Bonus	Bed	Bath	Width	Depth	Foundation	Price Category
2188 sq ft	1618 sq ft	570 sq ft	495 sq ft	3	2-1/2	54' 0"	57' 0"	Crawl Space*	E

Design Features

- A two-story great room and two-story foyer welcome natural light into this country classic.

- The large kitchen features a center-cooking island with counter and large breakfast area.

- Columns punctuate the interior spaces, and a separate dining room provides a formal touch.

- The semi-detached garage features a large bonus room above.

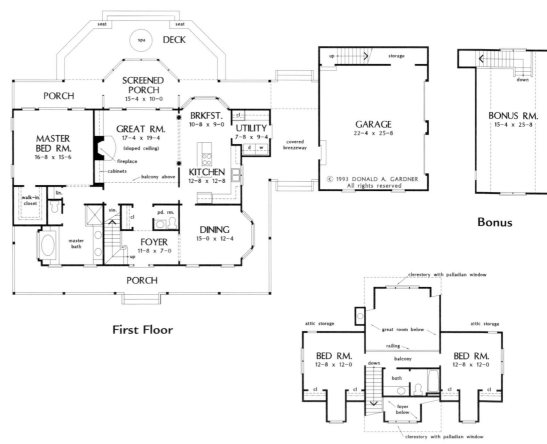

First Floor

Bonus

Second Floor

Rear Elevation

*Other options available. See page 513.

Baxendale — UDHDG01-822 — 1-866-525-9374

Total Living	First Floor	Bonus	Bed	Bath	Width	Depth	Foundation	Price Category
2195 sq ft	2195 sq ft	529 sq ft	4	3	71' 8"	54' 4"	Crawl Space*	E

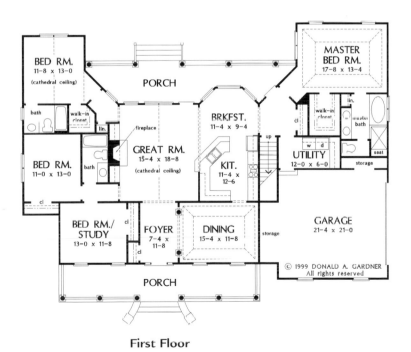

First Floor

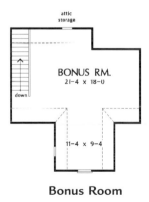

Bonus Room

Design Features

- At the heart of the home is a great room with cathedral ceiling and built-ins bordering the fireplace.
- The great room is open to the kitchen and breakfast room with bay window.
- A generous back porch extends living space to the outdoors.
- A split-bedroom design provides privacy for the master suite.

Rear Elevation

*Other options available. See page 513.

Admiralty Point — UDHDS01-6622 — 1-866-525-9374

© The Sater Design Collection, Inc.

Total Living	First Floor	Second Floor	Bonus	Bed	Bath	Width	Depth	Foundation	Price Category
2190 sq ft	2190 sq ft	N/A	N/A	3	2	58' 0"	54' 0"	Slab	F

Design Features

- The expansive great room offers a warming fireplace, built-in shelves and a place for an aquarium.

- A corner walk-in pantry, an eating bar open to the great room and morning nook brighten the kitchen.

- The master wing opens to the lanai while two walk-in closets surround a vestibule that leads from the bedroom to a luxurious bath.

- Lower-level recreation space may be developed into a home theater, game room or hobby area.

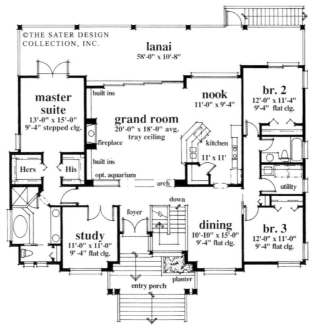

First Floor

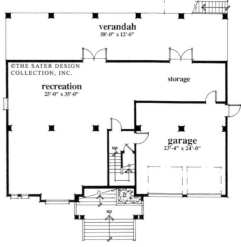

Lower Level

Rear Elevation

© The Sater Design Collection, Inc.

Tucker Town Way — UDHDS01-6692 — 1-866-525-9374

Total Living	First Floor	Lower Level	Bonus	Bed	Bath	Width	Depth	Foundation	Price Category
2190 sq ft	2190 sq ft	N/A	N/A	3	2	59' 8"	54' 0"	Slab	F

First Floor

Lower Level

Design Features

- The foyer opens to the grand room with fireplace.

- A well-crafted kitchen has wrapping counter space.

- A secluded master suite offers lanai access.

- The opulent master bath has twin lavatories.

- Two secondary bedrooms share a full bath.

Rear Elevation

Kinsley — UDHDS01-8030 — 1-866-525-9374

© The Sater Design Collection, Inc.

Total Living	First Floor	Second Floor	Bonus	Bed	Bath	Width	Depth	Foundation	Price Category
2191 sq ft	2191 sq ft	N/A	N/A	3	2-1/2	62' 10"	73' 6"	Opt. Basement/Slab	F

Design Features

- A dual-pitched hip roof, gently arched dormers, and a covered front porch enhance the front elevation.

- The great room features built-ins, a fireplace, art niche, a beamed ceiling and access to the veranda through three sets of French doors.

- The kitchen enjoys a stepped ceiling, island workstation and easy access to the breakfast nook and great room.

- Access to the veranda, dual walk-in closets, and a private foyer ensure privacy and comfort in the master suite.

Rear Elevation

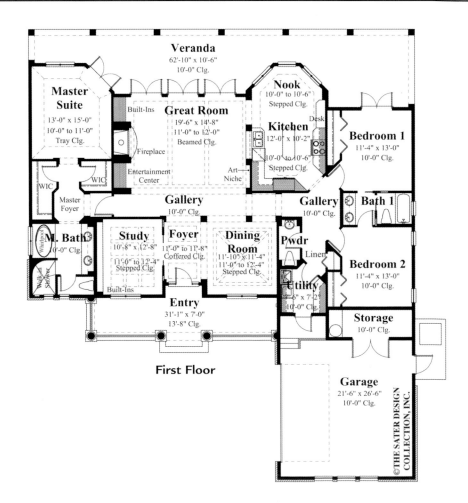

First Floor

© The Sater Design Collection, Inc.

Mercato — UDHDS01-8028 — 1-866-525-9374

Total Living	First Floor	Bonus	Bed	Bath	Width	Depth	Foundation	Price Category
2191 sq ft	2191 sq ft	N/A	3	2-1/2	62' 10"	73' 6"	Basement or Slab	F

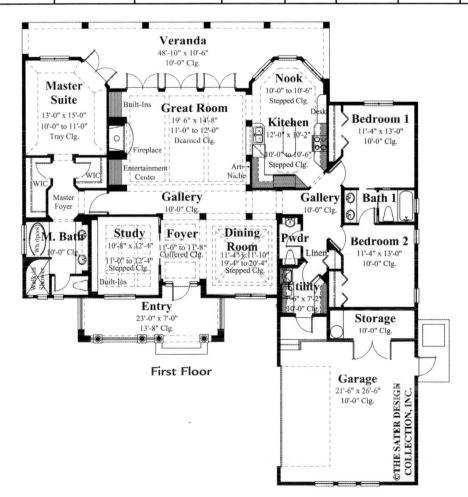

First Floor

Design Features

- An elegant covered porch is supported by tapered rope columns and a balustrade railing.
- A coffered ceiling foyer makes a grand entry into the home.
- A gallery provides a main corridor through the home.
- A row of triple French doors open the great room to the veranda.
- The great room is anchored by a massive fireplace and built-ins on either side.
- The master wing enjoys a private foyer.

Rear Elevation

Calhoun — UDHDG01-392 — 1-866-525-9374

© 1995 Donald A. Gardner Architects, Inc.

Total Living	First Floor	Bonus	Bed	Bath	Width	Depth	Foundation	Price Category
2192 sq ft	2192 sq ft	390 sq ft	4	2-1/2	74' 10"	55' 8"	Crawl Space*	E

Design Features

- Exciting extras, including tray and cathedral ceilings, add elegance to a comfortable, open plan.

- Sunlight fills the foyer from a vaulted dormer and streams into the great room.

- Secondary bedrooms are located on their own wing for ultimate homeowner privacy.

- The master suite, located separately, is highlighted by a tray ceiling and a skylit bath.

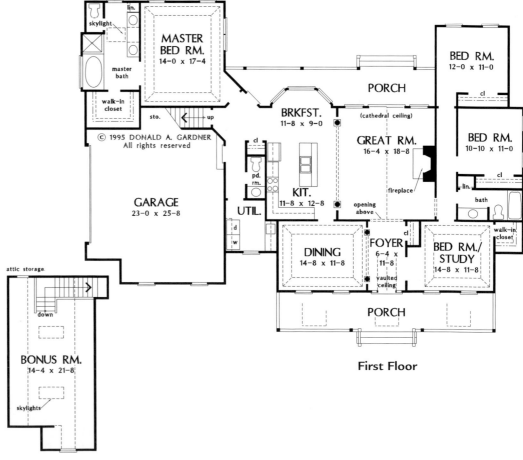

First Floor

Bonus Room

Rear Elevation

*Other options available. See page 513.

Summerhill — UDHDG01-1090 — 1-866-525-9374

Total Living	First Floor	Bonus	Bed	Bath	Width	Depth	Foundation	Price Category
2193 sq ft	2193 sq ft	387 sq ft	3	2	56' 4"	73' 0"	Crawl Space*	E

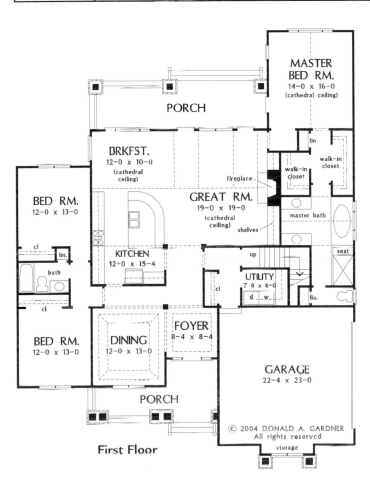

First Floor

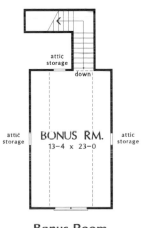

Bonus Room

Design Features

- An Arts-n-Crafts façade boasts elegant curb appeal as double dormers echo the dual-arched portico.
- Twin sets of tapered columns provide architectural detail to this lavish exterior.
- Vaulted ceilings in the great room offer generous vertical volume throughout the open living spaces.
- A vaulted ceiling, dual sinks and walk-in closets give the master suite additional flair.

Rear Elevation

*Other options available. See page 513.

Grammercy — UDHDG01-548 — 1-866-525-9374

© 1998 Donald A. Gardner, Inc.

Total Living	First Floor	Bonus	Bed	Bath	Width	Depth	Foundation	Price Category
2200 sq ft	2200 sq ft	338 sq ft	4	2-1/2	69' 3"	64' 5"	Crawl Space*	E

Design Features

- Keystone arches over windows, plus bold brick and stucco gables, make this home truly extraordinary.

- Eleven-foot ceilings grace the foyer, great room, dining room and screened porch.

- The kitchen, breakfast area and bedroom/study are expanded by cathedral ceilings.

- Interior columns add definition to the open great room and dining room.

- Two family bedrooms share a hall bath and nearby bonus room.

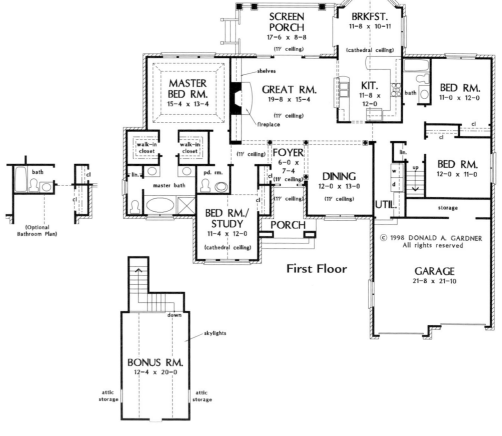

First Floor

Bonus Room

Rear Elevation

*Other options available. See page 513.

Gasden — UDHDG01-431 — 1-866-525-9374

Total Living	First Floor	Second Floor	Bonus	Bed	Bath	Width	Depth	Foundation	Price Category
2202 sq ft	1585 sq ft	617 sq ft	353 sq ft	3	2-1/2	65' 8"	42' 6"	Crawl Space*	E

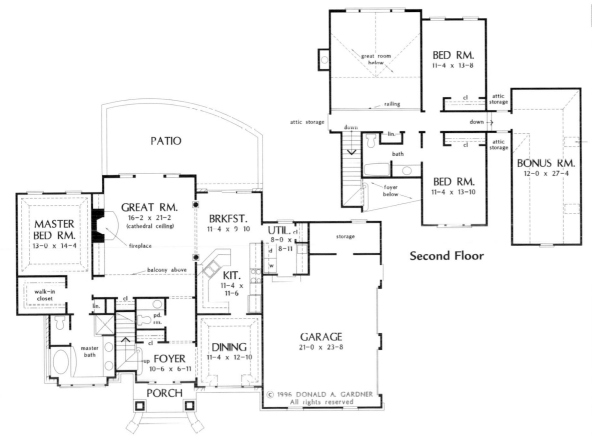

First Floor

Second Floor

Design Features

- Stone, stucco and refined styling add to the Old-World charm of this home.

- An open foyer accentuates a graceful stair and leads to the dining room.

- The great room features built-in cabinets and a wall of windows for extra drama.

- The first-floor master suite enjoys a tray ceiling.

- A skylit bonus room and attic storage are easily accessed from the second floor.

Rear Elevation

Donald A. Gardner Architects, Inc.

Pineville — UDHDG01-405 — 1-866-525-9374

Total Living	First Floor	Second Floor	Bonus	Bed	Bath	Width	Depth	Foundation	Price Category
2203 sq ft	1561 sq ft	642 sq ft	324 sq ft	3	2.5	68' 0"	50' 4"	Crawl Space*	E

Design Features

- Interior accent columns and a Palladian window distinguish the inviting two-story foyer.

- Transom windows over French doors brighten the dining room.

- Throughout the first floor, nine-foot ceilings add volume and drama.

- The master suite, secluded downstairs, features a space-amplifying tray ceiling.

- The second floor consists of two generous bedrooms with ample closet space.

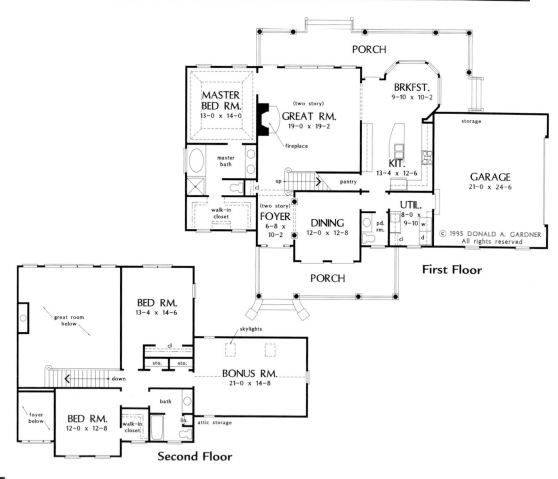

First Floor

Second Floor

Rear Elevation

© 2000 Donald A. Gardner, Inc.

Robinswood — UDHDG01-865 — 1-866-525-9374

Total Living	First Floor	Bonus	Bed	Bath	Width	Depth	Foundation	Price Category
2207 sq ft	2207 sq ft	441 sq ft	4	2-1/2	76' 9"	57' 4"	Crawl Space*	E

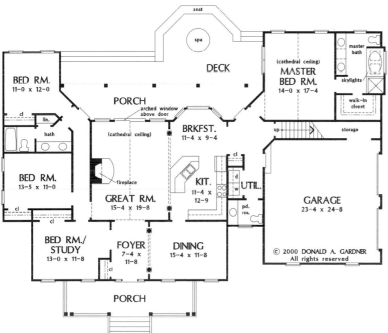

First Floor

BED RM.
11-0 x 12-0

PORCH
arched window
above door

seat

spa

DECK

(cathedral ceiling)
MASTER
BED RM.
14-0 x 17-4

master bath

skylights

walk-in closet

BRKFST.
11-4 x 9-4

bath

lin.

cl

BED RM.
13-5 x 11-0

(cathedral ceiling)

fireplace

GREAT RM.
15-4 x 19-8

KIT.
11-4 x 12-9

UTIL.

up

storage

GARAGE
23-4 x 24-8

cl

cl

cl

pd. rm.

d
w

© 2000 DONALD A. GARDNER
All rights reserved

BED RM./
STUDY
13-0 x 11-8

FOYER
7-4 x 11-8

DINING
15-4 x 11-8

cl

PORCH

BONUS RM.
14-4 x 24-8

down

attic storage

attic storage

Bonus Room

Design Features

- The curved transom and arched front porch are echoed in an overhead clerestory.
- A spacious rear porch and deck expand living areas outdoors.
- A cathedral ceiling tops the master bedroom, adding vertical volume.
- The master suite is complete with a walk-in closet, double vanity and skylit garden tub.

Rear Elevation

Lincoln Park — UDHFB01-3795 — 1-866-525-9374

© 2003 Frank Betz Associates, Inc.

Total Living	First Floor	Opt. Second Floor	Bed	Bath	Width	Depth	Foundation	Price Category
2211 sq ft	2211 sq ft	227 sq ft	4	3	57' 0"	66' 0"	Basement, Crawl Space or Slab	H

Design Features

- Shutters, shingles and siding wrap the colonial lines of this country cottage with a sweet disposition.
- Grand arches and columns frame the foyer and gallery, flanked by well-defined formal rooms.
- At the heart of the home, a spacious vaulted family room yields generous views of the back yard. Built-in cabinetry and a hearth create a warm ambience.
- A serving bar unites the living space with the kitchen and breakfast area, which leads outdoors.

Rear Elevation

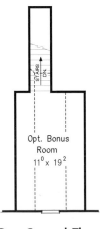

Opt. Second Floor

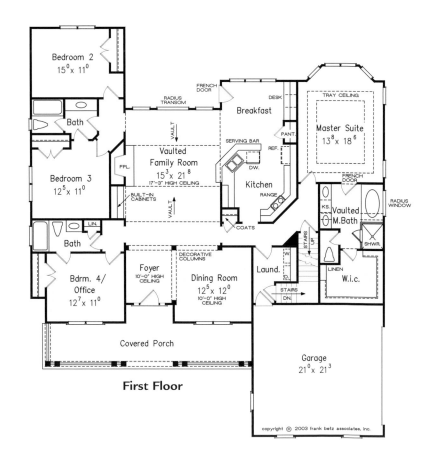

First Floor

Meadowsweet — UDHDG01-918 — 1-866-525-9374

Total Living	First Floor	Second Floor	Bonus	Bed	Bath	Width	Depth	Foundation	Price Category
2211 sq ft	1476 sq ft	735 sq ft	374 sq ft	4	2-1/2	48' 4"	51' 4"	Crawl Space*	E

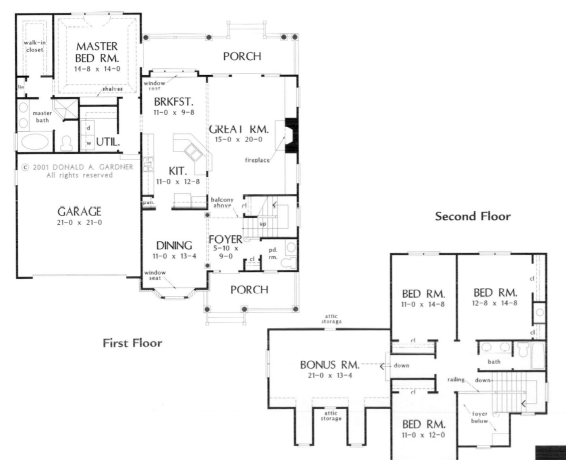

First Floor

Second Floor

Design Features

- A turret-styled bay window is show-cased on a wall of stone.

- Dormers and columns combine both country and traditional styles.

- The common rooms remain open, and the smart angled kitchen is the heart of the home.

- French doors access a rear porch from the great room and master suite.

- The U-shaped staircase has a decora-tive shelf for accessories.

Rear Elevation

Tessier — UDHFB01-3922 — 1-866-525-9374

© 2005 Frank Betz Associates, Inc.

Total Living	First Floor	Second Floor	Opt. Bonus	Bed	Bath	Width	Depth	Foundation	Price Category
2234 sq ft	1690 sq ft	544 sq ft	254 sq ft	3	2-1/2	55' 0"	48' 0"	Basement, Crawl Space or Slab	I

Design Features

- This main floor master suite plan possesses all the amenities of a much larger home.

- The spacious master bedroom encompasses one wing of the home.

- The keeping room with a fireplace is a special feature so many are looking for in their homes today.

- The back deck is the perfect place to relax at the end of the day.

First Floor

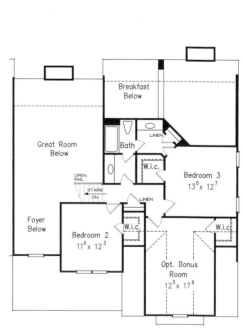

Second Floor

Rear Elevation

Roxbury — UDHDG01-722 — 1-866-525-9374

Total Living	First Floor	Second Floor	Bonus	Bed	Bath	Width	Depth	Walls/Foundation	Price Category
2235 sq ft	1701 sq ft	534 sq ft	274 sq ft	3	2-1/2	65' 4"	43' 5"	Crawl Space*	E

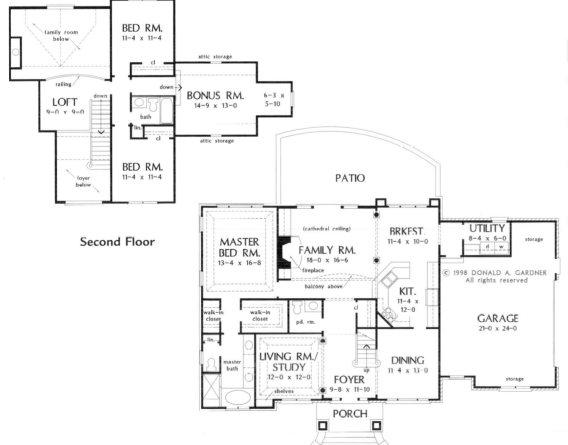

Second Floor

First Floor

Design Features

- Stone and stucco embellish the exterior of this stately traditional.

- Volume ceilings and architectural columns enhance its interior.

- Ceiling treatments cap the living room/study, family room and master bedroom.

- A second-floor loft with curved railing overlooks both the foyer and family room.

Rear Elevation

Elinor Park — UDHFB01-3943 — 1-866-525-9374

© 2005 Frank Betz Associates, Inc.

Total Living	First Floor	Opt. Second Floor	Bed	Bath	Width	Depth	Foundation	Price Category
2240 sq ft	2240 sq ft	369 sq ft	5	4	57' 0"	68' 0"	Basement or Crawl Space	H

Design Features

- The stone and brick façade of the *Elinor Park* are reminiscent of traditional homes of yesteryear.

- This one level home offers an open and airy floor plan, allowing easy transition from one room to another.

- The optional second floor also gives homeowners choices on how to finish this space.

- The deck on the rear of the home is the perfect place for entertaining.

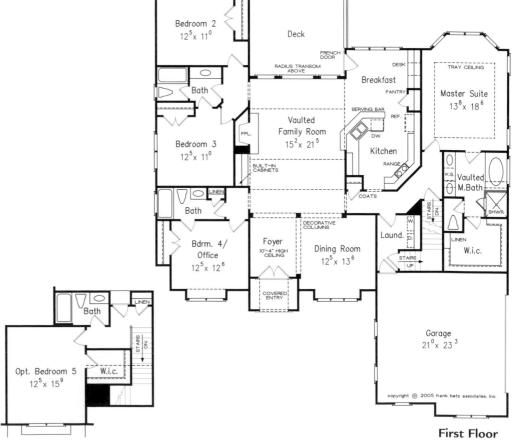

Rear Elevation

Opt. Second Floor

First Floor

© 2003 Donald A. Gardner, Inc.

Lilycrest — UDHDG01-1022 — 1-866-525-9374

Total Living	First Floor	Bonus	Bed	Bath	Width	Depth	Foundation	Price Category
2243 sq ft	2243 sq ft	332 sq ft	4	2	62' 0"	67' 2"	Crawl Space*	E

Design Features

- Twin dormers, multiple gables and bold columns create a lovely traditional exterior.
- A pass-thru with breakfast bar connects the kitchen to the great room, and built-ins flank the fireplace.
- The master suite features a bay window, which provides a comfortable sitting area.
- Perfect for outdoor entertaining, the rear porch includes a wet bar and skylights.
- The bonus room could provide additional recreation space.

First Floor

MASTER BED RM. 14-8 x 17-0
walk-in closet
walk-in closet
master bath
lin.
BRKFST. 10-0 x 9-0
skylights
PORCH
wet bar
shelves
(cathedral ceiling)
GREAT RM. 19-0 x 17-0
fireplace
KIT. 11-4 x 13-4
cl
BED RM. 11-0 x 13-0
BED RM. 13-0 x 11-0
cl
bath
UTIL. 7-4 x 7-0
d w
up
DINING 13-0 x 11-0
FOYER 6-4 x 11-0
BED RM./ STUDY 11-0 x 13-0
cl
cl
GARAGE 22-0 x 22-0
PORCH
© 2003 DONALD A. GARDNER All rights reserved
storage

Bonus Room

down
attic storage
BONUS RM. 14-10 x 22-0
(cathedral ceiling)
attic storage

Rear Elevation

Sullivan — UDHFB01-1224 — 1-866-525-9374

© 1998 Frank Betz Associates, Inc.

Total Living	First Floor	Second Floor	Opt. Bonus	Bed	Bath	Width	Depth	Walls/Foundation	Price Category
2246 sq ft	1688 sq ft	558 sq ft	269 sq ft	4	3	54' 0"	48' 0"	Basement, Crawl Space or Slab	I

Design Features

- The full brick façade, as well as the classic turret, have stood the test of time.

- A well-planned and thoughtful design accommodates the lifestyle of today's homeowner.

- The home is anchored by a vaulted great room, adjoining the kitchen and breakfast areas, allowing easy interaction between family and guests.

- An additional main-floor bedroom makes the ideal guest room or can also serve as a home office.

Rear Elevation

First Floor

Second Floor

Chatelaine — UDHDG01-550 — 1-866-525-9374

Total Living	First Floor	Bonus	Bed	Bath	Width	Depth	Foundation	Price Category
2250 sq ft	2250 sq ft	N/A	3	2-1/2	84' 10"	62' 4"	Crawl Space*	E

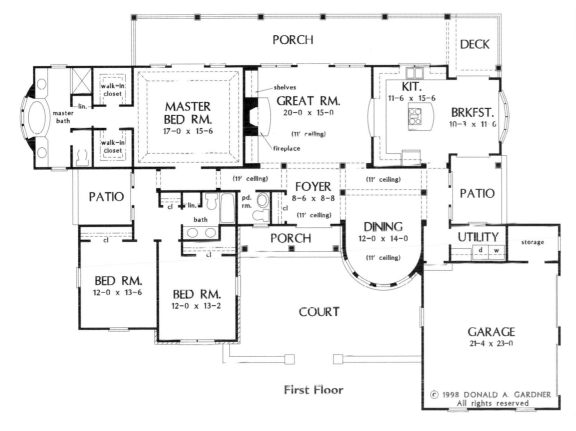

First Floor

Design Features

- The foyer, great room and dining room feature stately eleven-foot ceilings.

- Interior columns mark boundaries for the great room and dining room.

- The spacious kitchen features a pass-thru to the great room, where built-in shelves flank the fireplace.

- Cozy side decks and a large back porch add to the home's appeal.

Rear Elevation

Whiteheart — UDHDG01-926 — 1-866-525-9374

© 2001 Donald A. Gardner, Inc.

Total Living	First Floor	Bonus	Bed	Bath	Width	Depth	Foundation	Price Category
2252 sq ft	2252 sq ft	N/A	3	2	57' 8"	64' 4"	Crawl Space*	E

Design Features

- From metal and shingles to cedar shake and stone, this exterior blends with a variety of settings.
- With columns, sidelights and a transom, the front entry leads to an open interior.
- Columns and decorative ceilings define common rooms without enclosing them.
- The master bedroom's tray ceiling is arched to present the top of a circular-window transom.
- Note the large utility room and the versatile bedroom/study.

Rear Elevation

BRKFST.
12-4 x 8-4

PORCH

MASTER BED RM.
18-8 x 14-0

KITCHEN
14-4 x 14-0

GREAT RM.
23-0 x 17-8

fireplace
(vaulted ceiling)

walk-in closet

walk-in closet

lin.

master bath

UTIL.
9-8 x 10-8

d
w

DINING
12-0 x 14-0

FOYER
6-0 x 14-0

cl

BED RM./ STUDY
13-0 x 12-0

bath

walk-in closet

walk-in closet

© 2001 DONALD A. GARDNER
All rights reserved

PORCH

First Floor

GARAGE
21-0 x 21-0

BED RM.
12-0 x 13-0

storage

*Other options available. See page 513.

Please note: Home photographed may differ from blueprint.

Queenstown — UDHDG01-1066 — 1-866-525-9374

Total Living	First Floor	Bonus	Bed	Bath	Width	Depth	Foundation	Price Category
2264 sq ft	2264 sq ft	394 sq ft	3	2	57' 0"	73' 4"	Crawl Space	E

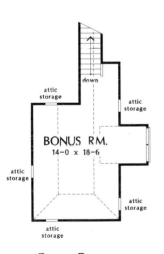

Bonus Room

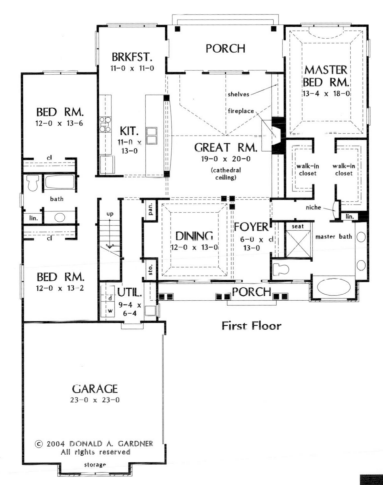

First Floor

Design Features

- Adding beauty and functionality, built-in cabinetry embraces the fireplace in the great room.
- A closet between the kitchen and dining room could be used as a reach-in pantry.
- Designed to pamper, the master suite features a Palladian-style window in the bedroom.
- An art niche, linen closet and porch access complete the master suite.

Rear Elevation

Walnut Grove — UDHFB01-3865 — 1-866-525-9374

© 2004 Frank Betz Associates, Inc.

Total Living	First Floor	Opt. Second Floor	Bed	Bath	Width	Depth	Foundation	Price Category
2275 sq ft	2275 sq ft	407 sq ft	3	3-1/2	59' 4"	69' 0"	Basement or Crawl Space	H

Design Features

- This design was created for the homeowner who wants upscale features on one level. Its cozy fieldstone exterior sets that stage for an equally impressive design inside.
- Two separate living spaces — the keeping and family rooms — give residents and guests alike options on where to gather.
- Double ovens and a serving bar in the kitchen make meal preparation and entertaining fun and easy.
- The master suite is private from the other bedrooms, and features a tray ceiling, a corner soaking tub and serene backyard views.

Rear Elevation

Opt. Second Floor

First Floor

Wisteria — UDHDG01-538 — 1-866-525-9374

Total Living	First Floor	Bonus	Bed	Bath	Width	Depth	Foundation	Price Category
2273 sq ft	2273 sq ft	342 sq ft	4	2-1/2	60' 8"	54' 10"	Crawl Space*	E

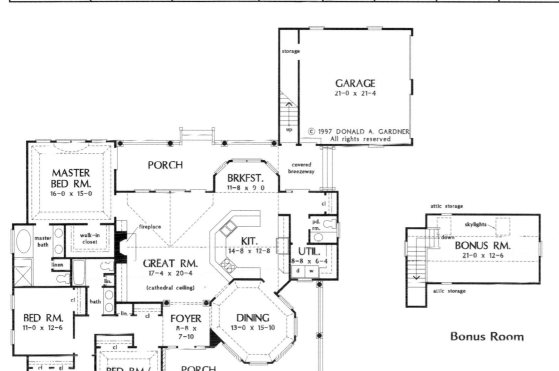

First Floor

Bonus Room

Design Features

- This home blends the wrapping porch of a country farmhouse with a brick and siding exterior.
- The great room shares its cathedral ceiling with a distinctly open and unusual kitchen.
- Built-ins flank the great room's fireplace for added convenience.
- The master suite includes a tray ceiling, arched picture window, and back-porch access.
- A flexible bedroom/study shines with a Palladian window and a graceful tray ceiling.

Rear Elevation

Durham Park — UDHFB01-3810 — 1-866-525-9374

© 2003 Frank Betz Associates, Inc.

Total Living	First Floor	Second Floor	Opt. Bonus	Bed	Bath	Width	Depth	Walls/Foundation	Price Category
2283 sq ft	1704 sq ft	579 sq ft	235 sq ft	3	2-1/2	55' 0"	58' 0"	Basement or Crawl Space	I

Design Features

- From the *Southern Living®* *Design Collection*

- The *Durham Park* exudes charm and character with its inviting stone and siding exterior.

- A bayed breakfast area adjoins the kitchen and accesses a tranquil screened porch and deck area.

- The master bedroom also has access to the deck and features its own private sitting area. A vaulted ceiling and decorative columns make this space distinct.

First Floor

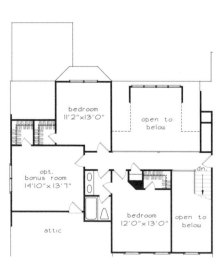

Second Floor

Rear Elevation

© 2005 Frank Betz Associates, Inc.

Kingsbridge — UDHFB01-3936 — 1-866-525-9374

Total Living	First Floor	Opt. Second Floor	Bed	Bath	Width	Depth	Foundation	Price Category
2289 sq ft	2289 sq ft	311 sq ft	3	3-1/2	57' 0"	70' 0"	Basement, Crawl Space or Slab	H

First Floor

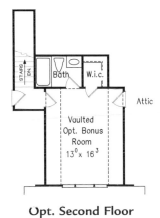

Opt. Second Floor

Design Features

- A brick elevation with columns makes this an inviting home.
- A keeping room is located just off the kitchen and breakfast room, and boasts a fireplace. This is a great place for families to end their day.
- The spacious family room has direct access to the covered porch and deck.
- The master suite and bath are spacious and open. A very large walk-in closet allows personal items to have their place.

Rear Elevation

Marchbanks — UDHDG01-855 — 1-866-525-9374

Total Living	First Floor	Bonus	Bed	Bath	Width	Depth	Foundation	Price Category
2290 sq ft	2290 sq ft	355 sq ft	4	3	53' 0"	80' 10"	Crawl Space*	E

Design Features

- Decorative wood brackets embellish the gables of this four-bedroom home.
- Tray ceilings create formality in several rooms: foyer, dining room, bedroom/study and master bedroom.
- A cathedral ceiling expands the great room and highlights a rear clerestory dormer.
- Bay windows enhance the dining room and breakfast area.
- French doors access the back porch via the great room, kitchen and master bedroom.

Rear Elevation

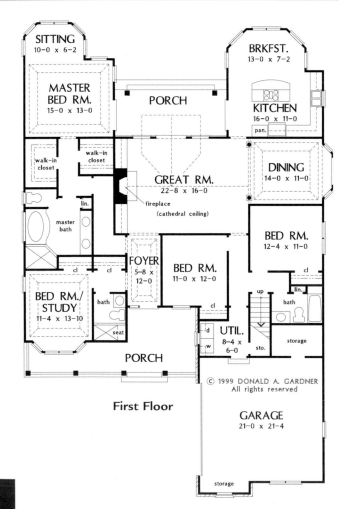

First Floor

© 1999 DONALD A. GARDNER
All rights reserved

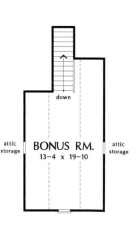

Bonus Room

*Other options available. See page 513.

Donald A. Gardner Architects, Inc.

Wicklow — UDHDG01-950 — 1-866-525-9374

Total Living	First Floor	Second Floor	Bonus	Bed	Bath	Width	Depth	Foundation	Price Category
2294 sq ft	1542 sq ft	752 sq ft	370 sq ft	3	2-1/2	44' 4"	54' 0"	Crawl Space*	E

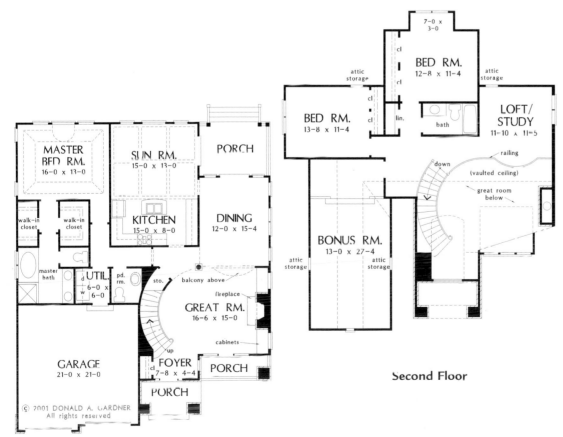

First Floor

Second Floor

Design Features

- A unique mixture of stone, siding and windows create character in this unique design.
- Columns, decorative railing and a metal roof add architectural interest to an intimate front porch.
- A rock entryway frames a French door flanked by sidelights and crowned with a transom.
- An elegant, curved staircase highlights the grand two-story foyer and great room.
- A delightful sunroom can be accessed from the dining room and is open to the kitchen.

Rear Elevation

Peachtree — UDHDG01-524 — 1-866-525-9374

Total Living	First Floor	Second Floor	Bonus	Bed	Bath	Width	Depth	Foundation	Price Category
2298 sq ft	1743 sq ft	555 sq ft	350 sq ft	4	3	78' 0"	53' 2"	Crawl Space*	E

Design Features

- Nine-foot ceilings are standard throughout the first and second floors of this classic country design.

- The foyer, great room and screened porch enjoy vaulted and cathedral ceilings.

- Bay windows perk up the dining room and breakfast area.

- The master suite features back-porch access, walk-in closet and a lavish bath.

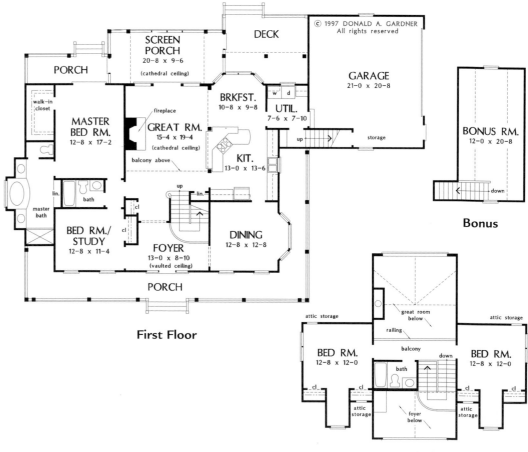

First Floor

Bonus

Second Floor

Rear Elevation

*Other options available. See page 513.

© 2001 Frank Betz Associates, Inc.

Bosworth — UDHFB01-3612 — 1-866-525-9374

Total Living	First Floor	Opt. Second Floor	Bed	Bath	Width	Depth	Foundation	Price Category
2296 sq ft	2296 sq ft	286 sq ft	4	3-1/2	61' 0"	58' 6"	Basement, Crawl Space or Slab	H

Opt. Second Floor

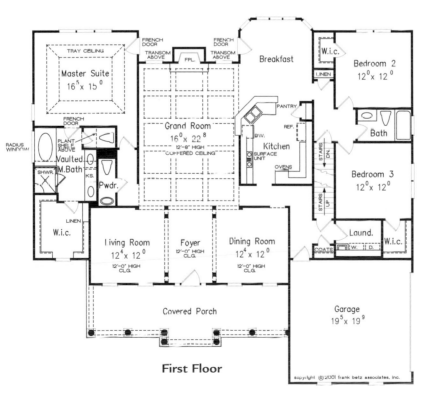

First Floor

copyright (c) 2001 frank betz associates, inc.

Design Features

- "Please, come in." No one can turn that invitation down once they see this impressive design.

- Living and dining rooms grace each side of the foyer.

- An extraordinary coffered ceiling canopies the sizeable grand room, with a fireplace and transom window as its backdrop.

- Sunshine beams into the breakfast area through a wall of windows, making this the perfect spot to start the day.

Rear Elevation

Weatherford — UDHDG01-1053 — 1-866-525-9374

© 2004 Donald A. Gardner, Inc.

Total Living	First Floor	Bonus	Bed	Bath	Width	Depth	Foundation	Price Category
2304 sq ft	2304 sq ft	361 sq ft	4	3	58' 4"	69' 8"	Crawl Space*	E

Design Features

- Board-n-batten siding accents a box-bay window set off by stone.

- A metal roof tops another bay window, while dormers, arches and columns create a dramatic entrance.

- The column and tray ceiling of the dining room opens to the grand cathedral ceiling of the great room.

- An angled counter is all that separates the kitchen from the breakfast nook.

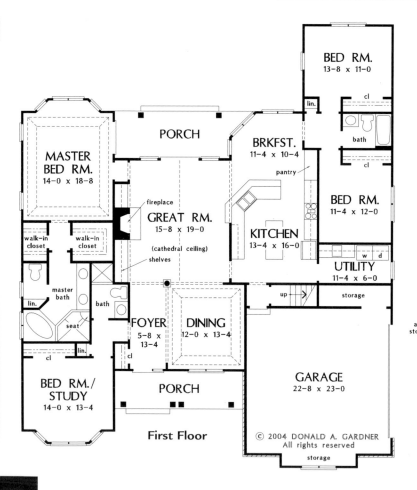

First Floor

© 2004 DONALD A. GARDNER
All rights reserved

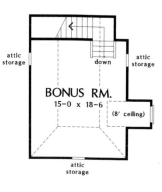

Bonus Room

Rear Elevation

*Other options available. See page 513.

Dunwood — UDHDG01-299 — 1-866-525-9374

Total Living	First Floor	Second Floor	Bonus	Bed	Bath	Width	Depth	Foundation	Price Category
2301 sq ft	1632 sq ft	669 sq ft	528 sq ft	3	2-1/2	72' 6"	46' 10"	Crawl Space*	E

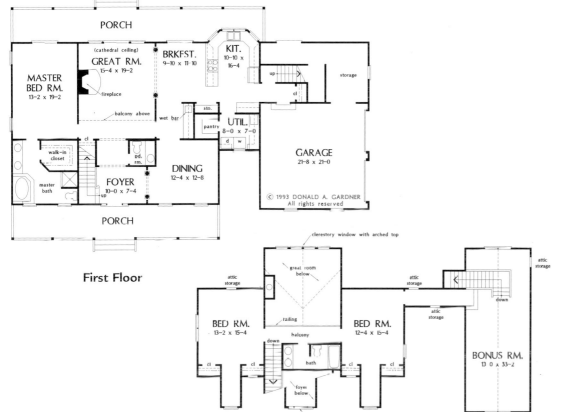

First Floor

Second Floor

Design Features

- An open floor plan plus bonus room make this home great for today's family.

- Columns visually separate the great room from the breakfast area and smart, U-shaped kitchen.

- A large utility room with walk-in pantry provides ultimate convenience.

- The privately located master suite accesses the back porch and features a luxurious bath.

Rear Elevation

Wentworth — UDHDG01-522 — 1-866-525-9374

Total Living	First Floor	Second Floor	Bonus	Bed	Bath	Width	Depth	Foundation	Price Category
2308 sq ft	1829 sq ft	479 sq ft	228 sq ft	4	3	63' 7"	50' 5"	Crawl Space*	E

Design Features

- This traditional home's foyer is enhanced by a graceful cathedral ceiling.

- Columns add definition to the casually elegant, open dining room.

- A cathedral ceiling in the great room creates a feeling of spaciousness.

- The kitchen is more than generous, featuring a center work island, pantry and breakfast counter.

First Floor

Second Floor

Rear Elevation

*Other options available. See page 513.

Photographed home may have been modified from original construction documents.

Waycross — UDHDG01-1039 — 1-866-525-9374

Total Living	First Floor	Second Floor	Bonus	Bed	Bath	Width	Depth	Walls/Foundation	Price Category
2665 sq ft	2006 sq ft	659 sq ft	527 sq ft	4	4	86'	49' 4"	Crawl Space*	F

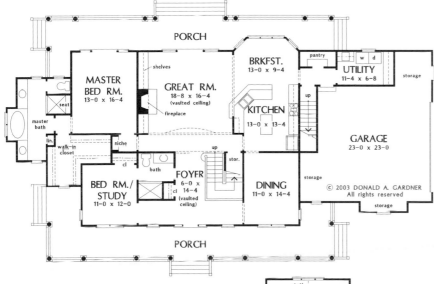

First Floor

Second Floor

Design Features

- Two massive porches, a prominent gable with a Palladian window and twin dormers showcase charm.

- An art niche, plant shelf, walk-in pantry and built-in cabinetry merge beauty with convenience.

- A striking staircase creates a grand focal point upon entry.

- The bonus room—with private staircase—provides space for a home office, gym or studio.

Rear Elevation

Medoro — UDHDS01-7035 — 1-866-525-9374

© The Sater Design Collection, Inc.

Total Living	First Floor	Bonus	Bed	Bath	Width	Depth	Foundation	Price Category
2329 sq ft	2329 sq ft	N/A	3 + Study	2-1/2	72' 0"	73' 4"	Crawl Space	F

Design Features

- An elevated covered front porch is topped with a trio of dormers.

- Open rooms and specialty ceilings add a spacious elegance.

- Interior columns set off the dining room and kitchen.

- The leisure room boasts a fireplace and views.

- The master suite has a private entry.

Rear Elevation

First Floor

© 2001 Donald A. Gardner, Inc.

Yankton — UDHDG01-933 — 1-866-525-9374

Total Living	First Floor	Bonus	Bed	Bath	Width	Depth	Foundation	Price Category
2330 sq ft	2330 sq ft	364 sq ft	3	2-1/2	62' 3"	60' 6"	Crawl Space*	E

© 2001 DONALD A. GARDNER
All rights reserved

First Floor

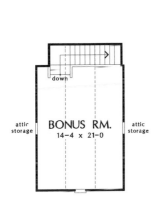

Bonus

Design Features

- This design takes a little of the Southeast and shares it with the rest of the regions.

- A metal roof accents the study's window.

- Columns are used to define the dining room without enclosing space.

- A convenient pass-thru connects the kitchen to the great room.

- Above the garage, the bonus room awaits expansion needs.

Rear Elevation

Savoy — UDHFB01-851 — 1-866-525-9374

© 1995 Frank Betz Associates, Inc.

Total Living	First Floor	Second Floor	Opt. Bonus	Bed	Bath	Width	Depth	Foundation	Price Category
2341 sq ft	1761 sq ft	580 sq ft	276 sq ft	4	3	56' 0"	47' 6"	Basement, Crawl Space or Slab	H

Design Features

- The hipped roofline and decorative quoin accents give interesting and eye-catching dimension to the *Savoy's* façade.

- The master suite encompasses an entire wing of the main level, giving homeowners ample space to unwind.

- An additional main-floor bedroom makes the perfect guest room or can be used as a home office.

- Two bedrooms share a divided bath upstairs.

First Floor

Second Floor

Rear Elevation

Hanley Hall — UDHFB01-1256 — 1-866-525-9374

Total Living	First Floor	Second Floor	Opt. Bonus	Bed	Bath	Width	Depth	Foundation	Price Category
2345 sq ft	1761 sq ft	584 sq ft	302 sq ft	4	3	56' 0"	47' 6"	Basement, Crawl Space or Slab	I

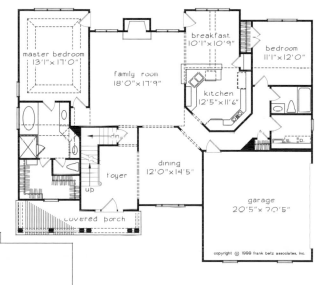

First Floor

Design Features

- From the *Southern Living® Design Collection*

- A spacious family room—with a two-story ceiling—is the focal point for activity.

- The kitchen also functions as the nucleus of the home; its openness allows the cook to interact with anyone in adjoining rooms.

- One bedroom with a full bath is located in its own corner of the plan.

Second Floor

Rear Elevation

Defoors Mill — UDHFB01-3712 — 1-866-525-9374

© 2002 Frank Betz Associates, Inc.

Total Living	First Floor	Second Floor	Opt. Bonus	Bed	Bath	Width	Depth	Foundation	Price Category
2351 sq ft	1803 sq ft	548 sq ft	277 sq ft	4	3	55' 0"	48' 0"	Basement, Crawl Space or Slab	H

Design Features

- A covered porch is situated on the front of the home and leads to a charming and practical floor plan.

- The master suite encompasses an entire wing of the home for comfort and privacy.

- An optional bonus room is available on the second floor

- Special details in this home include a handy island in the kitchen, decorative columns around the dining area and a coat closet just off the garage.

Second Floor

First Floor

Rear Elevation

Donald A. Gardner Architects, Inc.

© 1997 Donald A. Gardner Architects, Inc.

Jasmine — UDHDG01-509 — 1-866-525-9374

Total Living	First Floor	Bonus	Bed	Bath	Width	Depth	Foundation	Price Category
2349 sq ft	2349 sq ft	435 sq ft	4	3	83' 2"	56' 4"	Crawl Space*	E

Design Features

- This plan's front porch says, "welcome home," and inside, its comfortable design encourages relaxation.
- A center dormer lights the foyer, as columns punctuate the entry to the dining room and great room.
- The spacious kitchen has an angled countertop and is open to the breakfast bay.
- A second master suite features an optional arrangement for wheelchair accessibility.
- Two additional bedrooms share a third full bath with linen closet.

(optional handicapped accessible bath)

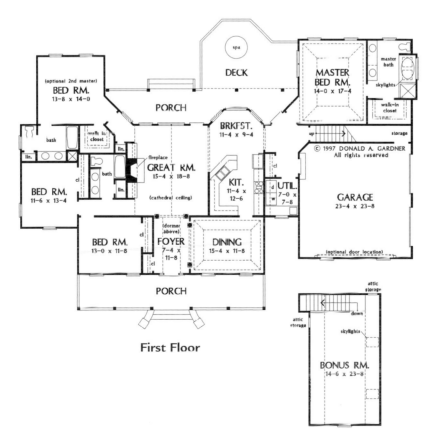

First Floor

BONUS RM.
14-6 x 23-8

Rear Elevation

Donald A. Gardner Architects, Inc.

Saddlebrook — UDHDG01-762 — 1-866-525-9374

© 1998 Donald A. Gardner, Inc.

Total Living	First Floor	Second Floor	Bonus	Bed	Bath	Width	Depth	Foundation	Price Category
2356 sq ft	1718 sq ft	638 sq ft	341 sq ft	4	3	71' 0"	42' 8"	Crawl Space*	E

Design Features

- Twin gables and a generous front porch give this graceful farmhouse stature and appeal.
- Vaulted and cathedral ceilings amplify the great room and master bedroom.
- The great room features a fireplace, built-ins, convenient rear staircase and balcony.
- The first-floor master suite enjoys his-and-her walk-in closets and a private bath with garden tub.
- Upstairs are two family bedrooms, separated by a loft with built-in bookshelves.

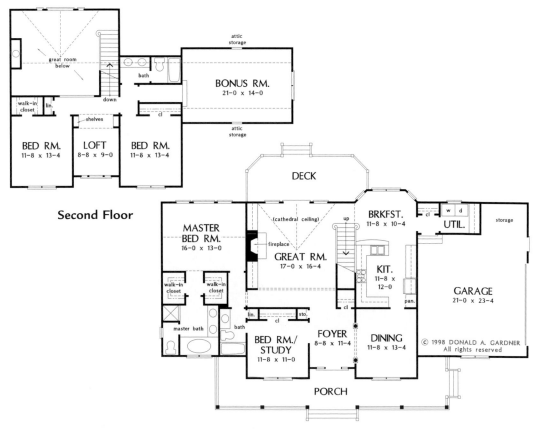

Second Floor

First Floor

© 1998 DONALD A. GARDNER
All rights reserved

Rear Elevation

*Other options available. See page 513.

© 2000 Donald A. Gardner, Inc.

Nottingham — UDHDG01-854 — 1-866-525-9374

Total Living	First Floor	Bonus	Bed	Bath	Width	Depth	Foundation	Price Category
2353 sq ft	2353 sq ft	353 sq ft	4	2	65' 8"	67' 10"	Crawl Space*	E

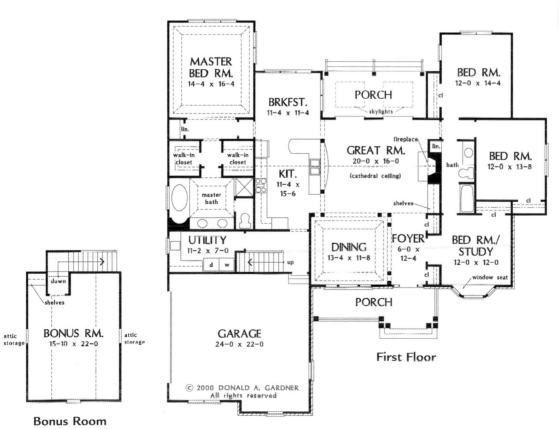

Bonus Room

First Floor

Design Features

- An exciting cathedral ceiling unifies the open great room and kitchen.

- The great room features a fireplace, built-in shelves and access to the skylit back porch.

- Note the spacious utility room with laundry sink and cabinets.

- Tray ceilings top the master bedroom and bath, which are separated by two walk-in closets.

Rear Elevation

Donald A. Gardner Architects, Inc.

Hayden — UDHDG01-1091 — 1-866-525-9374

Total Living	First Floor	Second Floor	Bonus	Bed	Bath	Width	Depth	Foundation	Price Category
2358 sq ft	2358 sq ft	N/A	324 sq ft	4	2	65' 8"	68' 10"	Crawl Space*	E

Design Features

- This Craftsman exterior produces ultimate curb appeal with a stone and cedar-shake façade.

- Metal roofs crown bay windows, while multiple gables create an exciting finish.

- Tray ceilings adorn the dining room and master bedroom, adding rich detail to both.

- A large kitchen pass-thru enables the openness of the floor plan to continue.

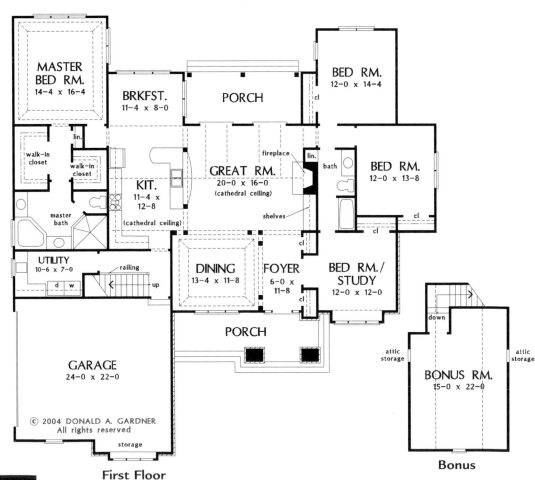

First Floor

Bonus

Rear Elevation

Juniper — UDHDG01-704 — 1-866-525-9374

Total Living	First Floor	Second Floor	Bonus	Bed	Bath	Width	Depth	Foundation	Price Category
2363 sq ft	1575 sq ft	788 sq ft	251 sq ft	4	3-1/2	65' 0"	49' 0"	Crawl Space*	E

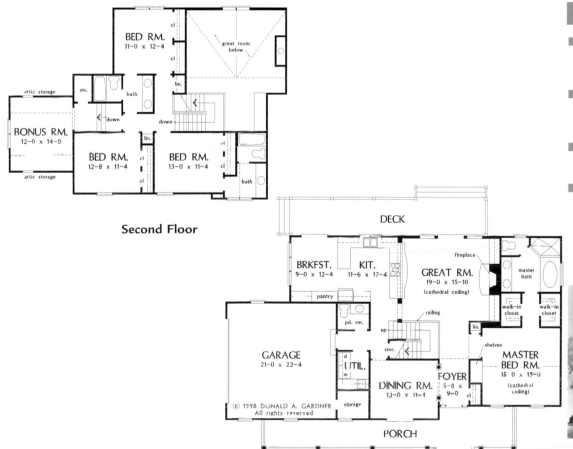

Second Floor

First Floor

Design Features

- Multiple gables and a gracious front porch add charm to this country farmhouse.

- The practical floor plan allows for easy traffic patterns around the U-shaped staircase.

- A space-enhancing cathedral ceiling tops the great room.

- The master suite on the first floor features a built-in entertainment center.

Rear Elevation

*Other options available. See page 513.

Bellavita — UDHDG01-1104 — 1-866-525-9374

Total Living	First Floor	Bonus	Bed	Bath	Width	Depth	Foundation	Price Category
2369 sq ft	2369 sq ft	N/A	3	2-1/2	56' 0"	70' 4"	Crawl Space*	E

Design Features

- This extraordinary exterior unites pizzazz with refinement.
- The Mediterranean façade with sweeping roof and dramatic entryway creates alluring curb appeal.
- Multiple sets of French doors and a fireplace accent the oversized great room.
- The breakfast room overlooks a screen porch complete with outdoor kitchen and built-in shelves.
- A large master bedroom exits onto the covered patio in the rear of the home, promoting privacy.

Rear Elevation

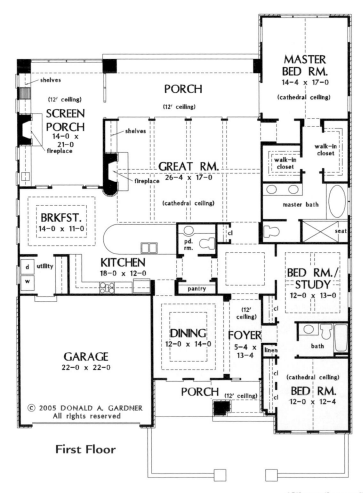

First Floor

*Other options available. See page 513.

© The Sater Design Collection, Inc.

Linden Place — UDHDS01-6805 — 1-866-525-9374

Total Living	First Floor	Second Floor	Bonus	Bed	Bath	Width	Depth	Foundation	Price Category
2374 sq ft	1510 sq ft	864 sq ft	N/A	3	3-1/2	44' 0"	49' 0"	Island Basement	F

Second Floor

First Floor

Lower Level

Design Features

- A widow's peak, transoms and a cozy porch with decorative fretwork and balusters invites visitors inside.

- The great room boasts a fireplace, built-in cabinets and two pairs of French doors that open to the rear porch.

- The master suite is enriched with a tray ceiling, tall windows and a pampering bath.

- To ensure privacy, the spare bedrooms are located on the upper level and each has its own full bath and private access to the upper deck.

Rear Elevation

Nicholas Park — UDHDS01-6804 — 1-866-525-9374

© The Sater Design Collection, Inc.

Total Living	First Floor	Second Floor	Bonus	Bed	Bath	Width	Depth	Foundation	Price Category
2374 sq ft	1510 sq ft	864 sq ft	N/A	3	3-1/2	44' 0"	49' 0"	Island Basement	F

Design Features

- Multiple porches, bold columns, transoms, decorative corbels and balustrades create an impressive front façade.

- An open arrangement of the two-story great room, gallery kitchen and dining room enhance the welcoming atmosphere of the home.

- The great room offers warmth by the fireplace, a built-in entertainment center and double French doors that lead out to the porch.

Second Floor

First Floor

Lower Level

Rear Elevation

Donald A. Gardner Architects, Inc.

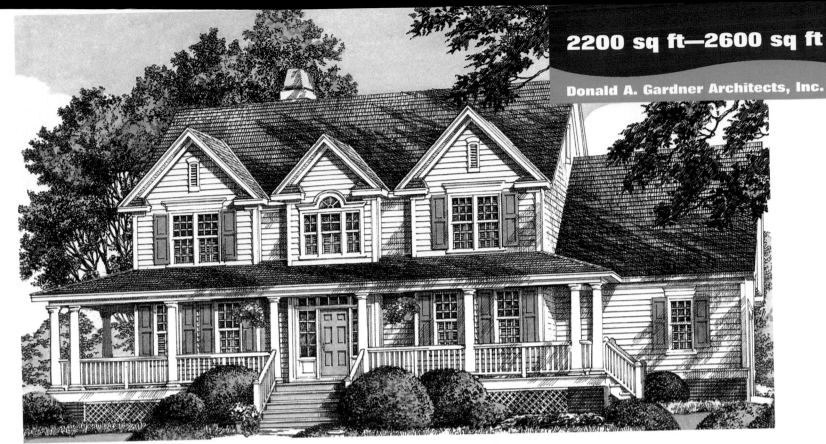

© 2002 Donald A. Gardner, Inc.

Brentwood — UDHDG01-998 — 1-866-525-9374

Total Livin									
2387 sq f									

Total Living	First Floor	Second Floor	Bonus	Bed	Bath	Width	Depth	Walls/Foundation	Price Category
2384 sq ft	1633 sq ft	751 sq ft	359 sq ft	3	3-1/2	69' 8"	44' 0"	Crawl Space*	E

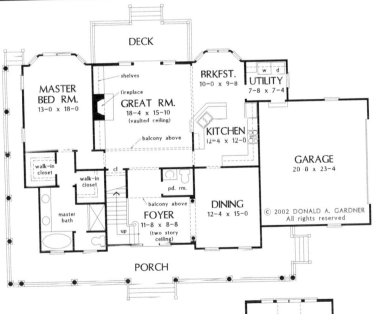

First Floor

Second Floor

Design Features

- This farmhouse captures Old-Time ambiance with a large wrapping porch and columns.

- A trio of gables and a side-entry garage add to the curb appeal.

- Filled with light by clerestory windows and French doors, this floor plan is efficient.

- A two-story ceiling extends from the foyer into the great room, while a balcony overlooks both areas.

- Upstairs, a loft separates two additional bedrooms and full baths.

Rear Elevation

*Other options available. See page 513.

2200 sq ft—2600 sq ft

Donald A. Gardner Architects, Inc.

Macg...

Hyde Park — UDHDG01-816 — 1-866-525-9374

© 1999 Donald A. Gardner, Inc.

Total Living	First Floor	Second Floor	Bonus	Bed	Bath	Width	Depth	Foundation	Price Category
2387 sq ft	1918 sq ft	469 sq ft	374 sq ft	4	3	73' 3"	43' 6"	Crawl Space*	E

Design Features

- A two-story ceiling adds height and drama to the formal foyer.

- The adjacent dining room is enriched by a box-bay window with lovely window seat.

- The vaulted great room features a stunning rear clerestory dormer and a fireplace.

- A second-floor balcony overlooks both the great room and foyer.

D

- The famil... breakfast...

- A conveni... window i... a warm, i...

- The room... orative tra... and an ex...

- Both upst... walk-in clo...

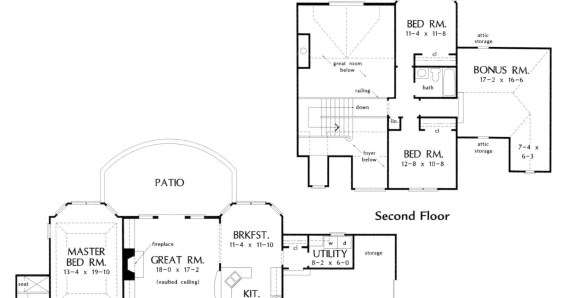

Second Floor

Rear Elevation

Rear Elevation

First Floor

*Other options available. See page 513.

© 1999 Frank Betz Associates, Inc.

Cornelia — UDHFB01-3482 — 1-866-525-9374

Total Living	First Floor	Opt. Bonus	Bed	Bath	Width	Depth	Foundation	Price Category
2388 sq ft	2388 sq ft	N/A	3	2-1/2	63' 0"	60' 0"	Basement, Crawl Space or Slab	H

First Floor

copyright © 1999 frank betz associates, inc.

GARAGE LOCATION WITH BASEMENT

Design Features

- The free-flowing main living areas of this design are incorporated into a split-bedroom layout, ensuring plenty of privacy to the homeowners.

- Its foyer and dining room are surrounded by decorative architectural columns, defining each space while maintaining its open and spacious feel.

- A living room just off the foyer would also function well as a study — perfect for the telecommuter or business owner.

- A bayed sitting area in the master suite has views to the backyard.

Rear Elevation

Catawba Ridge — UDHFB01-3823 — 1-866-525-9374

© 2003 Frank Betz Associates, Inc.

Total Living	First Floor	Second Floor	Opt. Bonus	Bed	Bath	Width	Depth	Walls/Foundation	Price Category
2389 sq ft	1593 sq ft	796 sq ft	238 sq ft	3	3-1/2	59' 8"	50' 6"	Basement, Crawl Space or Slab	I

Design Features

- From the *Southern Living®* *Design Collection*
- A cozy front porch graces the front of the home.
- The kitchen, breakfast area and family room are conveniently grouped together for easy family interaction.
- The master suite encompasses an entire wing of the home, giving the homeowner added privacy.

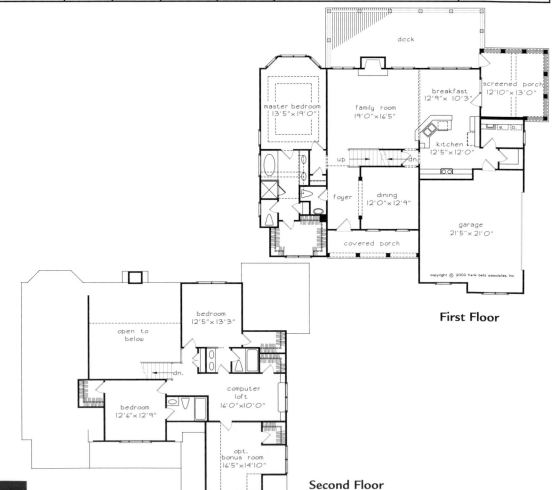

First Floor

Second Floor

Rear Elevation

© 2003 Frank Betz Associates, Inc.

Camden Lake — UDHFB01-3828 — 1-866-525-9374

Total Living	First Floor	Opt. Second Floor	Bed	Bath	Width	Depth	Foundation	Price Category
2395 sq ft	2395 sq ft	660 sq ft	4	3-1/2	62' 6"	77' 4"	Basement or Crawl Space	H

First Floor

Opt. Second Floor

Design Features

- One glance will tell you that this home is original and unique in its design and details. Beamed gables and cedar shake create an appealing Craftsman-style elevation.

- The pleasant surprises keep coming inside where entertainers will fall in love with this floor plan!

- The kitchen is adorned with many added extras that make it a fun place to be. Double ovens, a serving bar and a liberally sized pantry make it a user-friendly room.

Rear Elevation

Tullamore Square — UDHFB01-3801 — 1-866-525-9374

© 2003 Frank Betz Associates, Inc.

Total Living	First Floor	Second Floor	Opt. Bonus	Bed	Bath	Width	Depth	Foundation	Price Category
2398 sq ft	1805 sq ft	593 sq ft	255 sq ft	4	3	55' 0"	48' 0"	Basement, Crawl Space or Slab	H

Design Features

- This home is every bit as quaint as its name, with a cedar shake exterior accented with a rooftop cupola.

- A seated shower, soaking tub and his-and-her closets make the master bath feel like five-star luxury.

- A coat closet and a laundry room are placed just off the garage, keeping coats and shoes in their place.

- A second main-floor bedroom makes a great guest room or home office.

Second Floor

First Floor

Rear Elevation

Donald A. Gardner Architects, Inc.

Lewisville — UDHDG01-912 — 1-866-525-9374

Total Living	First Floor	Bonus	Bed	Bath	Width	Depth	Foundation	Price Category
2413 sq ft	2413 sq ft	417 sq ft	4	2-1/2	78' 8"	57' 8"	Crawl Space*	E

Design Features

- This design incorporates traditional and country elements to bring balance into everyday life.
- Although the bedrooms retain their privacy, the common rooms flow together.
- Even as the fireplace accents the great room, it can all be enjoyed from the kitchen or breakfast bay.
- From the foyer to the master suite, closet space is plentiful, and there's even storage in the garage.
- Other special features include built-in shelves and exterior columns.

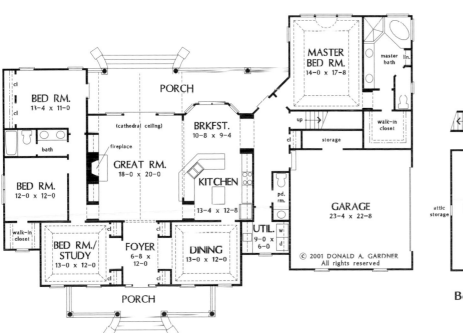

First Floor

Bonus Room

Rear Elevation

Clarkston — UDHFB01-3751 — 1-866-525-9374

© 2002 Frank Betz Associates, Inc.

Total Living	First Floor	Second Floor	Opt. Bonus	Bed	Bath	Width	Depth	Foundation	Price Category
2426 sq ft	1327 sq ft	1099 sq ft	290 sq ft	4	3	58' 0"	42' 6"	Basement, Crawl Space or Slab	H

Design Features

- A two-story foyer is encompassed by a dining room and study.

- Three bedrooms share the upper level of this design—the master suite and two secondary bedrooms that share a bath.

- A fourth bedroom with private bath is on the main level and makes perfect secluded guest accommodations.

- An optional bonus room on the upper level presents the opportunity to expand—ideal for a playroom, craft room or exercise area.

First Floor

Rear Elevation

Second Floor

© 2005 Frank Betz Associates, Inc.

Santa Monica — UDHFB01-3925 — 1-866-525-9374

Total Living	First Floor	Second Floor	Opt. Bonus	Bed	Bath	Width	Depth	Foundation	Price Category
2431 sq ft	1616 sq ft	815 sq ft	263 sq ft	3	3-1/2	55' 0"	49' 0"	Basement, Crawl Space or Slab	H

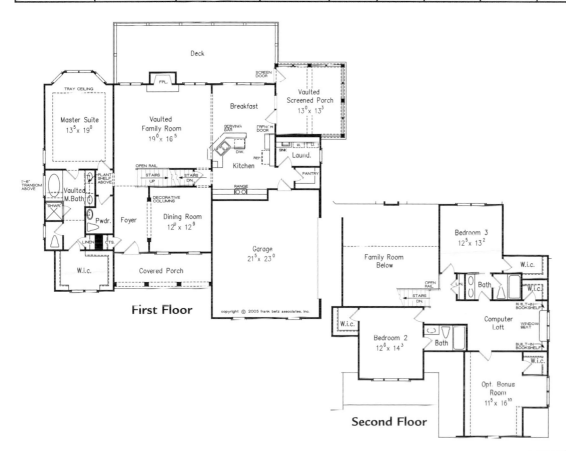

First Floor

Second Floor

Design Features

- Welcome home to the *Santa Monica*. The features of this home are generally reserved for much larger homes.

- The master suite resides on one wing of the home.

- Upstairs, there are two additional bedrooms, an optional bonus room and a computer loft.

- A vaulted screened porch and a deck allow for entertaining.

Rear Elevation

Blackstone — UDHFB01-3871 — 1-866-525-9374

© 2004 Frank Betz Associates, Inc.

Total Living	First Floor	Opt. Second Floor	Bed	Bath	Width	Depth	Foundation	Price Category
2434 sq ft	2434 sq ft	307 sq ft	5	4	63' 0"	64' 6"	Basement or Crawl Space	I

Design Features

- From the *Southern Living®* *Design Collection*

- A vaulted master suite is divided from the other bedrooms making a private haven for homeowners to enjoy.

- The breakfast area leads to a screened porch and oversized deck on the back of the home — perfect for outdoor entertaining.

- A mudroom buffers the living area from the garage, ensuring that coats and shoes stay in their place.

Opt. Second Floor

First Floor

Rear Elevation

Dobbins — UDHDG01-370 — 1-866-525-9374

Total Living	First Floor	Second Floor	Bonus	Bed	Bath	Width	Depth	Foundation	Price Category
2435 sq ft	1841 sq ft	594 sq ft	391 sq ft	4	3	82' 2"	48' 10"	Crawl Space*	E

Design Features

- This four-bedroom country home defines casual elegance with its front and back wrapping porches.

- An open two-level foyer with Palladian window leads to the expansive great room.

- Windows all around and bays in the master suite and breakfast area add space and light.

- The master suite features back-porch access, a walk-in closet and a luxurious bath.

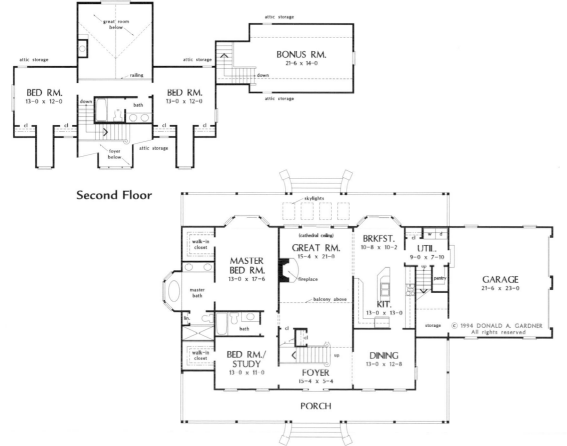

Second Floor

First Floor

Rear Elevation

Riverside — UDHDG01-269 — 1-866-525-9374

Total Living	First Floor	Second Floor	Bonus	Bed	Bath	Width	Depth	Foundation	Price Category
2436 sq ft	1766 sq ft	670 sq ft	N/A	4	3-1/2	59' 10"	53' 4"	Crawl Space*	E

Design Features

- This four-bedroom farmhouse celebrates sunlight with a Palladian window and screened porch.
- The center-island kitchen and breakfast area flow into the great room through an elegant colonnade.
- The first-level master suite opens to the screened porch through a bay area.
- A garden tub, double lavs and separate shower provide added luxury.
- Upstairs, two more bedrooms each have a private bath.

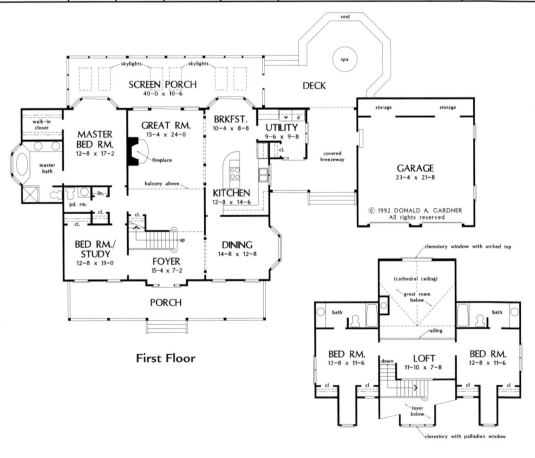

First Floor

Second Floor

Rear Elevation

*Other options available. See page 513.

© 2004 Frank Betz Associates, Inc.

Culbertson — UDHFB01-3860 — 1-866-525-9374

Total Living	First Floor	Second Floor	Opt. Bonus	Bed	Bath	Width	Depth	Walls/Foundation	Price Category
2443 sq ft	1214 sq ft	1229 sq ft	N/A	4	2-1/2	52' 4"	55' 10"	Basement or Crawl Space	H

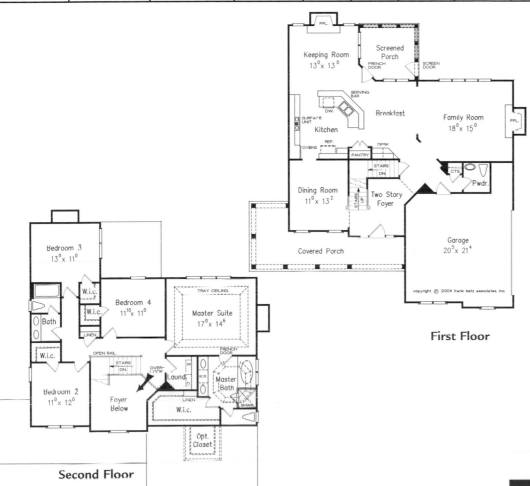

First Floor

Design Features

- The kitchen overlooks a keeping room with a fireplace, giving families a cozy place to gather for a board game.

- Double ovens, serving bar and an ample pantry accommodate the family.

- The family room is open to the breakfast area, allowing for easy traffic flow from one space to the next.

Rear Elevation

Second Floor

Lexington — UDHDS01-7065 — 1-866-525-9374

© The Sater Design Collection, Inc.

Total Living	First Floor	Second Floor	Bonus	Bed	Bath	Width	Depth	Foundation	Price Category
2454 sq ft	2454 sq ft	N/A	256	3	2	80' 6"	66' 6"	Crawl Space	F

Design Features

- The expansive great room and study boast built-ins and specialty ceilings as well as share a double-sided fireplace.

- Six sets of double French doors flood the kitchen, dining area and great room with sunlight.

- The openness of the kitchen, dining and great room create an inviting atmosphere.

- The master suite is placed away from the guest rooms and features "his-and-her" walk-in closets, a luxurious bath and a private entry.

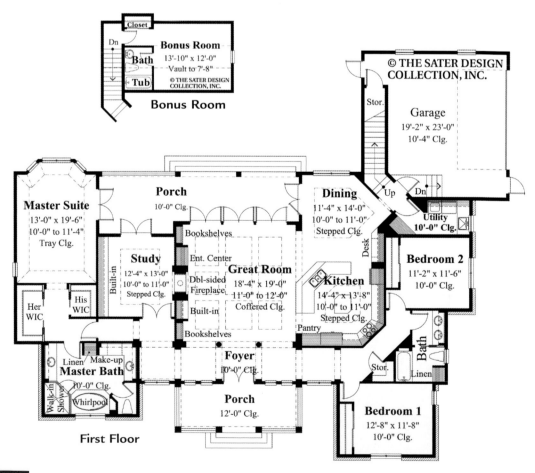

Rear Elevation

© The Sater Design Collection, Inc.

Madison — UDHDS01-7064 — 1-866-525-9374

Total Living	First Floor	Bonus	Bed	Bath	Width	Depth	Foundation	Price Category
2454 sq ft	2454 sq ft	256 sq ft	3 + Study	2	80' 6"	66' 0"	Crawl Space	F

Design Features

- A columned-lined entry porch leads through double doors to a broad foyer.

- The step-saver kitchen has a unique diamond shape.

- The pentagon-shaped dining room is positioned to take in rear views.

- The master bedroom boasts a bayed window and luxurious bath.

- An angled hallway leads to secondary bedrooms.

- The plan offers a bonus room over the garage.

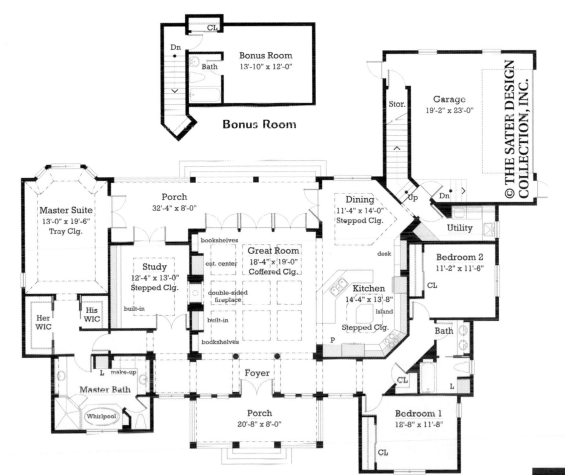

Bonus Room

First Floor

© THE SATER DESIGN COLLECTION, INC.

Rear Elevation

2200 sq ft—2600 sq ft

The Sater Design Collection, Inc.

Southhampton Bay — UDHDS01-6684 — 1-866-525-9374

© The Sater Design Collection, Inc.

Total Living	First Floor	Lower Level	Bonus	Bed	Bath	Width	Depth	Foundation	Price Category
2465 sq ft	2385 sq ft	80 sq ft	N/A	3	2-1/2	60' 4"	59' 4"	Slab	F

Design Features

- A cupola tops a classic pediment and low-pitched roof.

- A sunburst and sidelights set off the entry.

- The great room has a wall of built-ins for high-tech media.

- The master suite features a luxurious bath and dressing area.

- The lower level includes a game room and bonus room.

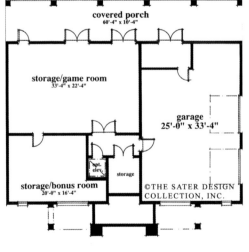

Lower Level

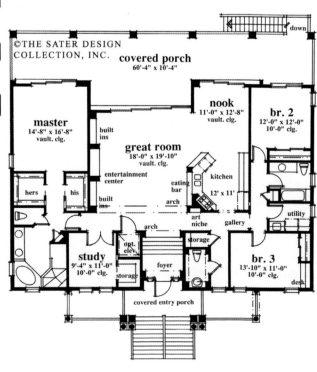

First Floor

Rear Elevation

Holloway — UDHDG01-1064 — 1-866-525-9374

Total Living	First Floor	Second Floor	Bonus	Bed	Bath	Width	Depth	Foundation	Price Category
2469 sq ft	1977 sq ft	492 sq ft	374 sq ft	4	3	75' 1"	44' 5"	Crawl Space*	E

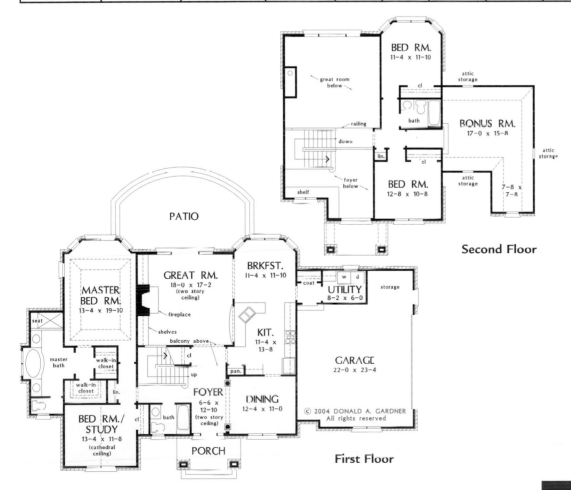

Second Floor

First Floor

Design Features

- The hip roof and strong use of brick reflect a popular traditional style.

- French doors open to a rear patio for outdoor entertaining and relaxation.

- Built-in cabinetry flanks the fireplace, and columns punctuate the dining room.

- A large bonus room provides space for a rec/media room, home gym or guest suite.

Rear Elevation

*Other options available. See page 513.

Devonhurst — UDHFB01-3806 — 1-866-525-9374

© 2003 Frank Betz Associates, Inc.

Total Living	First Floor	Opt. Second Floor	Bed	Bath	Width	Depth	Foundation	Price Category
2477 sq ft	2477 sq ft	555 sq ft	4	3-1/2	65' 4"	68' 0"	Basement or Crawl Space	H

Design Features

- Stepping inside you'll find a very open, unobstructed floor plan. The dining room is bordered by decorative columns, allowing effortless flow to the other living areas.

- The breakfast area and keeping room share open access to the kitchen — perfect for family gathering or parties.

- High ceilings always enhance the volume of a home, so vaults were incorporated into the keeping and family rooms.

Rear Elevation

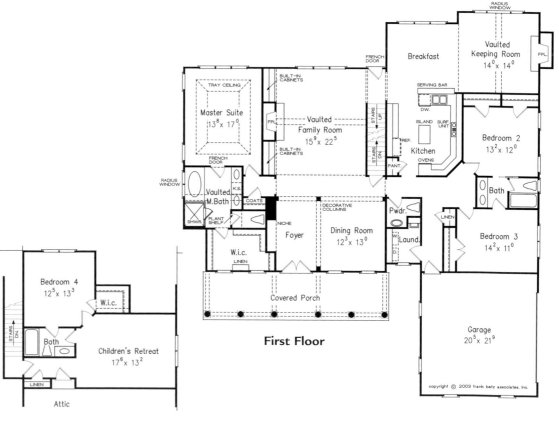

First Floor

Opt. Second Floor

copyright © 2003 frank betz associates, inc.

© 2005 Frank Betz Associates, Inc.

Pepperdine — UDHFB01-3933 — 1-866-525-9374

Total Living	First Floor	Opt. Second Floor	Bed	Bath	Width	Depth	Foundation	Price Category
2477 sq ft	2477 sq ft	546 sq ft	4	3-1/2	63' 0"	68' 0"	Basement, Crawl Space or Slab	H

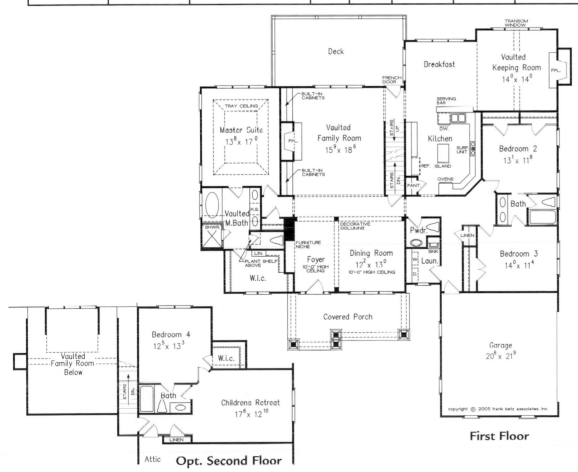

First Floor

Opt. Second Floor

Design Features

- The Craftsman style of the *Pepperdine* is as popular as ever.

- An optional second floor provides and additional bedroom, bathroom, closet and children's retreat.

- Decorative columns frame the dining room defining the space.

- The built-in cabinets flanking the fireplace are a special feature.

Rear Elevation

Carlton Square — UDHFB01-3588 — 1-866-525-9374

© 2001 Frank Betz Associates, Inc.

Total Living	First Floor	Second Floor	Opt. Bonus	Bed	Bath	Width	Depth	Foundation	Price Category
2481 sq ft	1961 sq ft	520 sq ft	265 sq ft	4	3	60' 0"	53' 0"	Basement or Crawl Space	G

Design Features

- A clean-lined combination of brick and siding creates a façade of understated simplicity.

- The interior spaces connect with ease, generating effortless traffic flow from one room to the next.

- Also on the main level, a bedroom can be easily converted into a home office—perfect for teleworkers or retirees.

- Optional bonus space is designed into the second floor.

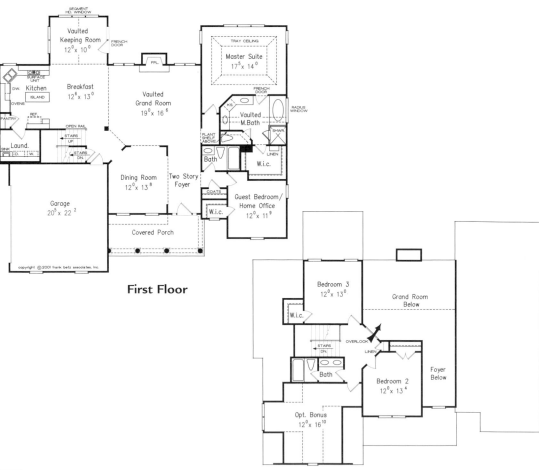

First Floor

Second Floor

Rear Elevation

Azalea Crossing — UDHDG01-849 — 1-866-525-9374

Total Living	First Floor	Second Floor	Bonus	Bed	Bath	Width	Depth	Foundation	Price Category
2482 sq ft	1706 sq ft	776 sq ft	414 sq ft	4	2-1/2	54' 8"	43' 0"	Crawl Space*	E

First Floor

Second Floor

Bonus

Design Features

- A relaxing front porch wraps this three-dormered, four-bedroom home in unbeatable curb appeal.

- An open, vaulted great room is the home's main attraction.

- Built-in bookshelves flank the fireplace, and French doors open to the rear deck.

- Bay windows expand the dining room, breakfast area and master bedroom.

- A lovely sitting area, generous walk-in closet and lavish bath enhance the master suite.

Rear Elevation

Heywood — UDHDG01-991 — 1-866-525-9374

Total Living	First Floor	Second Floor	Bonus	Bed	Bath	Width	Depth	Foundation	Price Category
2485 sq ft	1420 sq ft	1065 sq ft	411 sq ft	4	3	57' 8"	49' 0"	Crawl Space*	E

Design Features

- Twin dormers flank a prominent gable, and a Palladian-style window mimics the arched entryway.

- Numerous windows flood the home with natural light and allow wonderful views.

- French doors accent the bedroom/study as well as the great room.

- A striking fireplace highlights the great room, and the kitchen has plenty of workspace.

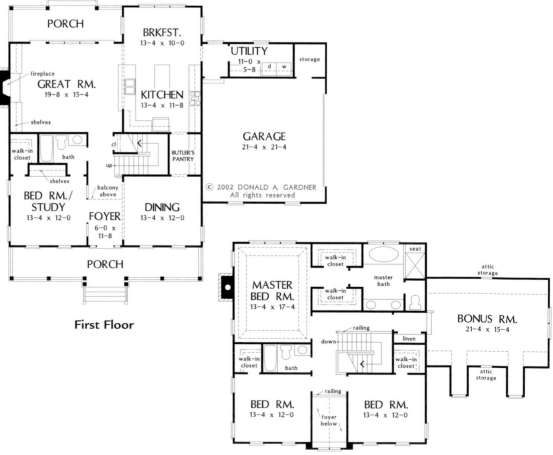

First Floor

Second Floor

Rear Elevation

*Other options available. See page 513.

© 2005 Frank Betz Associates, Inc.

Malibu — UDHFB01-3923 — 1-866-525-9374

Total Living	First Floor	Opt. Second Floor	Bed	Bath	Width	Depth	Foundation	Price Category
2487 sq ft	2487 sq ft	306 sq ft	4	3-1/2	61' 6"	67' 6"	Basement, Crawl Space or Slab	H

First Floor

Opt. Second Floor

Design Features

- The spaciousness of this Craftsman style *Malibu* plan must be seen to be believed.

- The living room can be used as such or French doors can be added connecting it to the master suite, making it a sitting room.

- A bedroom on the second floor can be added, utilizing the additional space.

- Coffered ceilings and built-in bookshelves enhance the look of the family room.

Rear Elevation

Marcella — UDHDS01-7005 — 1-866-525-9374

© The Sater Design Collection, Inc.

Total Living	First Floor	Bonus	Bed	Bath	Width	Depth	Foundation	Price Category
2487 sq ft	2487 sq ft	N/A	3 + Study	2	70' 0"	72' 0"	Slab/opt. Basement	F

Design Features

- A clever roofline is punctuated by shutters and a copper-topped office roof.

- Glass doors expand the dining and living rooms to the rear porch.

- The large kitchen maintains easy access to the dining room and nook.

- A study/office has built-in bookshelves and a front-yard view.

- The privacy of the master suite is protected by double entry doors.

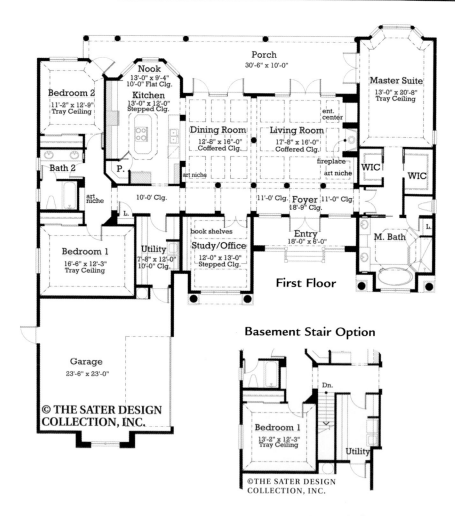

Rear Elevation

Trotterville — UDHDG01-984 — 1-866-525-9374

Total Living	First Floor	Second Floor	Bonus	Bed	Bath	Width	Depth	Foundation	Price Category
2490 sq ft	1687 sq ft	803 sq ft	N/A	4	2-1/2	52' 8"	67' 0"	Crawl Space*	E

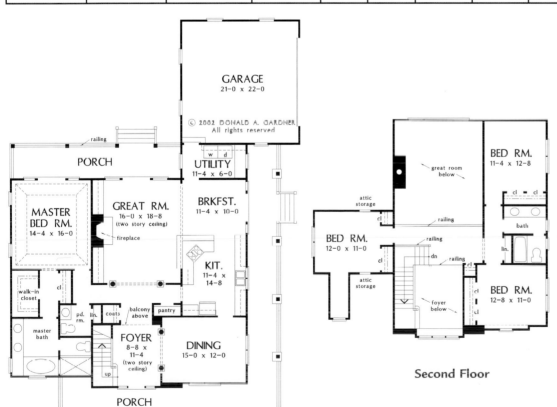

First Floor

Second Floor

Design Features

- A shed dormer, metal porch roof and gable with bracket display Craftsman charm.

- Two spacious porches welcome outdoor relaxation and entertaining.

- Columns accentuate the great room and dining room.

- Built-in cabinetry, French doors and a fireplace highlight the great room.

- Located for convenience, the utility/mud room connects the garage to the house.

Rear Elevation

Mission Hills — UDHDS01-6845 — 1-866-525-9374

© The Sater Design Collection, Inc.

Total Living	First Floor	Lower Level	Bonus	Bed	Bath	Width	Depth	Foundation	Price Category
2494 sq ft	2385 sq ft	109 sq ft	N/A	3	3	60' 0"	52' 0"	Island Basement	F

Design Features

- The study has double doors to the front balcony.
- Vaulted ceilings create openness throughout the living areas.
- Disappearing glass doors connect several rooms to a full-length veranda.
- A large utility room enjoys French doors to the balcony.
- A U-shaped kitchen has a center island and corner pantry.

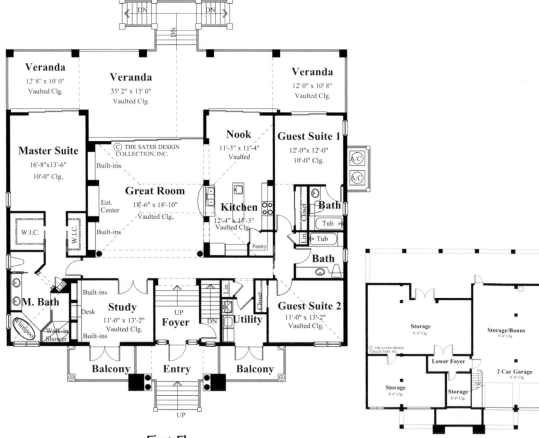

First Floor

Lower Level

Rear Elevation

© The Sater Design Collection, Inc.

Saint Martin — UDHDS01-6846 — 1-866-525-9374

Total Living	First Floor	Lower Level	Bed	Bath	Width	Depth	Foundation	Price Category
2494 sq ft	2385 sq ft	109 sq ft	3	3	60' 0"	52' 0"	Island Basement	F

First Floor

Design Features

- An open floor plan allows for easy movement between the kitchen, nook and great room.

- Built-ins, a vaulted ceiling and a wall of glass adorn the great room.

- The island kitchen has ample counter space, a large walk-in pantry and a work island with a prep sink.

- The master suite is secluded on the left side of the plan and features two walk-in closets and a pampering whirlpool master bath.

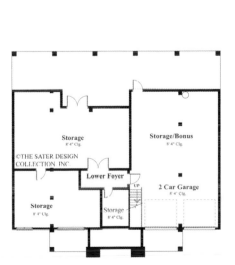

Lower Level

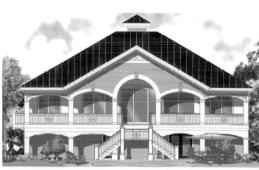

Rear Elevation

Lakeshore — UDHFB01-3752 — 1-866-525-9374

© 2002 Frank Betz Associates, Inc.

Total Living	First Floor	Second Floor	Opt. Bonus	Bed	Bath	Width	Depth	Foundation	Price Category
2507 sq ft	1483 sq ft	1024 sq ft	252 sq ft	4	3	55' 0"	47' 10"	Basement or Crawl Space	H

Design Features

- Thoughtful design details are apparent on the inside with functional amenities that make everyday living easier.

- A large island, double ovens and a butler's pantry take the work out of entertaining.

- The main-floor bedroom has access to a bath, making it ideal for accommodating guests.

- Radius windows keep the family room bright and sunny.

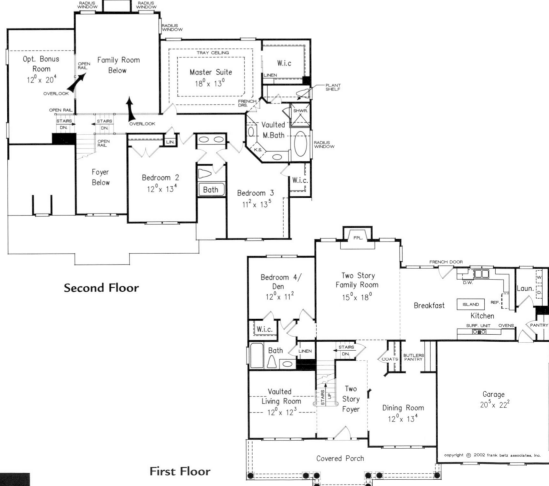

Second Floor

First Floor

Rear Elevation

© 1998 Donald A. Gardner, Inc.

Mulberry — UDHDG01-547 — 1-866-525-9374

Total Living	First Floor	Second Floor	Bonus	Bed	Bath	Width	Depth	Foundation	Price Category
2506 sq ft	1614 sq ft	892 sq ft	341 sq ft	4	2-1/2	71' 10"	50' 0"	Crawl Space*	F

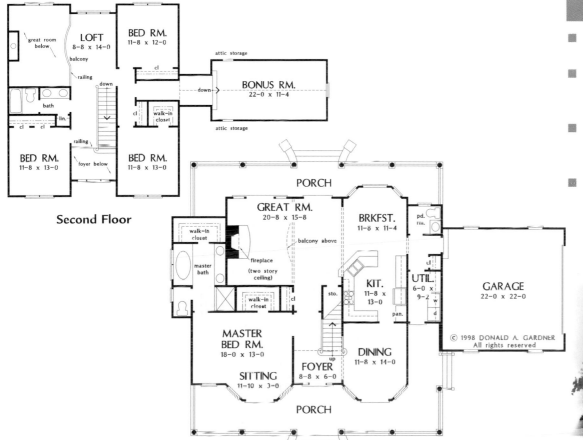

Second Floor

First Floor

Design Features

- The foyer and great room are each brightened by clerestory windows.

- Bay windows grace the dining room, breakfast area and master suite with sitting area.

- Generous front and back porches afford options for outdoor relaxation.

- Upstairs, three roomy bedrooms and a bonus room utilize a hall bath with linen closet.

Rear Elevation

*Other options available. See page 513.

Kerwin — UDHDG01-913 — 1-866-525-9374

Total Living	First Floor	Bonus	Bed	Bath	Width	Depth	Foundation	Price Category
2461 sq ft	2461 sq ft	397 sq ft	4	2	71' 2"	67' 2"	Crawl Space*	E

Design Features

- Turret-styled bay windows, an arched entryway and an elegant balustrade add timeless appeal.

- Separated from the kitchen, the great room features French doors leading to the rear porch with wet bar.

- Custom-styled details include tray ceilings as well as columns found in the foyer and master bath.

- A large utility room is equipped with cabinets, and for privacy, secondary spaces partition all of the bedrooms.

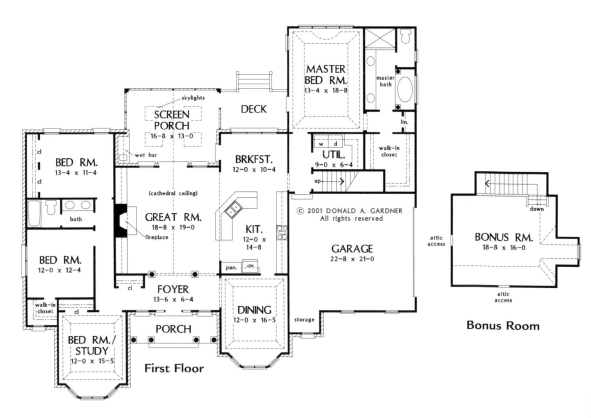

First Floor

Bonus Room

Rear Elevation

*Other options available. See page 513.

Edisto — UDHDG01-764 — 1-866-525-9374

Total Living	First Floor	Second Floor	Bonus	Bed	Bath	Width	Depth	Foundation	Price Category
2509 sq ft	1830 sq ft	679 sq ft	346 sq ft	4	4	81' 2"	48' 0"	Crawl Space*	F

Second Floor

Design Features

- A wrapping front porch creates a charming façade for this four-bedroom home.

- The vaulted foyer receives light from the center clerestory dormer.

- The master bedroom features a tray ceiling for added elegance and back-porch access.

- Another bedroom with walk-in closet and adjacent bath are nearby.

- Both upstairs bedrooms enjoy dormer windows, walk-in closets and private baths.

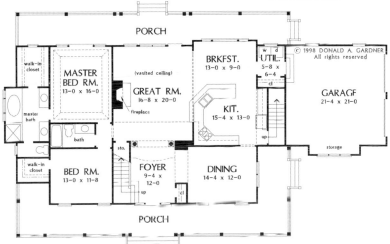

First Floor

Rear Elevation

Riveria dei Fiori — UDHDS01-6809 — 1-866-525-9374

© The Sater Design Collection, Inc.

Total Living	First Floor	Second Floor	Bonus	Bed	Bath	Width	Depth	Foundation	Price Category
2513 sq ft	1542 sq ft	971 sq ft	N/A	4	3	46' 0"	51' 0"	Island Basement	G

Design Features

- Elegant columns, balustrades, corbels, transoms and covered porches enhance the exterior.

- The great room features built-in cabinetry, a fireplace, glass doors opening to the rear porch and easy access to the dining room and kitchen.

- Located on the upper level away from the main living space, the master suite features a vaulted ceiling, spacious bath and a private sitting area that opens to the deck.

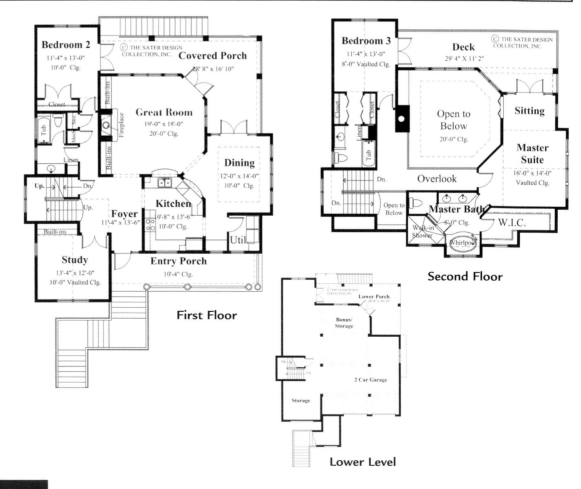

First Floor

Second Floor

Lower Level

Rear Elevation

Newcastle — UDHDG01-994 — 1-866-525-9374

Total Living	First Floor	Second Floor	Bonus	Bed	Bath	Width	Depth	Foundation	Price Category
2515 sq ft	1834 sq ft	681 sq ft	365 sq ft	3	3-1/2	50' 8"	66' 8"	Crawl Space*	F

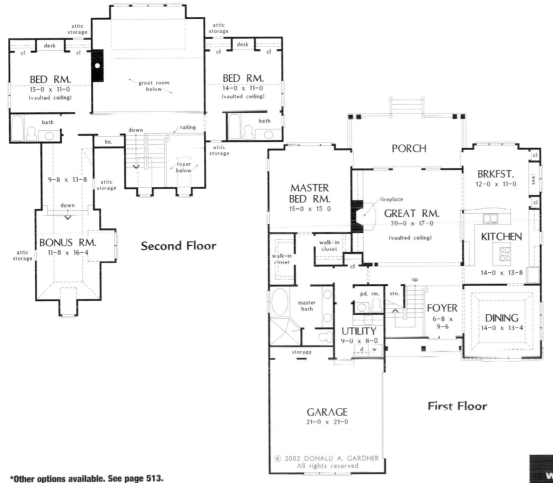

Second Floor

First Floor

Design Features

- With Old-World charm, this cottage's impressive exterior is made of stone and cedar shake.

- Inside, gathering rooms are open to each other and distinguished by columns.

- Both the foyer and great room have two-story ceilings that are brightened by dormers.

- The breakfast nook includes two pantries, while the kitchen features a cooktop island.

Rear Elevation

*Other options available. See page 513.

Bridgeport Harbor — UDHDS01-6685 — 1-866-525-9374

© The Sater Design Collection, Inc.

Total Living	First Floor	Second Floor	Bonus	Bed	Bath	Width	Depth	Foundation	Price Category
2520 sq ft	1305 sq ft	1215 sq ft	N/A	3	2-1/2	30' 6"	77' 6"	Slab/Island Basement	G

Design Features

- Wraparound porticos, charming shutters, dormers and a multitude of windows impress those who pass by.

- Built-ins, a fireplace, eating bar and four sets of French doors opening to the porch enhance the great room.

- The dining room enjoys expansive views through a bay window and easy access to the kitchen and great room.

- The upper level master suite features a spacious bath, and an observation deck with a place for sunning.

Rear Elevation

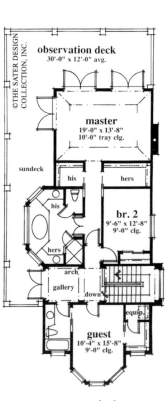

Second Floor

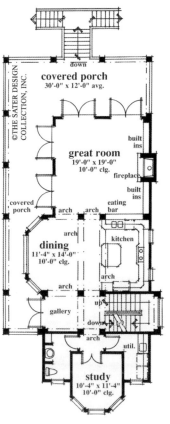

First Floor

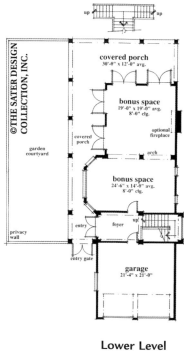

Lower Level

Southerland — UDHDG01-971 — 1-866-525-9374

Total Living	First Floor	Second Floor	Bonus	Bed	Bath	Width	Depth	Foundation	Price Category
2521 sq ft	1798 sq ft	723 sq ft	349 sq ft	4	3-1/2	66' 8"	49' 8"	Crawl Space*	F

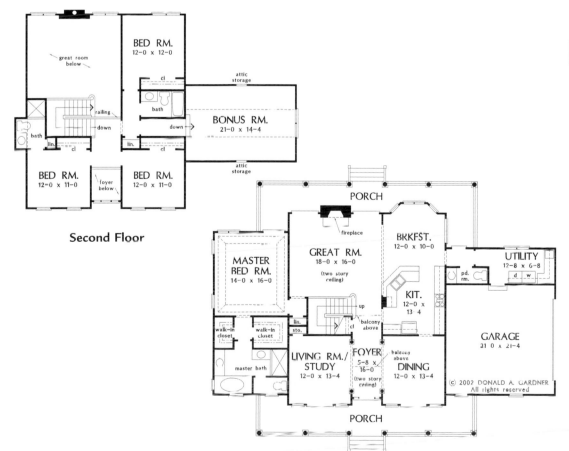

Second Floor

First Floor

Design Features

- Columns make a grand impression both inside and outside.

- Transoms above French doors brighten both the front and rear of the floor plan.

- The mud room/utility area is complete with a sink.

- An upstairs bedroom has its own bath and can be used as a guest suite.

Rear Elevation

Donald A. Gardner Architects, Inc.

Saint Clair — UDHDG01-284 — 1-866-525-9374

Total Living	First Floor	Bonus	Bed	Bath	Width	Depth	Foundation	Price Category
2526 sq ft	2526 sq ft	N/A	4	2-1/2	76' 11"	61' 6"	Crawl Space*	F

Design Features

- This stately home owes its refined demeanor to its elegant brick exterior.
- Light floods through the arched window in the dormer above the foyer.
- The great room leads directly to the sun room through glass doors.
- Privately situated, the master suite has a fireplace and access to the deck.

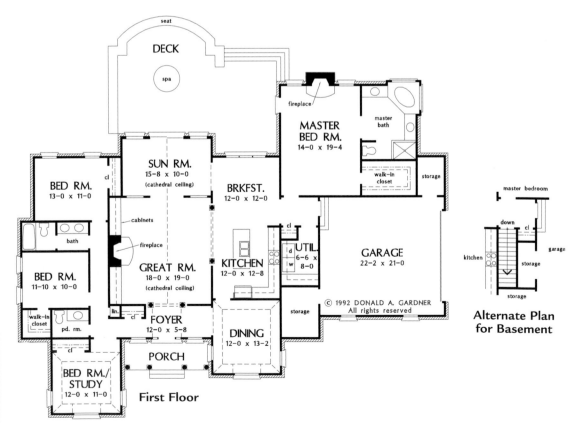

First Floor

Alternate Plan for Basement

Rear Elevation

*Other options available. See page 513.

© The Sater Design Collection, Inc.

Canterbury Trail — UDHDS01-6662 — 1-866-525-9374

Total Living	First Floor	Second Floor	Bonus	Bed	Bath	Width	Depth	Foundation	Price Category
2527 sq ft	1676 sq ft	851 sq ft	N/A	4	3-1/2	55' 0"	50' 0"	Slab	G

First Floor

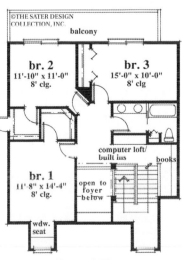

Second Floor

Design Features

■ Mirroring dormer windows, gables and a recessed triple arch entryway enhance the front façade.

■ Arches frame the great room, which features optional built-ins and a wall of glass opening to the veranda.

■ An ample kitchen has a walk-in pantry and island with eating bar

■ The master suite is tucked away from the spare bedrooms and features walk-in closets, a spacious bath and access to the veranda.

Rear Elevation

Hennefield — UDHFB01-3835 — 1-866-525-9374

© 2003 Frank Betz Associates, Inc.

Total Living	First Floor	Opt. Second Floor	Bed	Bath	Width	Depth	Foundation	Price Category
2548 sq ft	2548 sq ft	490 sq ft	4	3-1/2	63' 0"	67' 6"	Basement or Crawl Space	H

Design Features

- This one-level design is equipped with several added extras that make it original and unique.

- Just off the kitchen is a vaulted keeping room that is bright and comfortable with radius windows that allow the natural light to illuminate the room.

- Built-in cabinetry in the family room gives this area an appealing focal point, as well as ample storage and decorating opportunities.

First Floor

Opt. Second Floor

Rear Elevation

Plumstead — UDHDG01-874 — 1-866-525-9374

Total Living	First Floor	Bonus	Bed	Bath	Width	Depth	Foundation	Price Category
2544 sq ft	2544 sq ft	394 sq ft	4	2-1/2	62' 8"	82' 1"	Crawl Space*	F

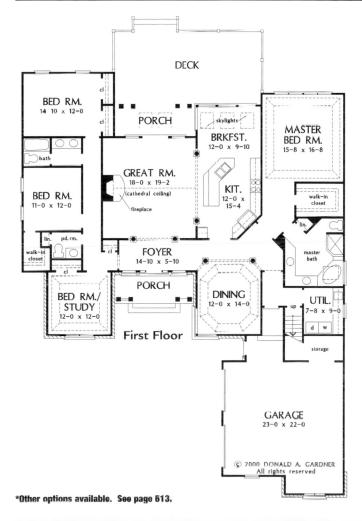

First Floor

DECK

BED RM.
14 10 x 12-0

PORCH

skylights

BRKFST.
12-0 x 9-10

MASTER
BED RM.
15-8 x 16-8

bath

GREAT RM.
18-0 x 19-2
(cathedral ceiling)
fireplace

KIT.
12-0 x 15-4

walk-in
closet

BED RM.
11-0 x 12-0

lin. pd. rm.

walk-in
closet

FOYER
14-10 x 5-10

master
bath

BED RM./
STUDY
12-0 x 12-0

PORCH

DINING
12-0 x 14-0

UTIL.
7-8 x 9-0

up

d   w

storage

GARAGE
23-0 x 22-0

attic
storage

down

BONUS RM.
15-0 x 22-0

Bonus Room

Design Features

- Refined elegance characterizes this stunning home with a dynamic open floor plan.
- Elegant columns separate the great room with cathedral ceiling from the angled kitchen with skylit breakfast area.
- Stunning tray ceilings enhance the bedroom/study and the dining room.
- The dining room is distinguished by two stately columns that grace the hallway to the kitchen and foyer.
- This home has plenty of closet and storage space, including a bonus room above the garage.

Rear Elevation

Coventry — UDHFB01-1103 — 1-866-525-9374

© 1997 Frank Betz Associates, Inc.

Total Living	First Floor	Second Floor	Opt. Bonus	Bed	Bath	Width	Depth	Foundation	Price Category
2551 sq ft	1972 sq ft	579 sq ft	256 sq ft	3	2-1/2	57' 4"	51' 2"	Basement, Crawl Space or Slab	H

Design Features

- A turret sitting room graces the master suite, which has its own wing on the main level.

- The vaulted ceilings add volume to the great room, keeping room and master bath.

- Windows across the rear of the home showcase backyard views.

- An informal keeping room is open to the breakfast nook and kitchen.

First Floor

Rear Elevation

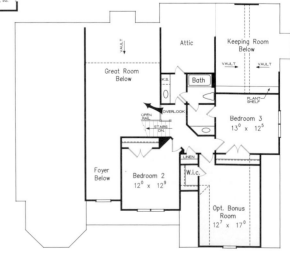

Second Floor

Donald A. Gardner Architects, Inc.

Rousseau — UDHDG01-451 — 1-866-525-9374

Total Living	First Floor	Second Floor	Bonus	Bed	Bath	Width	Depth	Foundation	Price Category
2549 sq ft	1904 sq ft	645 sq ft	434 sq ft	3	2-1/2	71' 2"	45' 8"	Crawl Space*	F

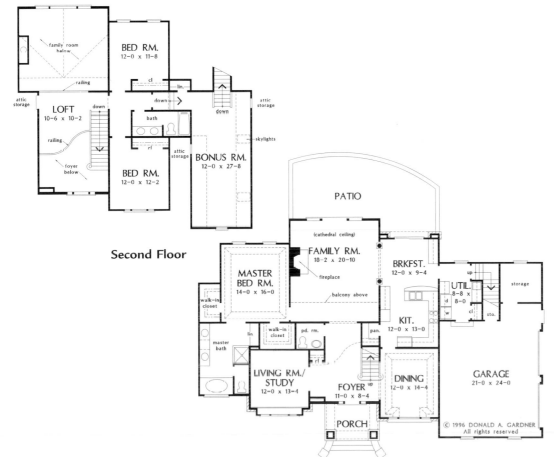

Second Floor

First Floor

Design Features

- This home is packed with visual excitement created by a stone and stucco exterior.

- The two-story great room has a fireplace, vaulted ceiling and over-looking balcony.

- The first-floor master suite features dual walk-in closets and a private bath with linen closet.

- Upstairs includes two bedrooms with full bath, bonus room, loft and attic storage.

Rear Elevation

La Posada — UDHDS01-6785 — 1-866-525-9374

© The Sater Design Collection, Inc.

Total Living	First Floor	Second Floor	Bonus	Bed	Bath	Width	Depth	Foundation	Price Category
2554 sq ft	2554 sq ft	N/A	N/A	4	3	60' 4"	78' 9"	Slab	G

Design Features

- Decorative pendants add one-of-a-kind detail to the entryway cornice.

- The kitchen, living and leisure room flow together and offer access to the lanai through disappearing glass walls.

- A stepped ceiling, work island, large walk-in pantry and eating bar enhance the kitchen.

- Owners will enjoy privacy in a master suite tucked to one side of the home that features built-ins, a tray ceiling, walk-in closet, spacious bath and access to the lanai.

Rear Elevation

© The Sater Design Collection, Inc.

Lunden Valley — UDHDS01-7050 — 1-866-525-9374

Total Living	First Floor	Bonus	Bed	Bath	Width	Depth	Foundation	Price Category
2555 sq ft	2555 sq ft	N/A	3 + Study	2-1/2	70' 0"	76' 6"	Crawl Space	G

First Floor

© THE SATER DESIGN COLLECTION, INC.

Design Features

- This home features a charming front porch which supports a distinctive front gable.

- A column-lined hall leads to private areas of the home.

- The master has rear-porch access.

- Natural light from the rear porch fills the great room and kitchen.

- A dining room and study border the foyer.

Rear Elevation

San Marino — UDHDS01-6833 — 1-866-525-9374

© The Sater Design Collection, Inc.

Total Living	First Floor	Second Floor	Bonus	Bed	Bath	Width	Depth	Foundation	Price Category
2433 sq ft	2433 sq ft	N/A	N/A	3	3	70' 2"	53' 0"	Island Basement	F

Design Features

- A balcony, sunburst transom window and dual staircases leading up to the recessed arch entry create an impressive front façade.

- The great room opens through columns in the central gallery hall.

- The kitchen has a food preparation island and a service counter that opens to the dining room.

- A tray ceiling watches over the master suite that boasts two walk-in closets, a spacious master bath and a wall of glass that opens to the private porch.

Rear Elevation

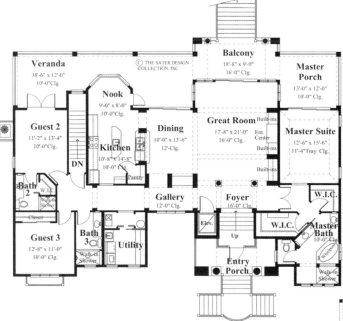

First Floor

Lower Level

© 2003 Frank Betz Associates, Inc.

Bainbridge Court — UDHFB01-3815 — 1-866-525-9374

Total Living	First Floor	Second Floor	Opt. Bonus	Bed	Bath	Width	Depth	Foundation	Price Category
2563 sq ft	1795 sq ft	768 sq ft	N/A	5	3	55' 0"	61' 0"	Basement, Crawl Space or Slab	I

First Floor

Second Floor

Design Features

- From the *Southern Living® Design Collection*
- The classic brick-and-siding exterior of the *Bainbridge Court* gives this home a time-honored elegant appeal.
- The staircase is strategically tucked away to keep the foyer open and roomy.
- A cozy screened porch adjoins the kitchen area and has access to an expansive deck, making a great space for grilling and entertaining.

Rear Elevation

Beckett — UDHDG01-357 — 1-866-525-9374

Total Living	First Floor	Second Floor	Bonus	Bed	Bath	Width	Depth	Foundation	Price Category
2563 sq ft	1907 sq ft	656 sq ft	467 sq ft	4	2-1/2	89' 10"	53' 4"	Crawl Space*	F

Design Features

- Bay windows and a screened porch make this four-bedroom home a haven for outdoor enthusiasts.

- The open foyer takes advantage of light from the central dormer with Palladian window.

- A grand gathering space emerges by opening the contemporary kitchen to the breakfast and great rooms.

- The versatile front bedroom can also be a study.

- A low maintenance exterior adds to the home's appeal.

Rear Elevation

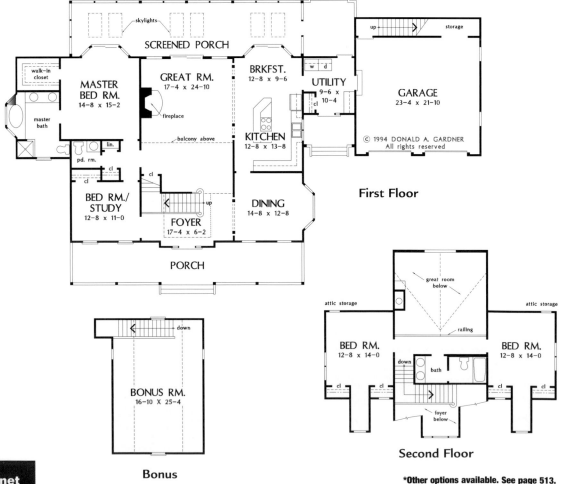

First Floor

Bonus

Second Floor

*Other options available. See page 513.

© The Sater Design Collection, Inc.

Walker Way — UDHDS01-6697 — 1-866-525-9374

Total Living	First Floor	Second Floor	Bonus	Bed	Bath	Width	Depth	Foundation	Price Category
2569 sq ft	1642 sq ft	927 sq ft	N/A	3	2-1/2	60' 0"	44' 6"	Slab with Pilings	G

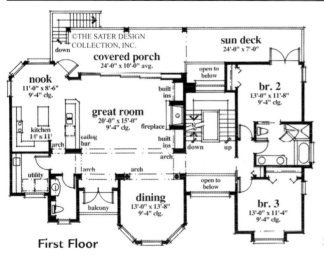

First Floor

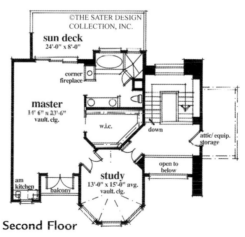

Second Floor

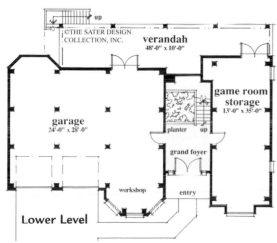

Lower Level

Design Features

- Charming balconies and a magnificent circle-head window set off a three-story turret on the front exterior.

- The gourmet kitchen opens to the morning nook, which boasts its own bay windows.

- Built-in cabinetry, fireplace, arches and a retreating wall of glass to the porch enhance the great room.

- The master retreat includes a private bayed study, corner fireplace, and a private sun deck.

Rear Elevation

2200 sq ft—2600 sq ft

Frank Betz Associates, Inc.

Ambrose — UDHFB01-3551 — 1-866-525-9374

© 2000 Frank Betz Associates, Inc.

Total Living	First Floor	Second Floor	Opt. Bonus	Bed	Bath	Width	Depth	Foundation	Price Category
2582 sq ft	2003 sq ft	579 sq ft	262 sq ft	4	3	54' 0"	60' 0"	Basement, Crawl Space or Slab	H

Design Features

- A distinctive turret with arched windows is the focal point of the façade on the *Ambrose*.

- A covered entry leads to an interesting and thoughtful layout inside.

- Family time is well spent in the large sunroom, situated just beyond the breakfast area.

- With its fireplace and built-in cabinetry, this room adds a comfortable and casual element to this home.

Rear Elevation

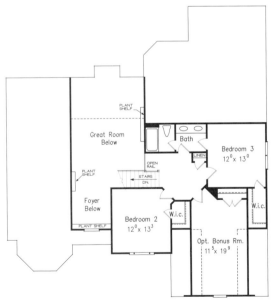

Second Floor

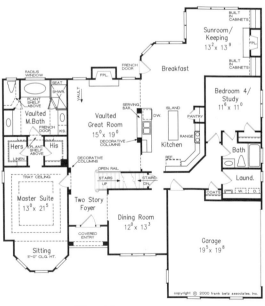

First Floor

Frank Betz Associates, Inc.

© 2002 Frank Betz Associates, Inc.

Oak Knoll — UDHFB01-3734 — 1-866-525-9374

Total Living	First Floor	Second Floor	Opt. Bonus	Bed	Bath	Width	Depth	Foundation	Price Category
2577 sq ft	1894 sq ft	683 sq ft	210 sq ft	4	3	57' 0"	53' 6"	Basement or Crawl Space	H

First Floor

Second Floor

Design Features

- This design was created to give homeowners living spaces that are supplementary to the traditional rooms found in most plans.

- The master bedroom is enhanced by a private sitting area with views overlooking the backyard.

- Just off the breakfast area is a bright and sunny keeping room with a radius window.

- Kids will appreciate having a private spot to study in the loft designed into the upper level of this home.

Rear Elevation

Peppermill — UDHDG01-1034 — 1-866-525-9374

Total Living	First Floor	Second Floor	Bonus	Bed	Bath	Width	Depth	Foundation	Price Category
2586 sq ft	1809 sq ft	777 sq ft	264 sq ft	4	3-1/2	70' 7"	48' 4"	Crawl Space*	F

Design Features

- A traditional brick exterior with two country porches creates a modern exterior.
- Bold columns and a metal roof welcome guests inside an equally impressive interior.
- Both the foyer and great room have two-story ceilings, and a tray ceiling tops the master bedroom.
- A bay window expands the breakfast nook, while French doors lead to the rear porch.
- The living room/study and bonus room add flexibility for changing needs.

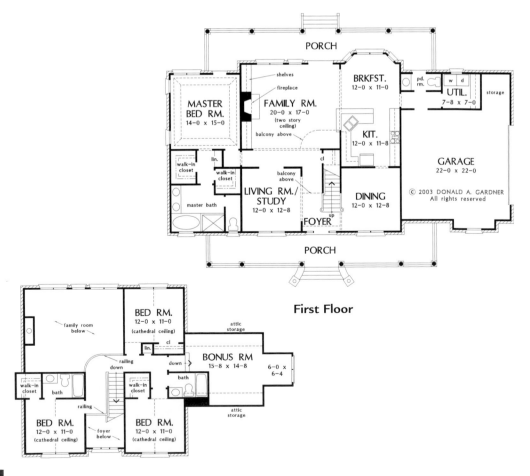

First Floor

Second Floor

Rear Elevation

*Other options available. See page 513.

© 2003 Frank Betz Associates, Inc.

Bakersfield — UDHFB01-3783 — 1-866-525-9374

Total Living	First Floor	Second Floor	Opt. Bonus	Bed	Bath	Width	Depth	Foundation	Price Category
2584 sq ft	1322 sq ft	1262 sq ft	N/A	4	3	48' 0"	50' 0"	Basement, Crawl Space or Slab	H

Second Floor

First Floor

Design Features

- Tapered columns and Mission-styled windows, combined with earthen stone and cedar shakes, make the *Bakersfield* reminiscent of the Craftsman era.

- A two-story foyer with an art niche creates an exciting first impression.

- The keeping room is strategically placed just off the kitchen for easy interaction from room to room.

- A bedroom connected to a full bath is incorporated into the main floor, making an ideal guest suite.

Rear Elevation

Greythorne — UDHFB01-3764 — 1-866-525-9374

© 2002 Frank Betz Associates, Inc.

Total Living	First Floor	Second Floor	Opt. Bonus	Bed	Bath	Width	Depth	Foundation	Price Category
2587 sq ft	2047 sq ft	540 sq ft	278 sq ft	4	3	60' 0"	56' 0"	Basement, Crawl Space or Slab	I

Design Features

- Thoughtful and creative design makes the *Greythorne* unique in both the layout and the details.

- The full-service kitchen has an attention-grabbing coffered ceiling.

- Accessible from both the master suite and the keeping room is a covered back porch.

- Window seats are incorporated into the master suite and the fourth bedroom.

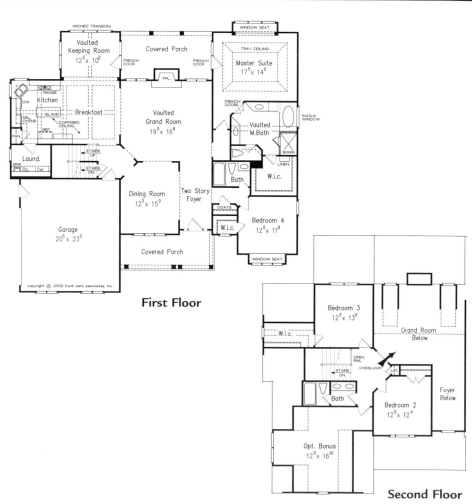

First Floor

Second Floor

Rear Elevation

Sunnybrook — UDHDG01-484 — 1-866-525-9374

Total Living	First Floor	Second Floor	Bonus	Bed	Bath	Width	Depth	Foundation	Price Category
2596 sq ft	1939 sq ft	657 sq ft	386 sq ft	4	3	80' 10"	55' 8"	Crawl Space*	F

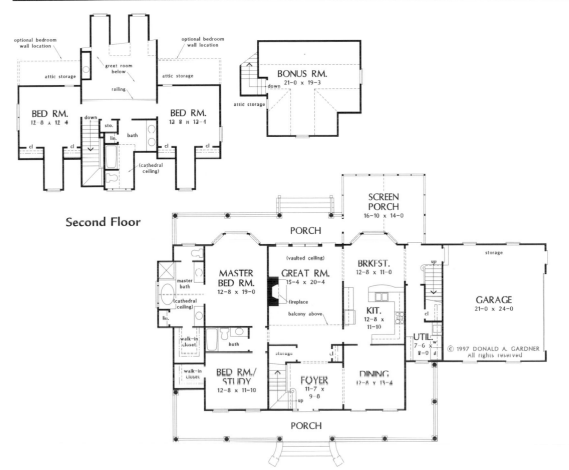

Second Floor

First Floor

Design Features

- This country farmhouse charms with its wrapping front porch and gabled dormers.

- The foyer gives way to a generous great room with fireplace, cathedral ceiling and balcony above.

- Nearby, a flexible bedroom/study has a walk-in closet and adjacent full bath.

- The first-floor master suite with sunny bay window features a private bath with cathedral ceiling.

- A bonus room over the garage completes the plan.

Rear Elevation

Bramwell — UDHDG01-1078 — 1-866-525-9374

© 2004 Donald A. Gardner, Inc.

Total Living	First Floor	Bonus	Bed	Bath	Width	Depth	Foundation	Price Category
2609 sq ft	2609 sq ft	431 sq ft	3	2	73' 10"	61' 7"	Crawl Space*	F

Design Features

- Two art niches lie just inside the foyer, and double-doors lead into the versatile bedroom/study.

- A double-sided fireplace visually and physically warms the great room and dining room.

- A patio and home office area fulfill the needs of today's active lifestyles with places to both relax and work.

- The breakfast nook accesses the patio and the screened porch through French doors.

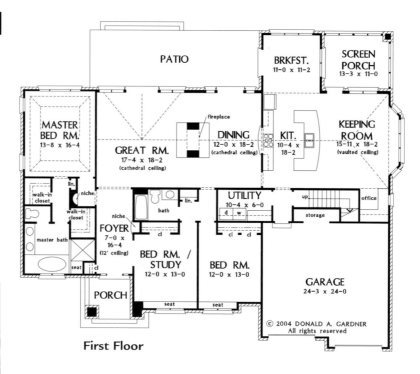

First Floor

Bonus Room

Rear Elevation

*Other options available. See page 513.

Donald A. Gardner Architects, Inc.

Charlevoix — UDHDG01-1086 — 1-866-525-9374

Total Living	First Floor	Bonus	Bed	Bath	Width	Depth	Foundation	Price Category
2607 sq ft	2607 sq ft	413 sq ft	4	3	77' 0"	58' 0"	Crawl Space*	F

Design Features

- A stone portico makes an impressive entry to this stone-and-siding home that showcases European charm.
- A coffered ceiling, window seat and double doors enhance the bedroom/study.
- A built-in desk turns the breakfast nook into a computer hub or a place to organize the grocery list.
- The butler's pantry, large walk-in pantry and serving bar add special touches that make this home live easily.

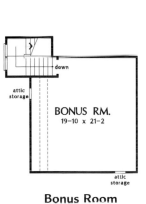

Bonus Room

First Floor

Rear Elevation

Magnolia — UDHDG01-544 — 1-866-525-9374

Total Living	First Floor	Second Floor	Bonus	Bed	Bath	Width	Depth	Foundation	Price Category
2617 sq ft	1878 sq ft	739 sq ft	383 sq ft	4	3	79' 8"	73' 4"	Crawl Space*	F

Design Features

- This Southern farmhouse features a wraparound porch and dormer windows for instant curb appeal.
- Illuminating the vaulted foyer is an arched clerestory window within the large, center dormer.
- The kitchen offers easy service to the great room by way of a convenient pass-thru.
- The master suite includes screened-porch access, a bay window and a splendid bath.
- The first-floor bedroom/study, with its own entrance, makes an ideal home office or guest room.

Rear Elevation

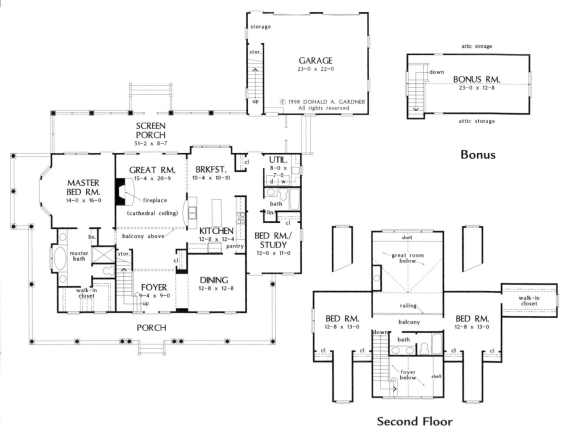

*Other options available. See page 513.

© 2004 Frank Betz Associates, Inc.

Kensington Park — UDHFB01-3910 — 1-866-525-9374

Total Living	First Floor	Second Floor	Opt. Bonus	Bed	Bath	Width	Depth	Foundation	Price Category
2619 sq ft	1755 sq ft	864 sq ft	N/A	4	3-1/2	56' 0"	53' 0"	Basement, Crawl Space or Slab	G

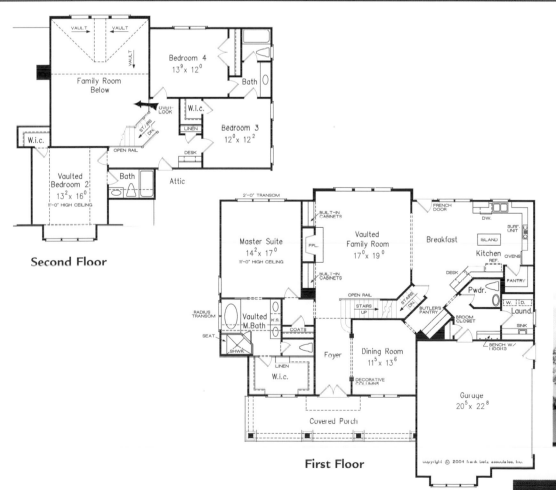

Second Floor

First Floor

Design Features

- The *Kensington Park* was designed to give families a home that interacts with their day-to-day living without sacrificing charm.

- Its kitchen, breakfast area and family room are all open to each other creating easy access.

- A butler's pantry connects the kitchen to the dining room adding convenience to entertaining.

- A mudroom is situated just off the garage and is equipped with a bench, wall hooks, a broom closet and access to the laundry room.

Rear Elevation

Blakeford — UDHFB01-3753 — 1-866-525-9374

© 2002 Frank Betz Associates, Inc.

Total Living	First Floor	Second Floor	Opt. Bonus	Bed	Bath	Width	Depth	Foundation	Price Category
2635 sq ft	1444 sq ft	1191 sq ft	186 sq ft	4	4	52' 4"	47' 4"	Basement, Crawl Space or Slab	I

Design Features

- Two story front porches give Southern charm to the façade of this smart design.

- Board-and-batten shutters and cedar shakes enhance the elevation with casual warmth.

- A main floor study can be easily converted into a fourth bedroom.

- The kitchen, breakfast and keeping rooms all gently join together to create one unified space.

- A covered porch serves as an outdoor extension of this space.

Rear Elevation

Second Floor

First Floor

2600 sq ft—3000 sq ft

Donald A. Gardner Architects, Inc.

© 2003 Donald A. Gardner, Inc.

Jeffcoat — UDHDG01-1031 — 1-866-525-9374

Total Living	First Floor	Bonus	Bed	Bath	Width	Depth	Foundation	Price Category
2636 sq ft	2636 sq ft	425 sq ft	3	2-1/2	67' 3"	69' 9"	Crawl Space*	F

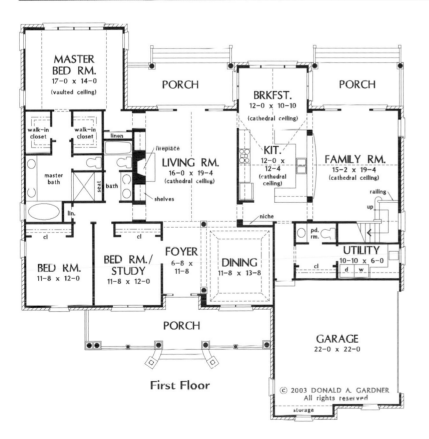

First Floor

© 2003 DONALD A. GARDNER
All rights reserved

Bonus Room

Design Features

- A dramatic barrel-vault entryway, grand columns and arched transoms create an elegant façade.

- Inside, the open floor plan features an abundance of windows, which usher in natural light and views.

- Columns and a tray ceiling define the dining room, and French doors lead to the bedroom/study.

- The family/media room is open to the kitchen and features a staircase leading to the bonus room.

- The master suite is complete with dual walk-in closets, a double vanity, garden tub and spacious shower.

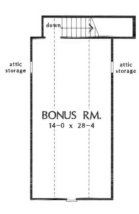

Rear Elevation

Michelle — UDHFB01-1013 — 1-866-525-9374

© 1996 Frank Betz Associates, Inc.

Total Living	First Floor	Second Floor	Opt. Bonus	Bed	Bath	Width	Depth	Foundation	Price Category
2643 sq ft	2015 sq ft	628 sq ft	315 sq ft	4	3	56' 0"	52' 6"	Basement, Crawl Space or Slab	H

Design Features

- Arched and bay windows complement vaulted and tray ceilings to make this home bright and cheery.

- Built-in bookshelves flanking the fireplace make wonderful areas for storage or display.

- The master suite has a tray ceiling and an arched window.

- A main-level secondary bedroom makes an ideal guest suite or home office.

Second Floor

First Floor

Rear Elevation

Briarcliff — UDHDG01-259 — 1-866-525-9374

Total Living	First Floor	Second Floor	Bonus	Bed	Bath	Width	Depth	Foundation	Price Category
2647 sq ft	1759 sq ft	888 sq ft	324 sq ft	4	3-1/2	85' 0"	53' 0"	Crawl Space*	F

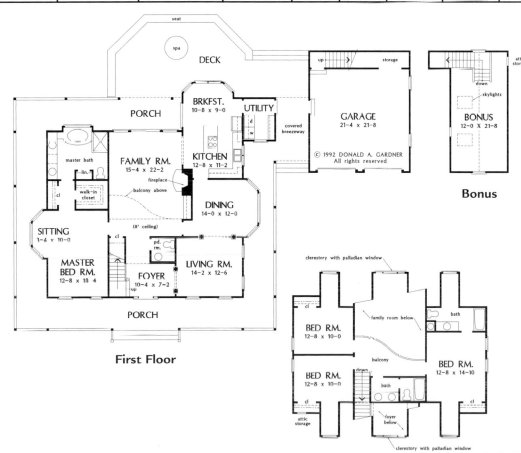

First Floor

Second Floor

Bonus

Design Features

- This spectacular country dream home is wrapped in porches and a massive deck.

- Front and rear Palladian windows let light flood this open plan.

- The family room with sloped ceiling receives added drama from an open, curved balcony.

- The first-floor master suite contains a sitting area, ample closet space and a luxurious bath.

- The bonus room provides extra elbow room to growing families.

Rear Elevation

Sommerset — UDHDS01-6827 — 1-866-525-9374

© The Sater Design Collection, Inc.

Total Living	First Floor	Second Floor	Bonus	Bed	Bath	Width	Depth	Foundation	Price Category
2650 sq ft	1296 sq ft	1354 sq ft	N/A	3	2-1/2	34' 0"	63' 2"	Slab	G

Design Features

- A gallery-style foyer leads to a powder room and a walk-in pantry.

- Wrapping counter space provides an overlook to a breakfast nook.

- French doors bring the outdoors into the dining and great rooms.

- Upstairs, the luxurious master suite has an octagonal sitting area and deck.

- Also opening to the upper deck are two more bedrooms and a study.

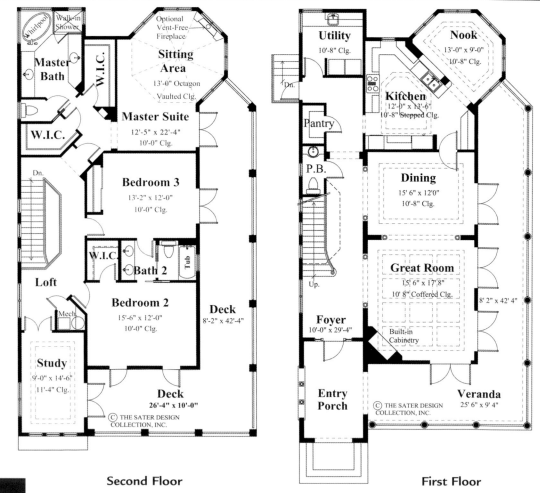

Rear Elevation

Second Floor

First Floor

Colridge — UDHDG01-1012-D — 1-866-525-9374

Total Living	First Floor	Basement	Bonus	Bed	Bath	Width	Depth	Foundation	Price Category
2652 sq ft	1732 sq ft	920 sq ft	N/A	3	3	70' 6"	59' 6"	Hillside Walkout	F

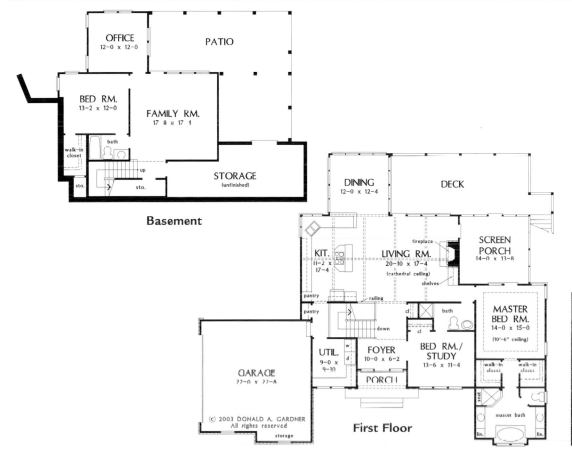

Design Features

- A mixture of exterior materials enhances the curb appeal of this hillside walkout.

- A large deck, screened porch and patio promote outdoor living.

- A cathedral ceiling with exposed beams crowns the kitchen and great room, creating volume.

- The master suite is complete with a tray ceiling in the bedroom and screened-porch access.

Rear Elevation

Esperane — UDHDS01-6759 — 1-866-525-9374

© The Sater Design Collection, Inc.

Total Living	First Floor	Bonus	Bed	Bath	Width	Depth	Foundation	Price Category
2654 sq ft	2654 sq ft	N/A	4	2	63' 8"	72' 8"	Slab	G

Design Features

- A slump-arch ceiling defines the elegant entryway.

- The living room is charming with its fireplace and built-ins.

- The kitchen and family room are ideal for entertaining.

- The master suite gets privacy and a luxe bathroom.

- Secondary bedrooms are tucked to the rear of the home.

- Full bath accesses three bedrooms and the lanai.

Rear Elevation

First Floor

© THE SATER DESIGN COLLECTION, INC.

Hollyhock — UDHDG01-864 — 1-866-525-9374

Total Living	First Floor	Second Floor	Bonus	Bed	Bath	Width	Depth	Foundation	Price Category
2661 sq ft	2065 sq ft	596 sq ft	483 sq ft	4	3-1/2	92' 0"	57' 8"	Crawl Space*	F

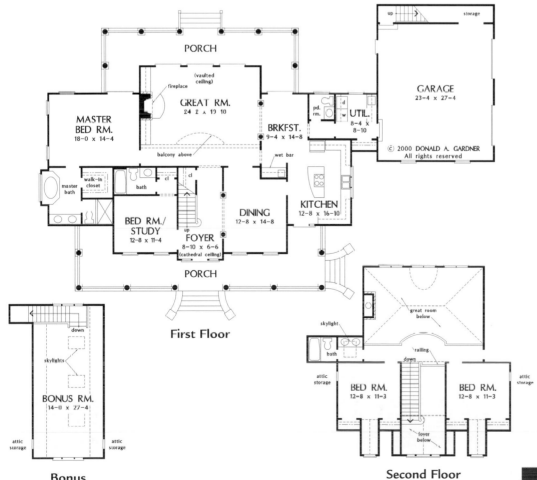

First Floor

Bonus

Second Floor

Design Features

- Sophistication abounds in this exquisite four-bedroom home with wrapping porches.

- A cathedral ceiling in the home's foyer makes a notable first impression.

- A large dormer with Palladian-style window adds to the drama.

- The expansive great room is enhanced by a vaulted ceiling and multiple doors that open onto the back porch.

- Note the nearby wet bar.

Rear Elevation

Rockingham — UDHDG01-1087 — 1-866-525-9374

© 2004 Donald A. Gardner, Inc.

Total Living	First Floor	Bonus	Bed	Bath	Width	Depth	Foundation	Price Category
2663 sq ft	2663 sq ft	404 sq ft	4	3	86' 10"	83' 9"	Crawl Space*	F

Design Features

- An arched portico mirrors the graceful shape of exterior windows in this stunning home.
- Multiple gables and twin dormers over the garage spark instant curb appeal.
- Numerous porches provide an abundance of space for entertaining and enjoying the outdoors.
- French doors accent the dining room, leading to both a screened porch and adjacent side porch.

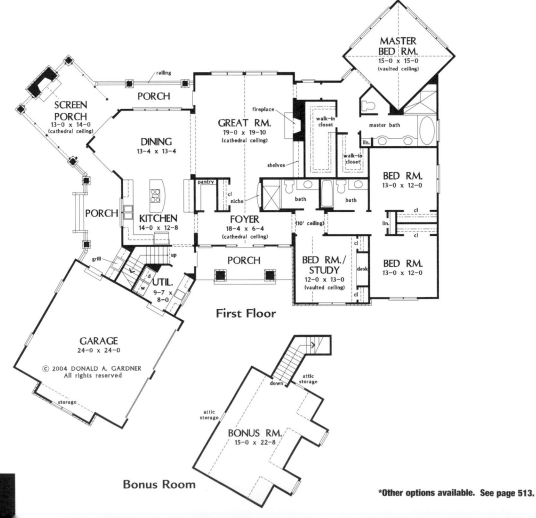

First Floor

Bonus Room

Rear Elevation

*Other options available. See page 513.

© 1993 Donald A. Gardner Architects, Inc.

Herndon — UDHDG01-302 — 1-866-525-9374

Total Living	First Floor	Bonus	Bed	Bath	Width	Depth	Foundation	Price Category
2663 sq ft	2663 sq ft	653 sq ft	4	2-1/2	72' 7"	71' 5"	Crawl Space*	F

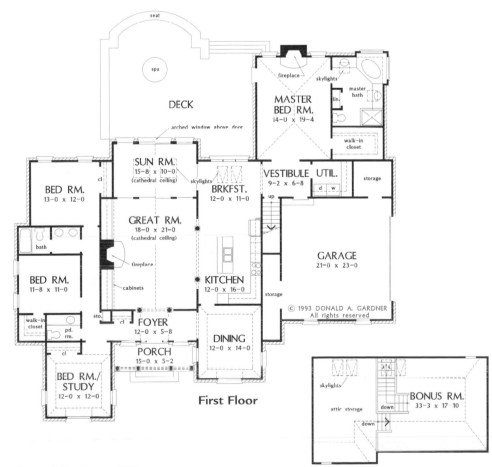

First Floor

Bonus Room

Design Features

- Arched windows, and interior and exterior columns give this four-bedroom home instant authority.
- An arched clerestory window channels light from the foyer to the great room.
- Graceful columns punctuate the open interior that connects the foyer, great room, kitchen and sunroom.
- Special ceiling treatments and skylights add volume throughout.
- The skylit bonus room makes a great play area for kids and provides easy access to attic storage.

Rear View

*Other options available. See page 513.

Photographed home may have been modified from original construction documents.

Donald A. Gardner Architects, Inc.

Riverbend — UDHDG01-225 — 1-866-525-9374

Total Living	First Floor	Second Floor	Bonus	Bed	Bath	Width	Depth	Foundation	Price Category
2677 sq ft	1734 sq ft	943 sq ft	N/A	4	3-1/2	55' 0"	44' 0"	Crawl Space*	F

Design Features

- A double-gabled roof, with front and rear Palladian windows, gives this plan a stately elegance.

- Vaulted ceilings in the foyer and great room reinforce the visual drama of the Palladian windows.

- The covered front porch and outstanding rear deck expand living space to the outdoors.

- The spacious first-floor master suite accesses the large sunroom from a luxurious master bath.

Second Floor

Rear Elevation

First Floor

*Other options available. See page 513.

© 2004 Donald A. Gardner, Inc.

East Haven — UDHDG01-1049 — 1-866-525-9374

Total Living	First Floor	Bonus	Bed	Bath	Width	Depth	Foundation	Price Category
2689 sq ft	2689 sq ft	409 sq ft	4	3	69' 8"	68' 10"	Crawl Space*	F

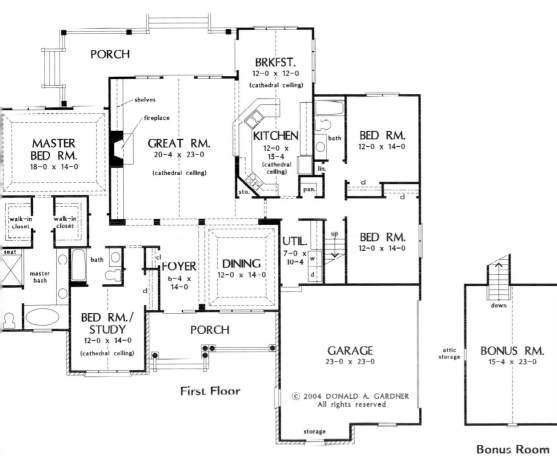

First Floor

© 2004 DONALD A. GARDNER
All rights reserved

Bonus Room

Design Features

- Arches and transoms contrast with gables and columns for a striking exterior.
- The front porch is designed to evoke the nostalgia of yesteryear.
- French doors access the rear porch from the master suite, great room and breakfast nook.
- Twin walk-in closets and a tray ceiling complement the master suite.
- The master bath includes a shower with seat, double vanity and garden tub.

Rear Elevation

Stonebridge — UDHDS01-6832 — 1-866-525-9374

© The Sater Design Collection, Inc.

Total Living	First Floor	Second Floor	Bonus	Bed	Bath	Width	Depth	Foundation	Price Category
2698 sq ft	1798 sq ft	900 sq ft	N/A	3	3-1/2	54' 0"	57' 0"	Crawl Space	G

Design Features

- Mirroring dormers, a stone gable entry, classic columns and rustic balustrades garner attention from those who pass-by.

- A coffered two-story sloped ceiling soars over the great room that features built-in cabinetry, easy access to the kitchen and is connected to the dining room by a two-sided fireplace.

- Secondary bedrooms are placed on the upper floor away from the master suite and feature walk-in closets and private baths.

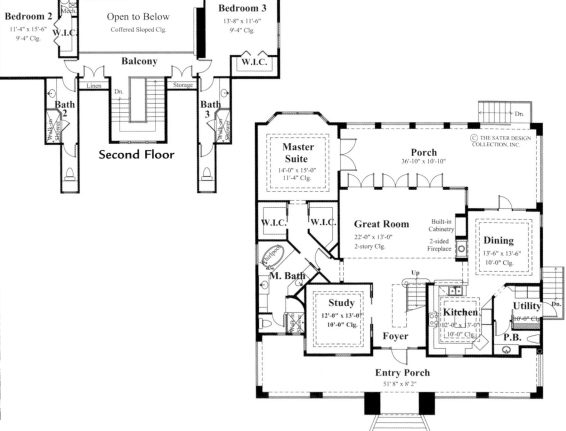

Rear Elevation

© 2005 Frank Betz Associates, Inc.

Barton Creek — UDHFB01-3928 — 1-866-525-9374

Total Living	First Floor	Opt. Second Floor	Bed	Bath	Width	Depth	Foundation	Price Category
2699 sq ft	2699 sq ft	418 sq ft	4	4-1/2	65' 0"	75' 4"	Basement, Crawl Space or Slab	H

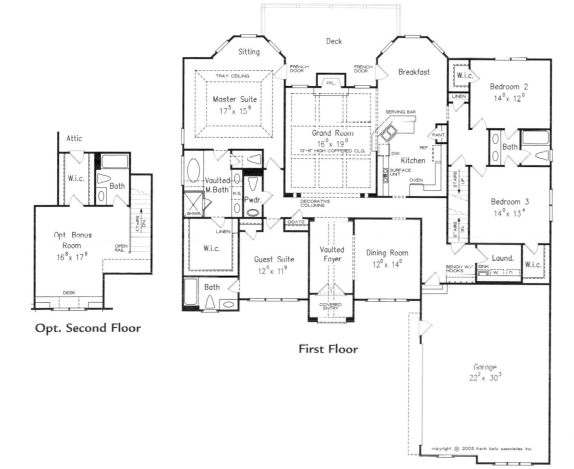

Opt. Second Floor

First Floor

Design Features

- The plaza entry plan with brick, stone and vertical siding fit into any neighborhood.

- The vaulted foyer opens up to a grand room, with coffered ceilings.

- A guest suite offers visitors a private bath.

- Two secondary bedrooms occupy one wing of the home, while an optional bonus room on the second floor gives homeowners room to grow.

Rear Elevation

Breyerton — UDHFB01-3766 — 1-866-525-9374

© 2002 Frank Betz Associates, Inc.

Total Living	First Floor	Second Floor	Opt. Bonus	Bed	Bath	Width	Depth	Foundation	Price Category
2723 sq ft	1847 sq ft	876 sq ft	N/A	4	3-1/2	56' 4"	50' 6"	Basement or Crawl Space	I

Design Features

- The *Breyerton* incorporates features that make everyday living more convenient.

- A keeping room is connected to the kitchen area, giving families that cozy, casual spot to reconnect at day's end.

- The coat closet and laundry room are located just inside the garage, making a handy drop spot for coats and shoes.

- The master suite is its own slice of heaven with a private sitting area, step-up jetted tub and seated shower.

First Floor

Second Floor

Rear Elevation

© The Sater Design Collection, Inc.

Bartolini — UDHDS01-8022 — 1-866-525-9374

Total Living	First Floor	Second Floor	Bonus	Bed	Bath	Width	Depth	Foundation	Price Category
2736 sq ft	2084 sq ft	652 sq ft	375 sq ft	3	2-1/2	60' 6"	94' 0"	Opt. Basement/Slab	G

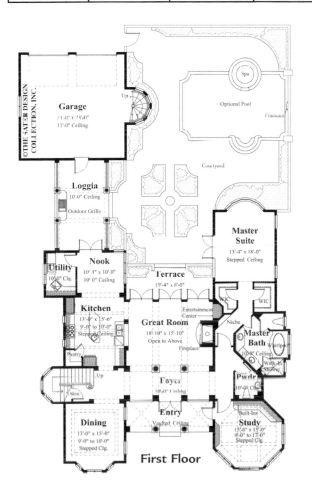

First Floor

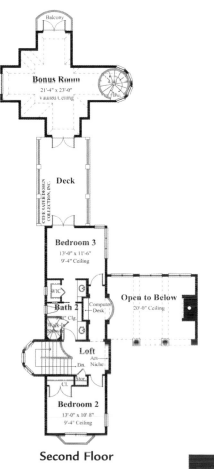

Second Floor

Design Features

- A graceful entry arcade leads to a grand foyer.

- Three sets of French doors are all that seperate the great room from a veranda and courtyard.

- The kitchen and morning nook open to a covered loggia.

- The secluded master suite has private courtyard access.

- The upper level harbors two bedroom suites and a bonus room.

Rear Elevation

Armaly — UDHDG01-1110 — 1-866-525-9374

Total Living	First Floor	Bonus	Bed	Bath	Width	Depth	Foundation	Price Category
2820 sq ft	2820 sq ft	473 sq ft	4	3	78' 1"	65' 5"	Crawl Space*	F

Design Features

- From a dynamic exterior to the sprawling interior, this floor plan is filled with exciting extras.
- Featuring a bay window, tray ceiling and separate dressing area, the master bedroom promotes relaxation.
- Coffered ceilings crown the dining room that includes a buffet niche for easy entertaining.
- The great room features a fireplace, cathedral ceiling and an impressive view of the back porch.
- The flexible floor plan includes a bedroom/study for extra guests.

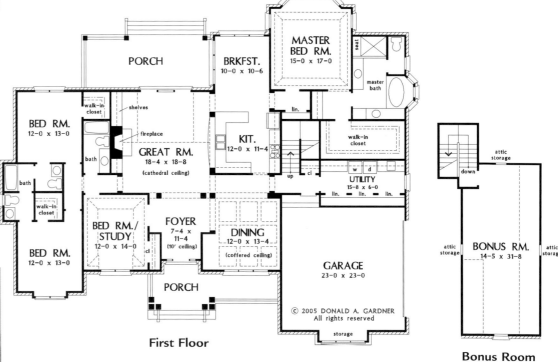

First Floor

Bonus Room

Rear Elevation

*Other options available. See page 513.

© The Sater Design Collection, Inc.

Montserrat — UDHDS01-6858 — 1-866-525-9374

Total Living	First Floor	Second Floor	Bonus	Bed	Bath	Width	Depth	Foundation	Price Category
2756 sq ft	1855 sq ft	901 sq ft	N/A	3	3-1/2	66' 0"	50' 0"	Island Basement	H

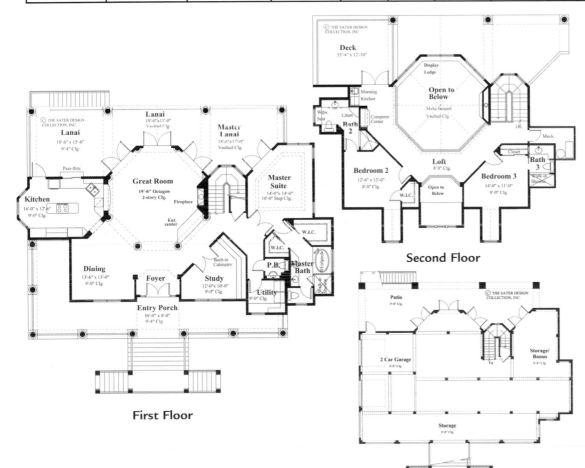

First Floor

Second Floor

Lower Level

Design Features

- The front elevation greets visitors with an inviting wraparound front porch, dormer windows and a widow's peak.

- The octagonal great room boasts a multi-faceted vaulted ceiling, fireplace, built-in entertainment center and three sets of French doors.

- The kitchen features a pass-thru to the lanai, an island workstation and access to the dining and great room.

- To ensure privacy, the master suite is tucked away from the guest bedrooms and main living areas.

Rear Elevation

2600 sq ft—3000 sq ft

Frank Betz Associates, Inc.

Arramore — UDHFB01-3869 — 1-866-525-9374

© 2004 Frank Betz Associates, Inc.

Total Living	First Floor	Second Floor	Opt. Bonus	Bed	Bath	Width	Depth	Foundation	Price Category
2792 sq ft	1365 sq ft	1427 sq ft	N/A	4	3	44' 0"	58' 0"	Basement, Crawl Space or Slab	H

Design Features

- Board-and-batten siding and shutters blend distinctively with brick and cedar shake.

- A furniture niche is incorporated into the foyer, perfect for a special piece.

- A bright and sunny keeping room is connected to the kitchen and breakfast areas.

- A children's retreat is included in the upper level of this design, giving kids plenty of space to play.

Rear Elevation

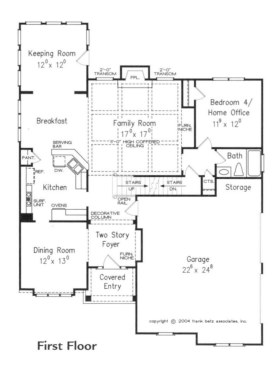

First Floor

Second Floor

Bennington — UDHDG01-1089 — 1-866-525-9374

Total Living	First Floor	Bonus	Bed	Bath	Width	Depth	Foundation	Price Category
2764 sq ft	2764 sq ft	306 sq ft	3	2-1/2	66' 4"	66' 1"	Crawl Space*	F

Design Features

- Stunning Palladian windows and columns frame the arched entryway to this impressive façade.

- A front-entry garage boasts convenience yet remains a striking focal point for the exterior.

- A large living room features twin sets of French doors that access an outdoor patio/porch.

- The family room flows naturally off the breakfast room, creating an additional gathering area.

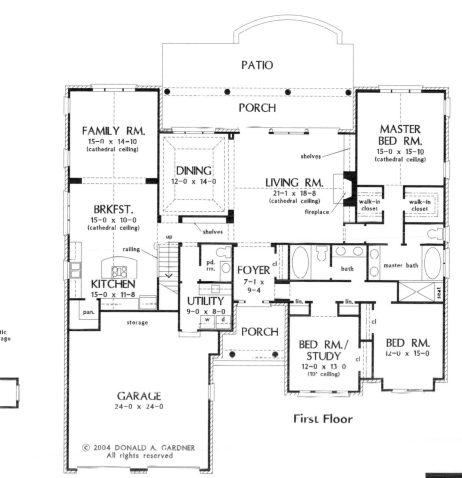

First Floor

Bonus Room

Rear Elevation

*Other options available. See page 513.

Burnside — UDHFB01-1018 — 1-866-525-9374

© 1996 Frank Betz Associates, Inc.

Total Living	First Floor	Second Floor	Opt. Bonus	Bed	Bath	Width	Depth	Foundation	Price Category
2764 sq ft	1904 sq ft	860 sq ft	388 sq ft	4	3-1/2	56' 0"	61' 6"	Basement or Crawl Space	H

Design Features

- The kitchen features a double oven, large pantry, center island and a serving bar adjoining the family room.

- Each of the four bedrooms has a walk-in closet.

- Other main-level rooms use nine-foot-high ceilings for an added sense of spaciousness.

- An optional bonus room above the garage adds 388 square feet of living space.

- Master suite luxuries include a tray ceiling in the bedroom, a private toilet compartment and a walk-in closet.

First Floor

Second Floor

Rear Elevation

© The Sater Design Collection, Inc.

Edmonton — UDHDS01-8023 — 1-866-525-9374

Total Living	First Floor	Second Floor	Bonus	Bed	Bath	Width	Depth	Foundation	Price Category
2769 sq ft	2117 sq ft	652 sq ft	375 sq ft	3	2-1/2	60' 6"	94' 0"	Opt. Basement/Slab	G

Design Features

- An elegant entry portico, sculpted arcades, terraces and a cupola adorn the exterior.

- A massive fireplace anchors the great room, which is extended by the veranda to the outdoors.

- The gourmet kitchen features a walk-in pantry, work island and easy access to the nook and great room.

- An interior door maintains privacy for the master suite, which begins with a sculpted art niche and extends to a private porch near the veranda and fountain.

First Floor

Second Floor

Rear Elevation

Cloverdale — UDHDS01-7058 — 1-866-525-9374

© The Sater Design Collection, Inc.

Total Living	First Floor	Second Floor	Bonus	Bed	Bath	Width	Depth	Foundation	Price Category
2775 sq ft	1874 sq ft	901 sq ft	382 sq ft	3	3-1/2	90' 0"	58' 6"	Opt. Basement/Crawl Space	G

Design Features

- Classic columns line the welcoming front porch.

- The octagonal-shaped great room boasts a row of French doors to the rear porch.

- A bay-window kitchen has serving counters to the great room and porch.

- Two upstairs bedrooms and a bonus room share a deck.

- The second-floor loft offers spectacular interior views.

Rear Elevation

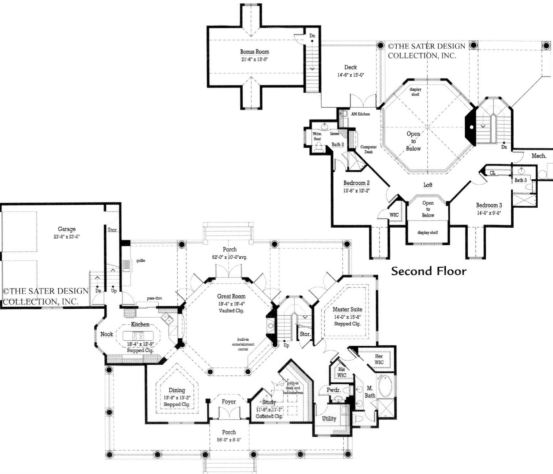

Second Floor

First Floor

© The Sater Design Collection, Inc.

Newberry — UDHDS01-7059 — 1-866-525-9374

Total Living	First Floor	Second Floor	Bonus	Bed	Bath	Width	Depth	Foundation	Price Category
2775 sq ft	1874 sq ft	901 sq ft	424 sq ft	3	3-1/2	90' 6"	61' 0"	Crawl Space/Opt. Basement	G

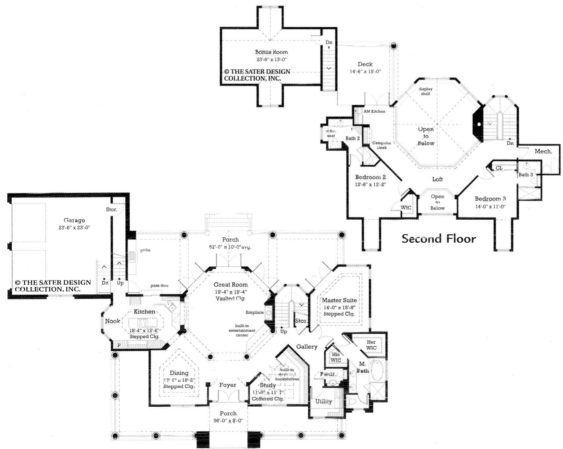

First Floor

Second Floor

Design Features

- The strategic placement of multi-pane windows, balusters, columns, mirrored dormers and stone chimneys add to the façade.

- A delightful bay-window kitchen provides easy access to formal and casual dining areas as well as the great room.

- The master suite features "his-and-her" walk-in closets, a spacious bath and opens onto the rear porch through double French doors.

Rear Elevation

2600 sq ft—3000 sq ft

Frank Betz Associates, Inc.

Heritage Pointe — UDHFB01-3946 — 1-866-525-9374

© 2005 Frank Betz Associates, Inc.

Total Living	First Floor	Second Floor	Opt. Bonus	Bed	Bath	Width	Depth	Foundation	Price Category
2766 sq ft	1959 sq ft	817 sq ft	271 sq ft	5	3	59' 0"	52' 0"	Basement or Crawl Space	H

Design Features

- The European look of the *Heritage Pointe* would be ideal for a mountain community.

- A teen loft on the second floor has a window seat and the option to include a closet.

- The master suite occupies one wing of the home and features a vaulted ceiling.

- The vaulted family room has built-in bookshelves, a fireplace and views to rear of the home.

First Floor

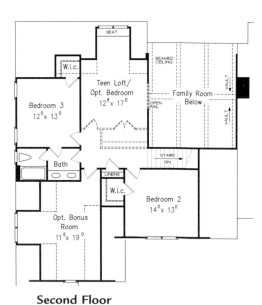

Second Floor

Rear Elevation

© 1998 Frank Betz Associates, Inc.

Lake Placid — UDHFB01-1131 — 1-866-525-9374

Total Living	First Floor	Second Floor	Opt. Bonus	Bed	Bath	Width	Depth	Foundation	Price Category
2792 sq ft	1980 sq ft	812 sq ft	255 sq ft	4	3-1/2	60' 6"	51' 2"	Basement, Crawl Space or Slab	I

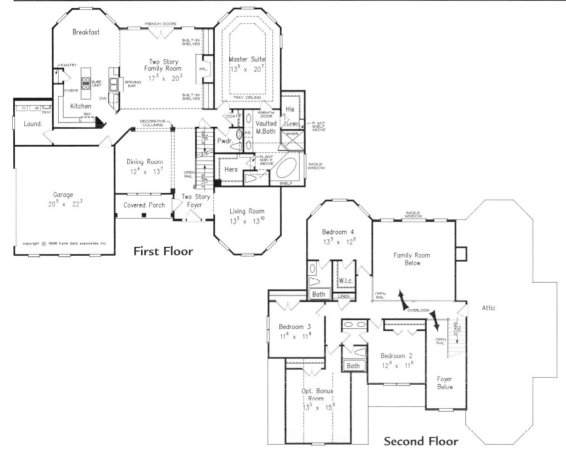

First Floor

Second Floor

Design Features

- Broad bay windows brighten the living room, breakfast room, master suite and a secondary bedroom.

- The two-story family room is enhanced with French doors to the backyard and a fireplace flanked by built-in shelves.

- The bonus room on the upper level can be a fifth bedroom.

Rear Elevation

Capistrano — UDHFB01-3920 — 1-866-525-9374

© 2005 Frank Betz Associates, Inc.

Total Living	First Floor	Second Floor	Opt. Bonus	Bed	Bath	Width	Depth	Foundation	Price Category
2795 sq ft	1919 sq ft	876 sq ft	167 sq ft	4	3-1/2	56' 0"	51' 0"	Basement, Crawl Space or Slab	I

Design Features

- The brick front porch and columns of the *Capistrano* is a perfect backdrop for a tranquil spot to end the day.

- The master suite resides on the main level and encompasses one side of the home.

- The breakfast area, kitchen and keeping room are arranged in such a way that makes entertaining a breeze.

- The second floor houses three additional bedrooms and an optional bonus room.

Rear Elevation

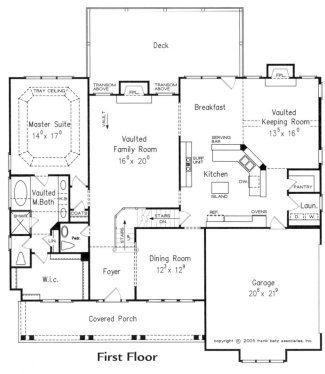

First Floor

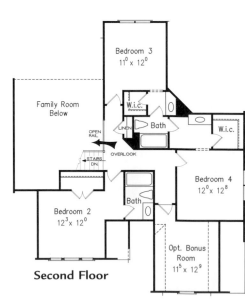

Second Floor

Frank Betz Associates, Inc.

© 1995 Frank Betz Associates, Inc.

Balmoral — UDHFB01-925 — 1-866-525-9374

Total Living	First Floor	Second Floor	Opt. Bonus	Bed	Bath	Width	Depth	Foundation	Price Category
2806 sq ft	1952 sq ft	854 sq ft	N/A	4	2-1/2	56' 6"	50' 6"	Basement or Crawl Space	I

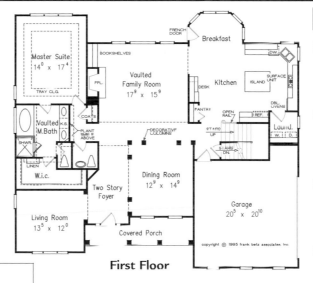

First Floor

Design Features

- A traditional design style is recognized in the *Balmoral*, with a combination of brick and stucco on the front elevation.

- The kitchen is generously sized and highly functional, incorporating a built-in desk, pantry, island and double ovens.

- Decorative columns create a soft border around the dining area, defining its space but keeping the floor plan open and roomy.

- The master suite resides on the main level, a popular design feature.

Second Floor

Rear Elevation

Royal Palm — UDHDS01-6727 — 1-866-525-9374

© The Sater Design Collection, Inc.

Total Living	First Floor	Bonus	Bed	Bath	Width	Depth	Foundation	Price Category
2823 sq ft	2823 sq ft	N/A	3	2-1/2	65' 0"	85' 4"	Slab	G

Design Features

- Triple arches supported by tapered columns present a symmetrical Mediterranean façade.
- The columned porch leads to a view-oriented foyer.
- Two angled walls of disappearing glass open the living room.
- The master includes a gallery foyer and private garden bath.
- The leisure room has two walls of pocketing doors.

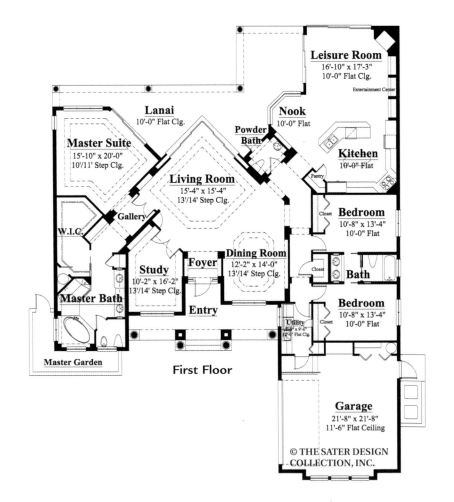

First Floor

Rear Elevation

Edgewater — UDHDG01-1009 — 1-866-525-9374

Total Living	First Floor	Bonus	Bed	Bath	Width	Depth	Foundation	Price Category
2818 sq ft	2818 sq ft	N/A	4	3	70' 0"	69' 10"	Crawl Space*	F

Design Features

- This home has plenty of Craftsman character with a low-maintenance exterior.

- Art niches, fireplaces and built-in cabinetry add beauty and convenience.

- The kitchen has a handy pass-thru to the great room.

- The spacious deck accommodates outdoor living.

- The master suite has a bay sitting area and French doors that lead to the deck.

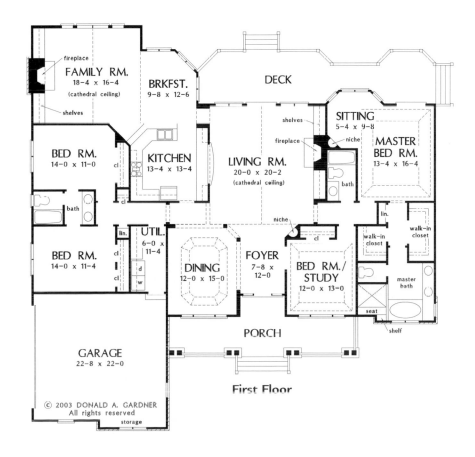

First Floor

Rear Elevation

*Other options available. See page 513.
Photographed home may have been modified from original construction documents.

www.ultimatehomeplans.net   355

Springdale — UDHDG01-419 — 1-866-525-9374

Total Living	First Floor	Second Floor	Bonus	Bed	Bath	Width	Depth	Foundation	Price Category
2832 sq ft	1483 sq ft	1349 sq ft	486 sq ft	4	2-1/2	66' 10"	47' 8"	Crawl Space*	F

Design Features

- Columns between the foyer and living room/study hint at the extras in this four-bedroom estate.
- Transom windows over French doors open up the living room/study to the front porch.
- A generous family room accesses the covered back porch.
- Nine-foot ceilings amplify the first floor.
- All bedrooms are upstairs, including a deluxe master suite with a tray ceiling.

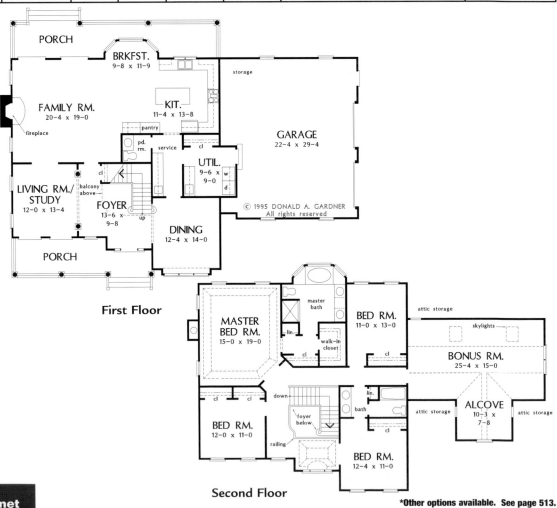

First Floor

Second Floor

Rear Elevation

*Other options available. See page 513.

© 1994 Donald A. Gardner Architects, Inc.

Mercer — UDHDG01-372 — 1-866-525-9374

Total Living	First Floor	Second Floor	Bonus	Bed	Bath	Width	Depth	Foundation	Price Category
2833 sq ft	2162 sq ft	671 sq ft	345 sq ft	4	3	61' 11"	54' 8"	Crawl Space*	F

Design Features

- Although impressive and airy, this elegant executive home stays warm from dual fireplaces.

- Rear bays expand space and maximize natural light.

- The master suite has an angled entrance for privacy and includes a sitting bay and lavish bath.

- Extra room is added by a skylit bonus room and ample attic storage.

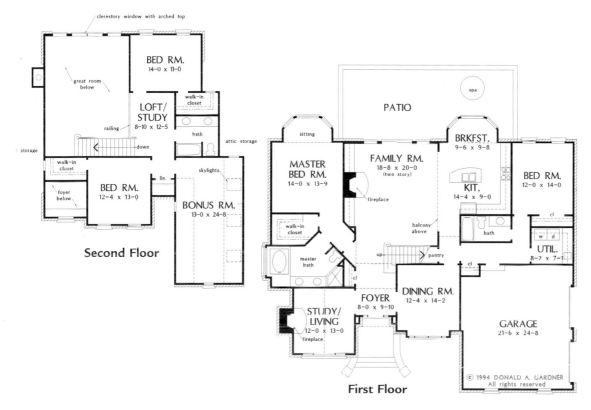

Second Floor

First Floor

© 1994 DONALD A. GARDNER
All rights reserved

Rear Elevation

Gentry — UDHFB01-913 — 1-866-525-9374

© 1995 Frank Betz Associates, Inc.

Total Living	First Floor	Second Floor	Opt. Bonus	Bed	Bath	Width	Depth	Foundation	Price Category
2840 sq ft	1347 sq ft	1493 sq ft	243 sq ft	5	4-1/2	58' 4"	46' 6"	Basement, Crawl Space or Slab	I

Design Features

- French Country warmth is often achieved by blending European stucco and stacked stone, like on the *Gentry*.
- Formal living and dining rooms border the two-story foyer, giving it a time-honored flair.
- The two-story family room is anything but traditional, surrounded by arched openings and decorative columns.
- Family gatherings just got easier in the oversized kitchen, complete with double ovens and a large prep island.

Rear Elevation

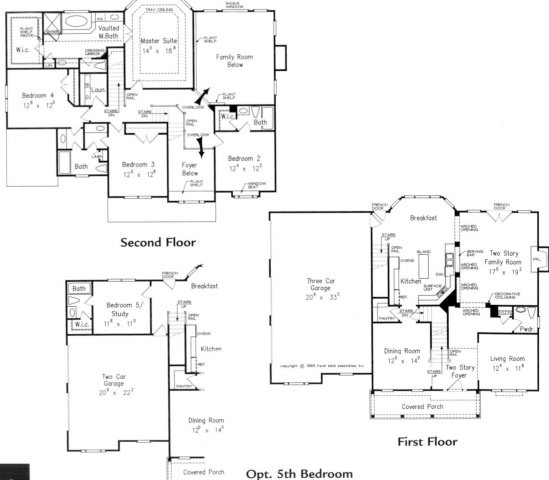

Second Floor

Opt. 5th Bedroom

First Floor

Donald A. Gardner Architects, Inc.

Sedona Ridge — UDHDG01-986-B — 1-866-525-9374

Total Living	First Floor	Second Floor	Bonus	Bed	Bath	Width	Depth	Foundation	Price Category
2843 sq ft	2843 sq ft	N/A	N/A	3	2-1/2	89' 2"	92' 1"	Slab	F

First Floor

Design Features

- This Southwestern enchanter showcases a stucco exterior with parapet walls and a tile roof.

- French doors and windows usher in light, while columns and a fireplace complement the great room.

- The rear loggia's fireplace is perfect to set the mood for alfresco dining and entertaining.

- The spacious kitchen features an angled stovetop island.

- Note the powder room and hall niche.

Rear Elevation

Montpelier — UDHDG01-483 — 1-866-525-9374

© 1997 Donald A. Gardner Architects, Inc.

Total Living	First Floor	Second Floor	Bonus	Bed	Bath	Width	Depth	Foundation	Price Category
2869 sq ft	2249 sq ft	620 sq ft	308 sq ft	4	3-1/2	69' 6"	52' 0"	Crawl Space*	F

Design Features

- A clerestory window and detailed square columns lend drama to the arched and gabled entryway.

- Inside, luxury abounds with a formal living room with fireplace and box-bay window.

- The open, two-story family room boasts a fireplace with built-in cabinets on either side.

- Additionally, this plan offers a convenient second master suite on the first floor.

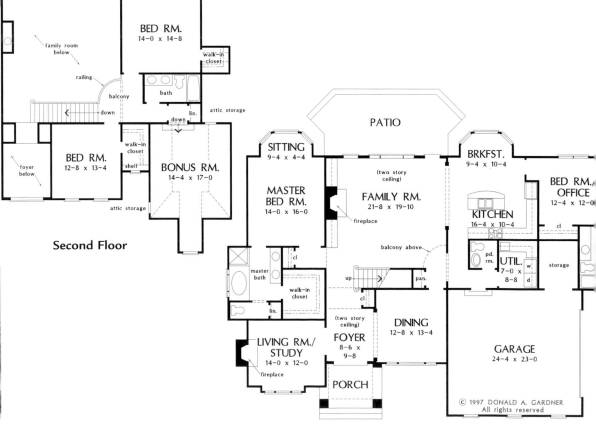

Second Floor

First Floor

Rear Elevation

*Other options available. See page 513.

© The Sater Design Collection, Inc.

Wulfert Point — UDHDS01-6688 — 1-866-525-9374

Total Living	First Floor	Second Floor	Bonus	Bed	Bath	Width	Depth	Foundation	Price Category
2873 sq ft	1293 sq ft	1154 sq ft	426 sq ft	4	3-1/2	50' 0"	90' 0"	Slab	G

Design Features

- Louvered shutters, circle-head windows, gentle arches and decorative columns enhance the exterior.

- A Charleston-style courtyard includes a lap pool, spa, sundeck and fountain.

- The great room features built-in cabinetry, a TV niche, fireplace and three sets of French doors that open to the covered porch.

- Spacious walk-in closets, a luxurious bath and three sets of French doors leading to the covered balcony enhance the master retreat.

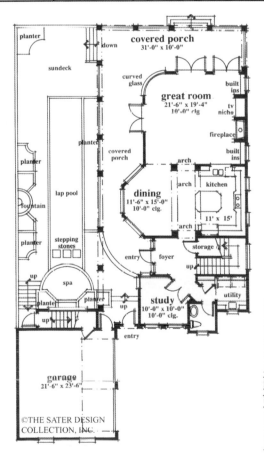

First Floor

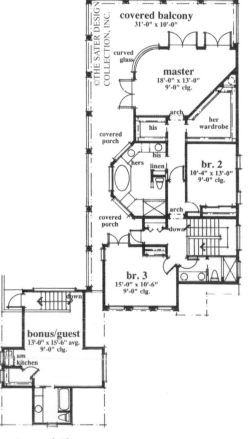

Second Floor

Rear View

Photographed home may have been modified from original construction documents.

Galleon Bay — UDHDS01-6620 — 1-866-525-9374

© The Sater Design Collection, Inc.

Total Living	First Floor	Second Floor	Bonus	Bed	Bath	Width	Depth	Foundation	Price Category
2875 sq ft	2066 sq ft	809 sq ft	N/A	3 + Study	3-1/2	64' 0"	45' 0"	Slab/Island Basement	H

Design Features

- A double stepped entry staircase and curved balcony compliment the high arched entryway of the front elevation.

- The open floor plan creates flow between the kitchen, dining and grand room.

- The gourmet kitchen features ample counter and storage space, a breakfast nook and interacts with the veranda for outdoor cooking and eating.

- The master suite enjoys a vaulted ceiling, walk-in closet, a private sundeck and a three-sided fireplace.

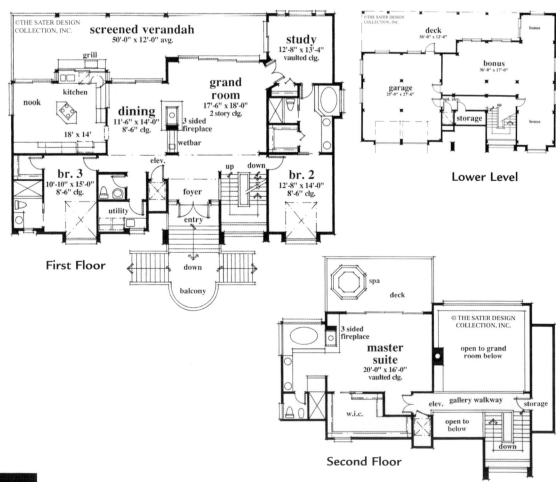

Rear Elevation

Frank Betz Associates, Inc.

© 2004 Frank Betz Associates, Inc.

Stoney River — UDHFB01-3866 — 1-866-525-9374

Total Living	First Floor	Opt. Second Floor	Bed	Bath	Width	Depth	Foundation	Price Category
2876 sq ft	2876 sq ft	393 sq ft	3	3-1/2	65' 4"	85' 6"	Basement or Crawl Space	H

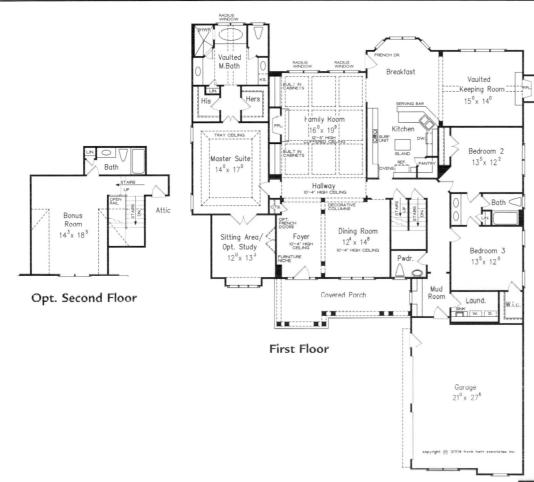

Opt. Second Floor

First Floor

Design Features

- A furniture niche in the foyer creates a place for that special piece that will make an attractive first impression.

- Coffered ceilings and built-in cabinetry in the family room make this room the natural center-point of the home.

- A vaulted keeping room adjoins the kitchen area, providing an additional cozy gathering spot.

- The master suite is accommodating in every sense of the word, with its private sitting room, his-and-her closets, and soaking tub.

Rear Elevation

Savannah Sound — UDHDS01-6698 — 1-866-525-9374

© The Sater Design Collection, Inc.

Total Living	First Floor	Second Floor	Bonus	Bed	Bath	Width	Depth	Foundation	Price Category
2879 sq ft	1684 sq ft	1195 sq ft	N/A	3	3	45' 0"	52' 0"	Island Basement	G

Design Features

- Asymmetrical rooflines, a grand turret, two-story bay windows and a widow's peak create an impressive front exterior.

- Guests can convene around the wet bar and a corner fireplace that connect the dining and great room.

- The gourmet kitchen boasts a center island with an eating bar and windowed wrapping counter.

- The upper-level master suite features a private master balcony, morning kitchen and a two-sided fireplace.

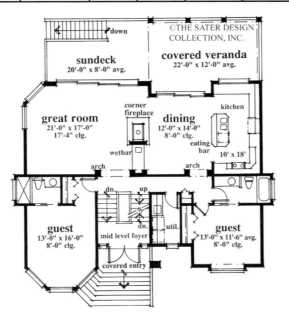

First Floor

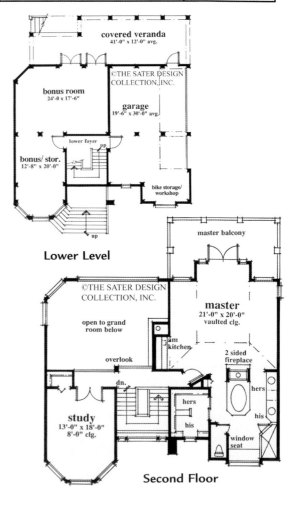

Lower Level

Second Floor

Rear Elevation

Greenlaw — UDHFB01-3559 — 1-866-525-9374

Total Living	First Floor	Second Floor	Opt. Bonus	Bed	Bath	Width	Depth	Foundation	Price Category
2884 sq ft	2247 sq ft	637 sq ft	235 sq ft	4	4	64' 0"	55' 2"	Basement, Crawl Space or Slab	I

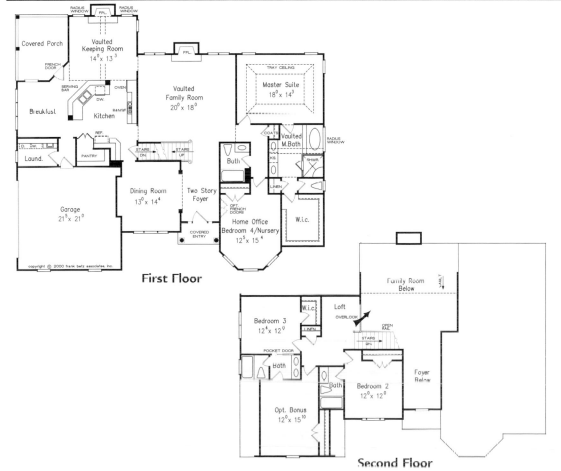

First Floor

Second Floor

Design Features

- The *Greenlaw* is a wonderful design for today's growing and active family.

- A vaulted keeping room, breakfast area, kitchen and covered porch come together to create a comfortable core of the home where family and company will likely gather most frequently.

- The home office can be effortlessly converted into a nursery with easy access from the master suite.

Rear Elevation

Prescott Ridge — UDHFB01-3746 — 1-866-525-9374

© 2002 Frank Betz Associates, Inc.

Total Living	First Floor	Second Floor	Bonus	Bed	Bath	Width	Depth	Foundation	Price Category
2885 sq ft	2052 sq ft	833 sq ft	N/A	5	4	59' 0"	55' 6"	Basement or Crawl Space	H

Design Features

- Original and thoughtful design talent went into every detail of the *Prescott Ridge*.

- The kitchen is complete with a cooktop island and double ovens.

- A window seat creates the back wall of the keeping room, adding charm and comfort.

- The keeping room shares a two-sided fireplace with the neighboring two-story great room.

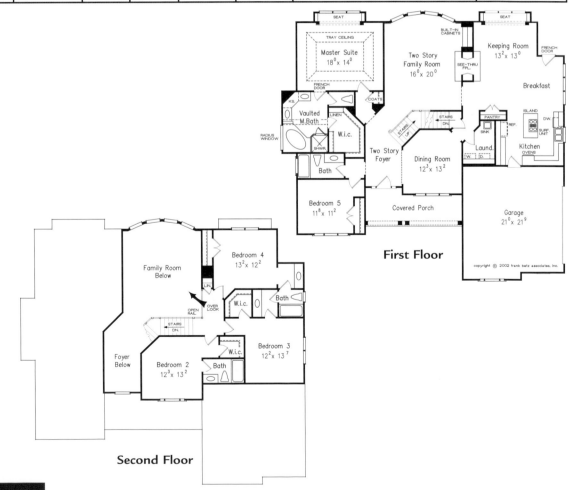

First Floor

Second Floor

Rear Elevation

© The Sater Design Collection, Inc.

Ansel Arbor — UDHDS01-7023 — 1-866-525-9374

Total Living	First Floor	Second Floor	Bonus	Bed	Bath	Width	Depth	Foundation	Price Category
2889 sq ft	2151 sq ft	738 sq ft	534 sq ft	3	2-1/2	99' 0"	56' 0"	Opt. Basement/Crawl Space	G

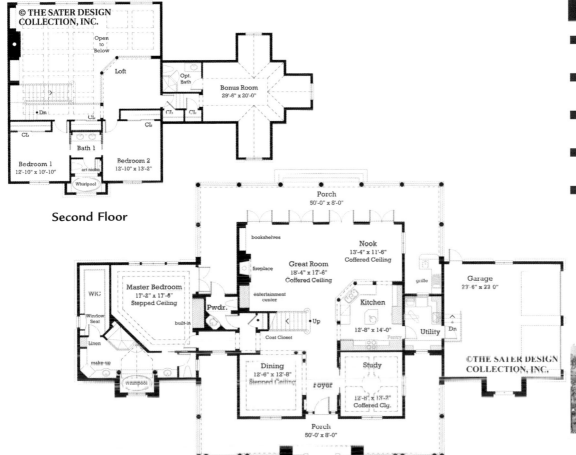

Second Floor

First Floor

Design Features

- Wraparound front and rear porches join the home's wings.
- Speciality ceilings and interior columns provide light and elegance.
- The study opens through pocket doors off the foyer.
- The master suite features a projected whirlpool tub.
- Two bedrooms with an adjoining bath are near the great room.

Rear Elevation

2600 sq ft—3000 sq ft

Frank Betz Associates, Inc.

Candler Park — UDHFB01-3777 — 1-866-525-9374

© 2003 Frank Betz Associates, Inc.

Total Living	First Floor	Second Floor	Opt. Bonus	Bed	Bath	Width	Depth	Foundation	Price Category
2900 sq ft	2262 sq ft	638 sq ft	252 sq ft	4	4	64' 0"	56' 4"	Basement, Crawl Space or Slab	I

Design Features

- A covered front porch gives a warm welcome to guests as they enter the *Candler Park*.

- A two-story foyer extends the friendly greeting.

- Accessorizing the dining room will be fun and easy with a furniture niche and decorative columns.

- A main-floor bedroom makes the perfect nursery, with easy access to the master suite.

Second Floor

First Floor

Rear Elevation

© The Sater Design Collection, Inc.

Kinsey — UDHDS01-6756 — 1-866-525-9374

Total Living	First Floor	Bonus	Bed	Bath	Width	Depth	Foundation	Price Category
2907 sq ft	2907 sq ft	N/A	3	2-1/2	65' 0"	84' 0"	Slab	G

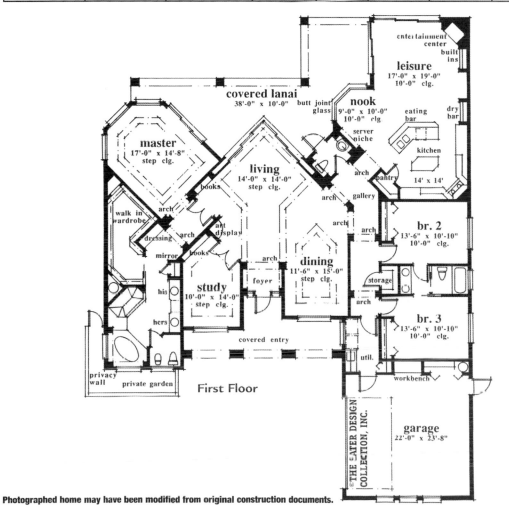

First Floor

Design Features

- Elegant columns line both the front and rear of the home.
- Two walls of pocketing glass doors border the living room.
- Arches lead past the cabana powder bath to the kitchen.
- The kitchen features a pantry and prep island.
- The master bath has a garden tub that takes in private views.
- The breakfast nook is bright with walls of glass.

Rear View

Nadine — UDHDS01-7047 — 1-866-525-9374

© The Sater Design Collection, Inc.

Total Living	First Floor	Second Floor	Bonus	Bed	Bath	Width	Depth	Foundation	Price Category
2923 sq ft	2215 sq ft	708 sq ft	420 sq ft	3	3	75' 4"	69' 10"	Opt. Basement/Crawl Space	G

Design Features

- Columns and coffered ceilings enlarge the interior spaces.

- The grand room features triple French doors and a fireplace.

- Built-ins and walk-in closets complete two upstairs bedrooms.

- An over-the-garage bonus room houses a bath.

- A bay-window breakfast nook and central island create an ideal kitchen.

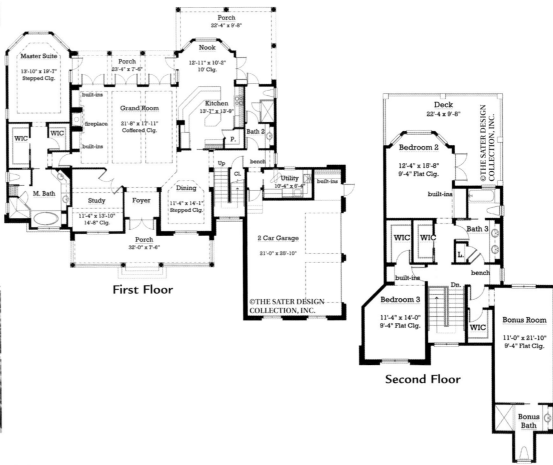

First Floor

Second Floor

Rear Elevation

Thorne Bay — UDHDG01-1074 — 1-866-525-9374

Total Living	First Floor	Second Floor	Bonus	Bed	Bath	Width	Depth	Foundation	Price Category
2934 sq ft	2934 sq ft	N/A	975 sq ft	4	3	85' 4"	57' 8"	Crawl Space*	F

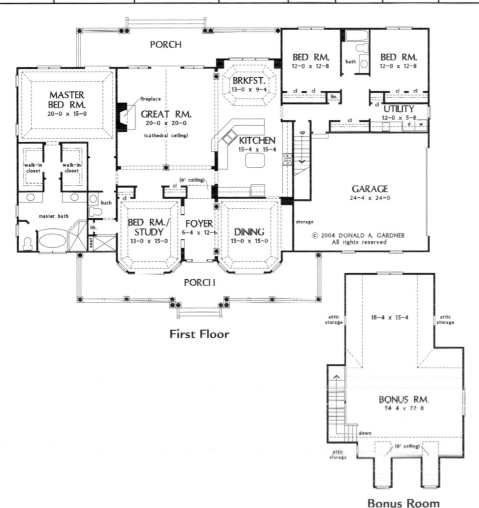

First Floor

Bonus Room

Design Features

■ A massive front porch, prominent gable and decorative bracket evoke sophistication.

■ An angled counter separates the kitchen from the great room and breakfast nook.

■ A vaulted ceiling caps the great room, expanding visual space.

■ Two large walk-in closets provide plenty of storage.

■ The common rooms divide the master suite from the secondary bedrooms.

Rear Elevation

Rockledge — UDHDG01-875-D — 1-866-525-9374

Total Living	First Floor	Second Floor	Basement	Bonus	Bed	Bath	Width	Depth	Foundation	Price Category
2949 sq ft	1682 sq ft	577 sq ft	690 sq ft	459 sq ft	4	3-1/2	79' 0"	68' 2"	Hillside Walkout	F

Design Features

- Stone and siding combine to give this Craftsman design striking curb appeal.

- A portico sets the tone with a gentle arch and four stately columns.

- A clerestory above the front entrance floods the two-story foyer with natural light.

- Inside, Old-World charm gives way to an open, family-efficient floor plan.

- A family room also sports a fireplace and patio access.

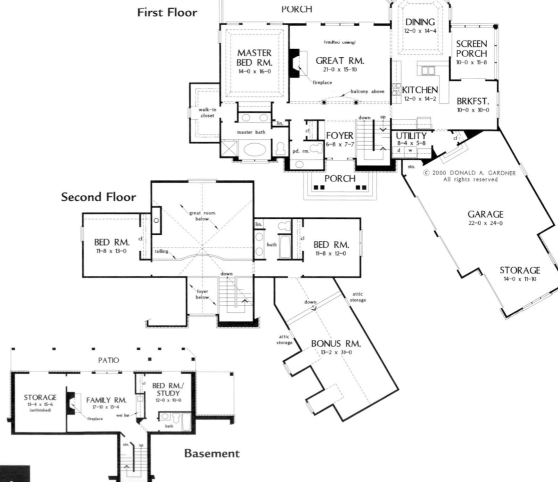

Rear Elevation

© 1999 Donald A. Gardner, Inc.

Peekskill — UDHDG01-780-D — 1-866-525-9374

Total Living	First Floor	Second Floor	Basement	Bonus	Bed	Bath	Width	Depth	Foundation	Price Category
2953 sq ft	1662 sq ft	585 sq ft	706 sq ft	575 sq ft	4	3-1/2	81' 4"	68' 8"	Hillside Walkout	F

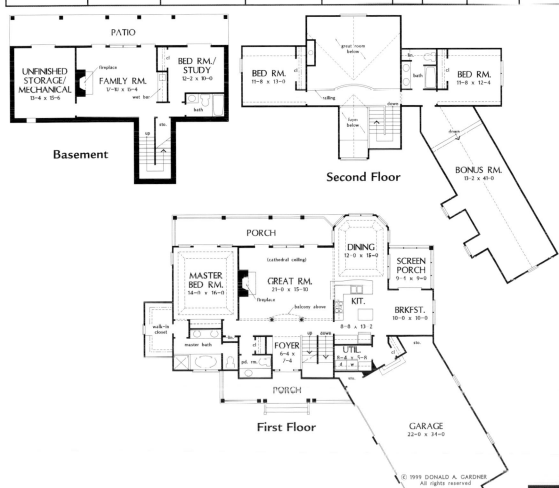

Basement

Second Floor

First Floor

Design Features

- A stunning center dormer with arched window embellishes the exterior.

- The dormer's arched window floods light into the foyer with built-in niche.

- A generous back porch extends the great room, which features a vaulted ceiling.

- The master bedroom, which has a tray ceiling, enjoys back-porch access.

- Note the huge bonus room over the three-car garage.

Rear Elevation

Vandenberg — UDHDG01-746-D — 1-866-525-9374

© 1998 Donald A. Gardner, Inc.

Total Living	First Floor	Basement	Bonus	Bed	Bath	Width	Depth	Foundation	Price Category
2956 sq ft	1810 sq ft	1146 sq ft	N/A	4	3	68' 4"	60' 10"	Hillside Walkout	F

Design Features

- This hillside home combines stucco, stone and cedar shake for exceptional Craftsman character.

- The breakfast and dining rooms enjoy screened-porch access.

- The master bedroom includes a tray ceiling, a lovely private bath and walk-in closet.

- A versatile bedroom/study and full bath are nearby.

- Downstairs are two more bedrooms, each with an adjacent covered patio.

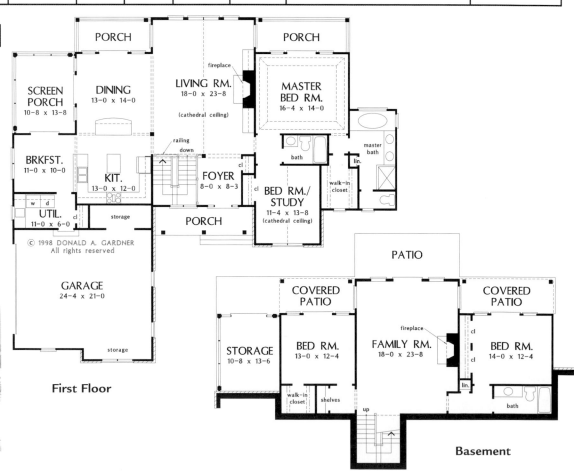

First Floor

Basement

Rear Elevation

© The Sater Design Collection, Inc.

Hemingway Lane — UDHDS01-6689 — 1-866-525-9374

Total Living	First Floor	Second Floor	Lower Level	Bed	Bath	Width	Depth	Foundation	Price Category
2957 sq ft	1642 sq ft	1165 sq ft	150 sq ft	5	3-1/2	44' 6"	58' 0"	Slab with Pilings	G

Design Features

- A widow's peak, mirroring dormers, Doric columns and a glass-paneled arched entry adorn the exterior.

- The living/dining room area enjoys a fireplace, built-in cabinetry, French doors leading to the sundeck and a two-story picture window.

- The kitchen features a walk-in pantry, ample storage space and a food prep island.

- The upper level features four secondary bedrooms and a central computer loft.

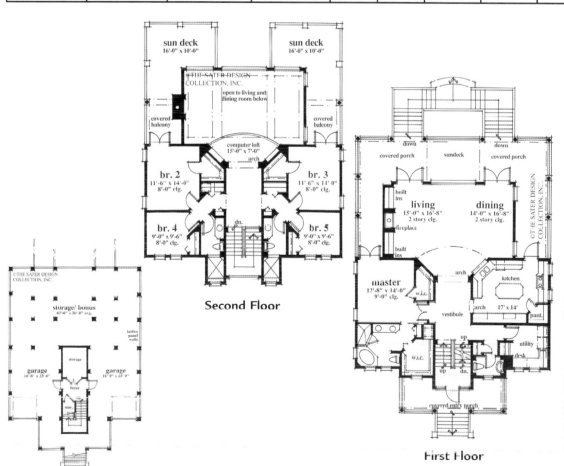

Second Floor

Lower Level

First Floor

Rear Elevation

Nantucket Sound — UDHDS01-6693 — 1-866-525-9374

© The Sater Design Collection, Inc.

Total Living	First Floor	Second Floor	Lower Level	Bed	Bath	Width	Depth	Foundation	Price Category
2957 sq ft	1642 sq ft	1165 sq ft	150 sq ft	3	3-1/2	44' 6"	58' 0"	Post/Pier/Slab	G

Design Features

- A faux widow's walk complements the observation balcony and two sundecks, together allowing panoramic views front and back.

- A cozy fireplace framed by built-ins invites gatherings.

- The gourmet kitchen features an island prep area, walk-in pantry and a pass-thru counter.

- Upstairs, a gallery loft leads to a balcony overlook and two secondary bedrooms.

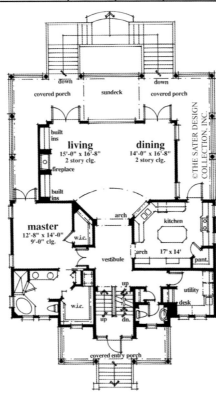

First Floor

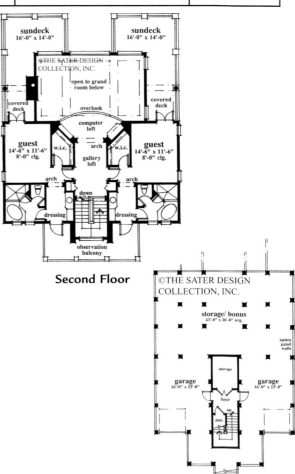

Second Floor

Lower Level

Rear Elevation

© 1999 Frank Betz Associates, Inc.

Morningside — UDHFB01-1257 — 1-866-525-9374

Total Living	First Floor	Second Floor	Opt. Bonus	Bed	Bath	Width	Depth	Foundation	Price Category
2970 sq ft	2074 sq ft	896 sq ft	209 sq ft	4	3-1/2	63' 0"	56' 0"	Basement, Crawl Space or Slab	I

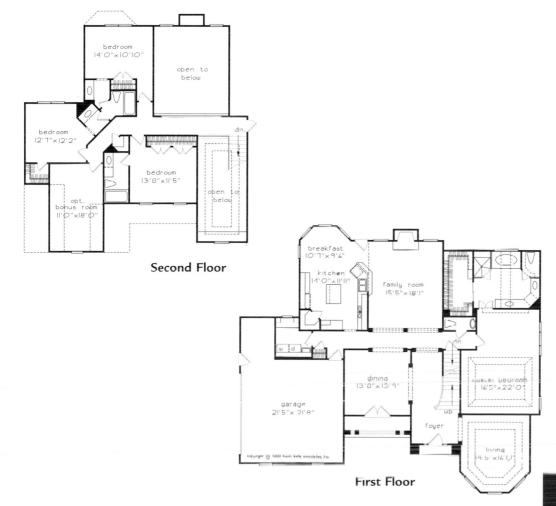

Second Floor

First Floor

Design Features

- From the *Southern Living® Design Collection*
- Architectural features include arched openings and columns framing the dining and family rooms.
- A bay with large windows brings light into the living room.
- The family room, kitchen and breakfast room are grouped together for convenience.

Rear Elevation

Queenstown Harbor — UDHDS01-6663 — 1-866-525-9374

© The Sater Design Collection, Inc.

Total Living	First Floor	Bonus	Bed	Bath	Width	Depth	Foundation	Price Category
2978 sq ft	2978 sq ft	N/A	3	3-1/2	84' 0"	90' 0"	Slab	G

Design Features

- A fourteen-foot high classic entry provides elegant curb appeal.

- The family wing hosts the kitchen, nook and leisure rooms with plenty of patio access.

- The kitchen has ample counter and pantry space.

- The owner's wing includes a library and convenient powder bath.

- An enhanced utility room offers all the most up-to-date conveniences.

Rear Elevation

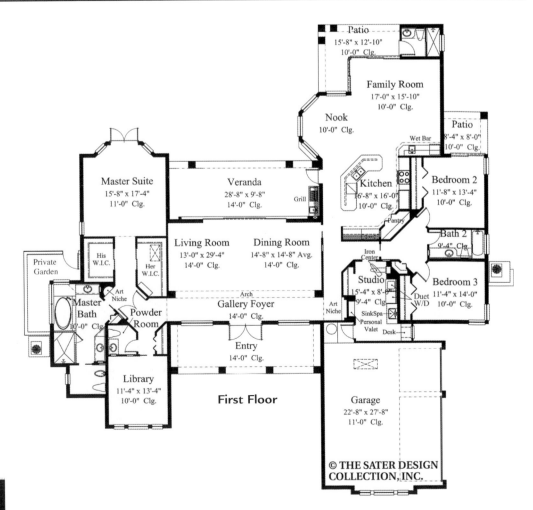

© 2004 Frank Betz Associates, Inc.

River Forest — UDHFB01-3903 — 1-866-525-9374

Total Living	First Floor	Second Floor	Opt. Bonus	Bed	Bath	Width	Depth	Foundation	Price Category
2978 sq ft	2031 sq ft	947 sq ft	340 sq ft	5	4	78' 0"	62' 6"	Basement or Crawl Space	I

First Floor

Second Floor

Design Features

- From the *Southern Living® Design Collection*

- Stacked stone, board-and-batten accents and carriage doors all contribute to the casually elegant demeanor of the *River Forest*.

- Beauty and function are coupled together to create a smart and attractive floor plan inside.

- A coffered ceiling canopies the family room adding character and dimension to the room.

Rear Elevation

Frank Betz Associates, Inc.

Montaigne — UDHFB01-3731 — 1-866-525-9374

© 2002 Frank Betz Associates, Inc.

Total Living	First Floor	Second Floor	Opt. Bonus	Bed	Bath	Width	Depth	Foundation	Price Category
2983 sq ft	1897 sq ft	1086 sq ft	N/A	4	3-1/2	62' 4"	50' 0"	Basement or Crawl Space	H

Design Features

- Shutters, native stone and shingles create the right mix of rugged and refined elements.
- A gallery foyer defined by arches and columns grants vistas that extend from the entry to the back property.
- Twin windows flank a centered fireplace in the family room.
- One wing of the home is dedicated to the owners' retreat, with a sitting area in the bedroom.

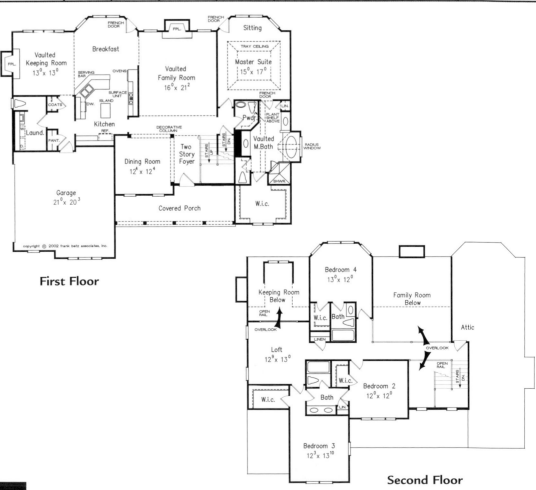

First Floor

Second Floor

Rear Elevation

Saint Thomas — UDHDG01-1081 — 1-866-525-9374

Total Living	First Floor	Bonus	Bed	Bath	Width	Depth	Foundation	Price Category
2984 sq ft	2984 sq ft	273 sq ft	4	3	60' 6"	76' 6"	Crawl Space*	F

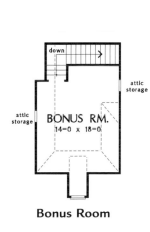

Bonus Room

First Floor

Design Features

- Keystone arches, curved transoms and stucco banding showcase attention to detail.

- Custom features include built-in cabinetry and desk, and ceiling treatments throughout.

- While the porch features a wet bar, two art niches highlight the master suite.

- Elegant columns, twin vanities, a garden tub, shower and private privy complete the master bath.

Rear Elevation

Royal Troon Lane — UDHDS01-6633 — 1-866-525-9374

© The Sater Design Collection, Inc.

Total Living	First Floor	Bonus	Bed	Bath	Width	Depth	Foundation	Price Category
2986 sq ft	2986 sq ft	N/A	4	3-1/2	82' 8"	76' 4"	Slab	G

Design Features

- The unique angled entry to this home is perfect for a corner lot.
- Decorative ceilings adorn the living and dining rooms.
- The step-down living room offers a two-sided fireplace, with enough room for sitting and a piano.
- The courtyard is perfect for a large covered pool area.

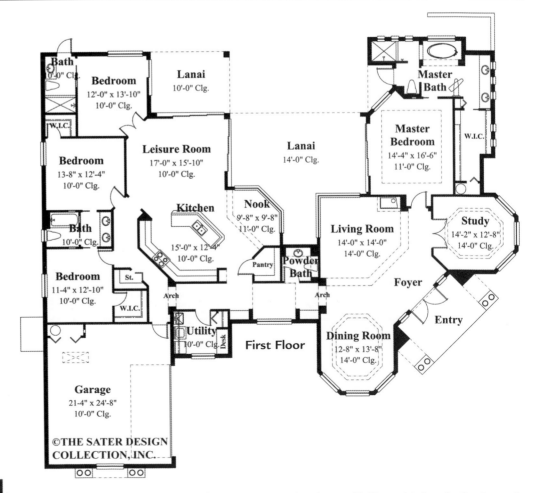

Pool & Lanai View

Photographed home may have been modified from original construction documents.

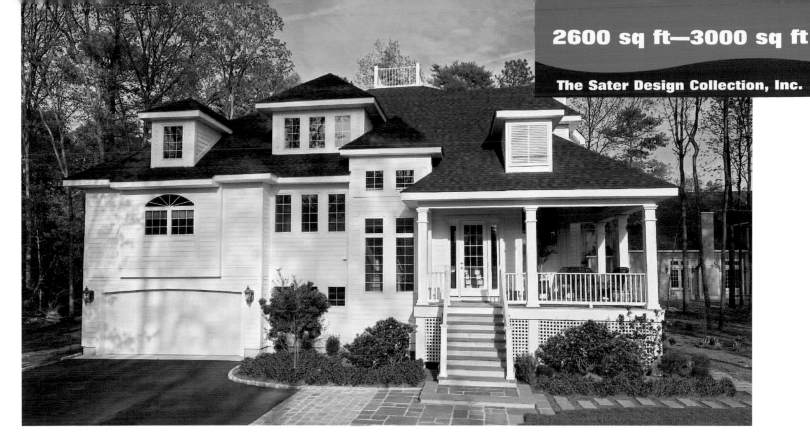

© The Sater Design Collection, Inc.

Montego Bay — UDHDS01-6800 — 1-866-525-9374

Total Living	First Floor	Second Floor	Bonus	Bed	Bath	Width	Depth	Foundation	Price Category
2988 sq ft	2096 sq ft	892 sq ft	N/A	3	3-1/2	58' 0"	54' 0"	Island Basement	G

Design Features

- An arched foyer leads into a great room with coffered ceiling and fireplace.

- The large kitchen has a center island with cooktop and a bayed dining nook.

- The main-floor master suite has a pampering bath and a walk-in shower.

- Upstairs, each of the two bedrooms has a walk-in closet.

- A loft provides bonus space overlooking the great room below.

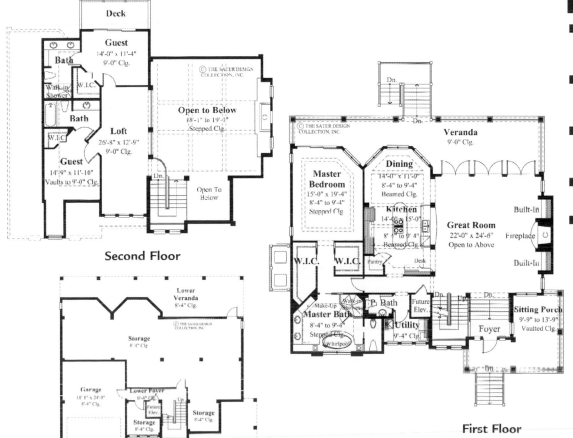

Second Floor

Lower Level

First Floor

Rear Elevation

VANAUER STUDIO

Hembree — UDHDG01-1111 — 1-866-525-9374

© 2005 Donald A. Gardner, Inc.

Total Living	First Floor	Bonus	Bed	Bath	Width	Depth	Foundation	Price Category
2991 sq ft	2991 sq ft	371 sq ft	3	2-1/2	55' 7"	90' 3.5"	Crawl Space*	F

Design Features

- Open spaces are plentiful in this rambling floor plan.
- Featuring an optional pool and lanai, this plan was designed to be unique and beautiful.
- A spacious great room with striking fireplace becomes an immediate gathering spot.
- Columns outline the dining room, which is enhanced by a tray ceiling.
- Overlooking the courtyard, the breakfast area flows into a generous family room.

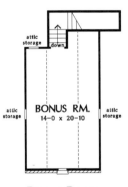

Bonus Room

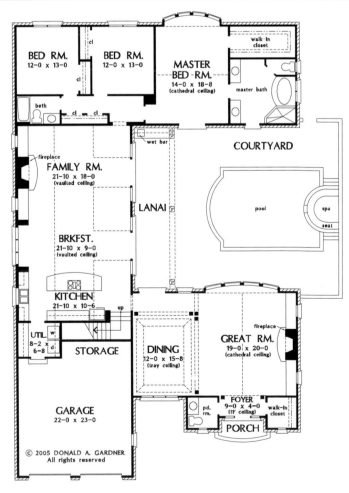

Rear Elevation

*Other options available. See page 513.

© 2002 Frank Betz Associates, Inc.

Westhampton — UDHFB01-3767 — 1-866-525-9374

Total Living	First Floor	Second Floor	Opt. Bonus	Bed	Bath	Width	Depth	Foundation	Price Category
3012 sq ft	1974 sq ft	1038 sq ft	N/A	4	3-1/2	72' 0"	57' 0"	Basement or Crawl Space	I

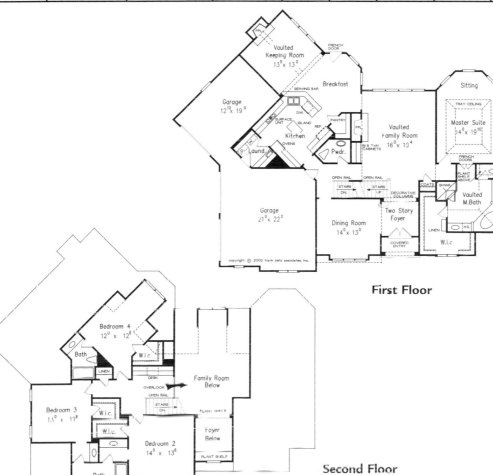

First Floor

Second Floor

Design Features

- A cozy keeping room is situated adjacent to the kitchen, creating uncommon angles rarely found in stock home plans.

- The master suite is secluded on the main level and features a bayed sitting area—a great spot to unwind.

- Three additional bedrooms have private access to bathing areas and walk-in closets.

- A built-in desk is incorporated to the upper floor, giving children a perfect place to do homework or crafts.

Rear Elevation

Belmeade — UDHDG01-1097 — 1-866-525-9374

© 2005 Donald A. Gardner, Inc.

Total Living	First Floor	Bonus	Bed	Bath	Width	Depth	Foundation	Price Category
3064 sq ft	3064 sq ft	746 sq ft	3	2-1/2	78' 4"	86' 3"	Crawl Space*	G

Design Features

- With abundant custom-styled amenities, this plan was designed to impress.
- The stately exterior delivers instant curb appeal with dual columns framing the stone entryway.
- A spacious master suite enjoys a private wing.
- The well-appointed common areas include columns, high ceilings, and built-in shelves.
- A walk-in pantry, art niche and large secondary bedrooms complete the floor plan.

Rear Elevation

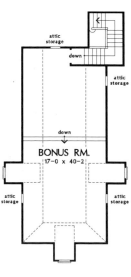

Bonus Room

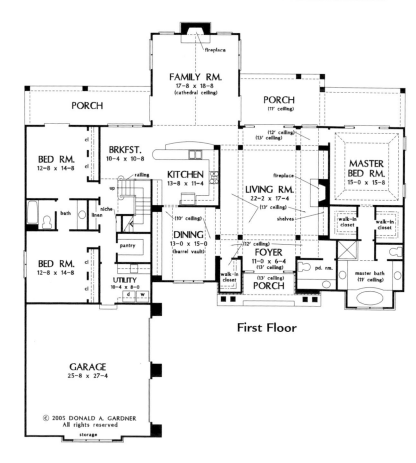

First Floor

*Other options available. See page 513.

© 2005 Donald A. Gardner, Inc.

Clarkson — UDHDG01-1117 — 1-866-525-9374

Total Living	First Floor	Second Floor	Bonus	Bed	Bath	Width	Depth	Foundation	Price Category
3080 sq ft	3080 sq ft	N/A	498 sq ft	4	4-1/2	75' 7"	72' 3"	Crawl Space*	G

Design Features

- This home is perfect for families who want a large square-footage home on one floor.

- The massive utility area provides room for more than just washing clothes.

- A screen porch with cathedral ceiling adds nice architectural detail.

- Featuring a rear porch, the master bedroom includes an easy way to access Mother Nature.

- The open kitchen, breakfast and morning rooms become one giant open space.

First Floor

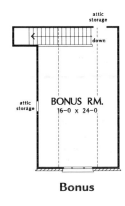

Bonus

Rear Elevation

Donald A. Gardner Architects, Inc.

Jerivale — UDHDG01-1033 — 1-866-525-9374

© 2003 Donald A. Gardner, Inc.

Total Living	First Floor	Second Floor	Bonus	Bed	Bath	Width	Depth	Foundation	Price Category
3647 sq ft	2766 sq ft	881 sq ft	407 sq ft	3	3-1/2	92' 5"	71' 10"	Crawl Space*	H

Design Features

- Four towering columns frame the dramatic barrel-vault entrance.

- Cedar shake, stone and siding complement a metal roof over the front porch.

- The two-story foyer has impressive views of the study, dining room, living room and balcony.

- Built-ins, three fireplaces and a walk-in pantry add special touches.

- Every bedroom has walk-in closets.

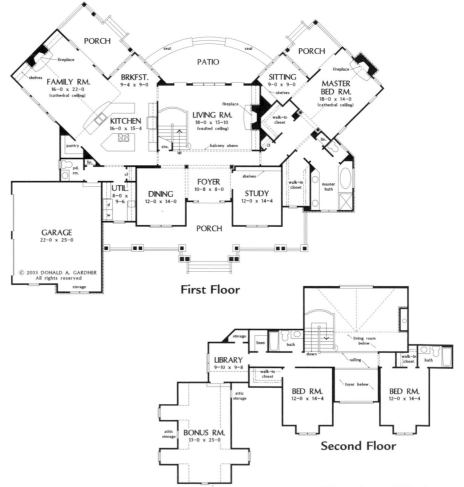

First Floor

Second Floor

Rear Elevation

*Other options available. See page 513.

Northampton — UDHFB01-1005 — 1-866-525-9374

Total Living	First Floor	Scoond Floor	Opt. Bonus	Bed	Bath	Width	Depth	Foundation	Price Category
3083 sq ft	2429 sq ft	654 sq ft	420 sq ft	3	3-1/2	63' 6"	71' 4"	Basement, Crawl Space or Slab	I

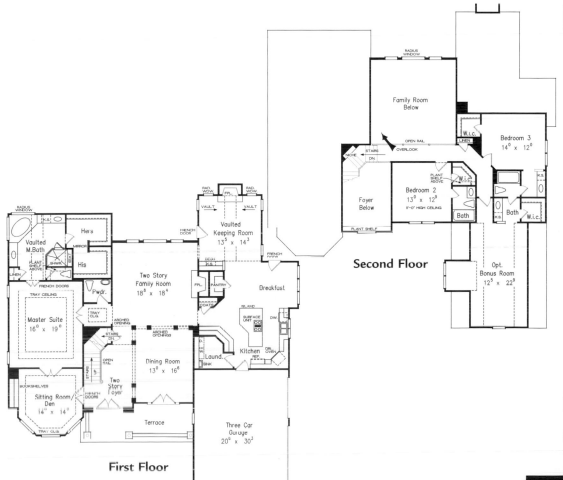

Design Features

- This home's façade features a turret and a terrace area, giving it phenomenal curb appeal.

- The dining room is defined by architectural columns.

- The turreted room makes a beautiful study, but can be easily altered to make a stunning sitting area for the master bedroom.

- The kitchen overlooks a vaulted keeping room.

Rear Elevation

Sunset Beach — UDHDS01-6848 — 1-866-525-9374

© The Sater Design Collection, Inc.

Total Living	First Floor	Second Floor	Bonus	Bed	Bath	Width	Depth	Foundation	Price Category
3096 sq ft	2083 sq ft	1013 sq ft	N/A	4	3-1/2	74' 0"	88' 0"	Crawl Space	H

Design Features

- A gazebo-style front porch accents this country villa.

- The entry leads to the grand foyer and sweeping radius staircase.

- The main level master suite boasts a private lanai.

- A study has a window seat and built-in cabinetry.

- A bayed breakfast nook and butler's pantry complete the kitchen.

Second Floor

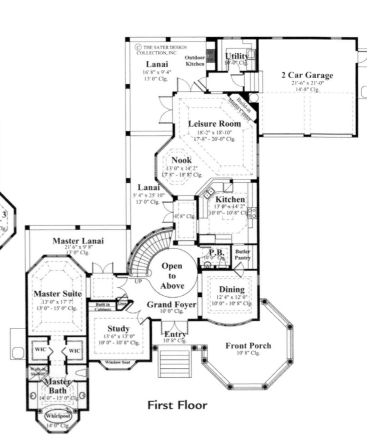

First Floor

Rear Elevation

© 2005 Frank Betz Associates, Inc.

Tillman — UDHFB01-3953 — 1-866-525-9374

Total Living	First Floor	Second Floor	Opt. Bonus	Bed	Bath	Width	Depth	Foundation	Price Category
3125 sq ft	2399 sq ft	726 sq ft	425 sq ft	4	4	58' 4"	72' 0"	Basement or Crawl Space	I

Second Floor

First Floor

Design Features

- With vertical siding, cedar shakes, stone and brick the *Tillman* embodies all the elements of a truly classic home.

- The foyer boasts decorative columns to frame the entryway.

- The open floor plan allows an easy flow from room to room, making entertaining a breeze.

- A vaulted covered porch and deck allow homeowners to enjoy the outdoors regardless of the weather.

Rear Elevation

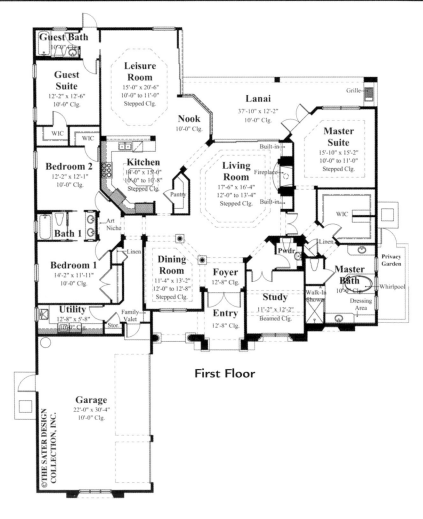

Porta Rossa — UDHDS01-8058 — 1-866-525-9374

© The Sater Design Collection, Inc.

Total Living	First Floor	Bonus	Bed	Bath	Width	Depth	Foundation	Price Category
3166 sq ft	3166 sq ft	N/A	4 + Study	3-1/2	67' 0"	91' 8"	Slab	H

Design Features

- An elaborate entry turret highlights the façade and gives a Spanish Colonial feel.

- A high beamed ceiling lends character to the study.

- The master boasts a step-up spa-style tub with a private garden view.

- Two secondary bedrooms share a full bath.

- The guest suite is tucked away in the far corner of the plan and has a cabana-style bath that also serves the pool and patio.

Rear Elevation

First Floor

Hickory Ridge — UDHDG01-916 — 1-866-525-9374

Total Living	First Floor	Second Floor	Bonus	Bed	Bath	Width	Depth	Foundation	Price Category
3167 sq ft	2194 sq ft	973 sq ft	281 sq ft	4	3-1/2	71' 11"	54' 4"	Crawl Space*	G

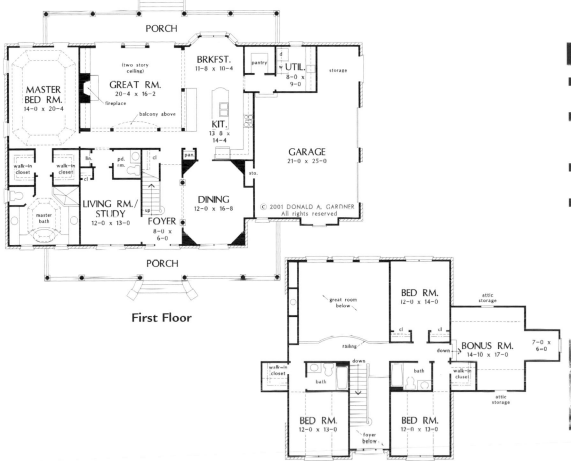

First Floor

Second Floor

Design Features

- Twin gables, sidelights and an arched entryway accent the façade.
- Decorative ceiling treatments, bay windows and French doors adorn the interior.
- Details include counter space, walk-in pantry, built-ins and storage areas.
- Supported by columns, a curved balcony overlooks the stunning two-story great room.

Rear Elevation

*Other options available. See page 513.

Dogwood Ridge — UDHAL01-5005 — 1-866-525-9374

Total Living	First Floor	Basement	Bonus	Bed	Bath	Width	Depth	Foundation	Price Category
3201 sq ft	2090 sq ft	1111 sq ft	N/A	3	3-1/2	71' 1"	78' 6"	Hillside Walkout	O

Design Features

- This hillside walkout boasts a rear wall of glasswork on both floors.

- A patio, and rear and screened porches take living outdoors.

- The open floor plan distinguishes rooms by ceiling treatments and columns.

- For added convenience and future planning, an elevator makes living easier.

- Along with the master suite, the secondary bedrooms take advantage of the natural scenery.

Rear Elevation

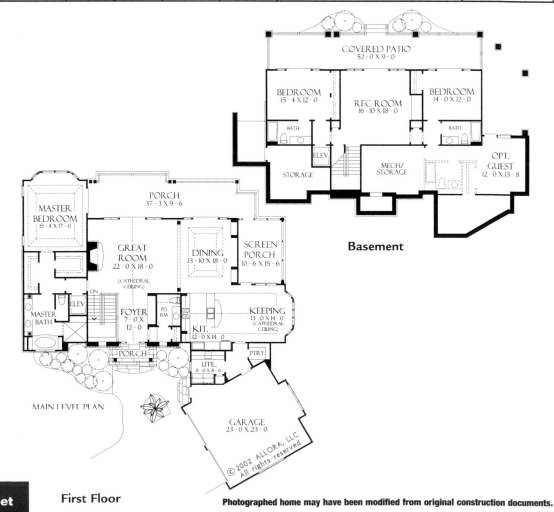

Basement

First Floor

Total Living	First F
3367 sq ft	2562 s

Touchstone — UDHDG01-1099-D — 1-866-525-9374

Total Living	First Floor	Basement	Bonus	Bed	Bath	Width	Depth	Foundation	Price Category
3213 sq ft	2143 sq ft	1070 sq ft	N/A	4	4	73' 9"	60' 0"	Hillside Walkout	G

Design Features

- The walkout basement also includes two bedrooms with full baths.

- Sweeping gables and a stone façade add drama to the exterior.

- A tray ceiling and bay window compliment the master suite, which also features walk-in closets.

- The lofty living room overlooks a rear deck and gracefully flows into the dining room and kitchen.

- Hugged by a bay window, the breakfast room includes a walk-in pantry.

First Floor

DECK

DINING
16–0 x 11-11
(cathedral ceiling)

SCREEN PORCH
11-6 x 11-10

MASTER BED RM.
14–0 x 20-8

LIVING RM.
20–0 x 17-10
(cathedral ceiling)

fireplace

KITCHEN
16–0 x 9-7

BRKFST.
14–0 x 11-4

niche

walk-in closet

walk-in closet

FOYER
7-8 x 7-8

BED RM./ STUDY
13–0 x 12-0

bath

UTIL
7-8 x 8-4

master bath

PORCH

GARAGE
23–0 x 23–0

STORAGE

Second Floor

great room below

(vaulted ceiling)

bath

railing

foyer below

BED RM.
13–0 x 12-0
(cathedral ceiling)

Basement

PATIO

BED RM.
13-2 x 11-8

FAMILY RM.
20-4 x 17-8

BED RM.
12-10 x 11-8

fireplace

walk-in closet

bath

bath

Rear Elevation

Donald A. Gardner /

Frank Betz Associates, Inc.

Tuscany —

Total Living	First Flo...
3219 sq ft	2477 sq...

Design Fea...

- Built-ins in the great... counter space in the... room add convenien...

- The family-efficient f... be witnessed in the k... pass-thru.

- The kitchen has rear-... for outdoor entertai...

- Ceiling treatments hi... master bedroom, bec... breakfast area and lo...

- The bonus room can... home theatre, playro...

Rear Elevation

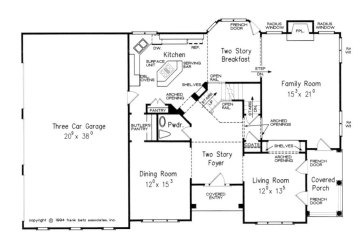

Carmichael — UDHFB01-770 — 1-866-525-9374

© 1994 Frank Betz Associates, Inc.

Total Living	First Floor	Second Floor	Opt. Bonus	Bed	Bath	Width	Depth	Foundation	Price Category
3262 sq ft	1418 sq ft	1844 sq ft	N/A	4	3-1/2	63' 0"	41' 0"	Basement, Crawl Space or Slab	I

Design Features

- A two-story breakfast area adjoins the sizeable kitchen.

- Entertaining is easy and convenient with a butler's pantry connecting the dining room to the kitchen.

- Decorative shelves are creatively tucked between the living room and family room.

- The master retreat is complete with private sitting area and two-sided fireplace.

First Floor

Second Floor

Rear Elevation

© The Sater Design Collection, Inc.

Isabel — UDHDS01-6938 — 1-866-525-9374

Total Living	First Floor	Second Floor	Bonus	Bed	Bath	Width	Depth	Foundation	Price Category
3273 sq ft	3273 sq ft	N/A	467 sq ft	3	3	88' 4"	104' 4"	Slab	O

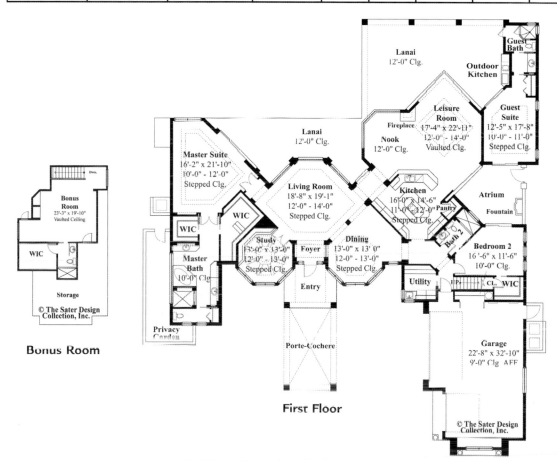

Bonus Room

First Floor

© The Sater Design Collection, Inc.

Design Features

- A gable porte-cochere provides a gracious sentry to this stunning home, which features an arched entryway, transoms and a side-entry garage.

- The gourmet kitchen includes a walk-in pantry, stove top work island and an eating bar.

- A vaulted ceiling soars above the leisure room, which features a fireplace and disappearing walls of glass.

- The master suite sits under a stepped ceiling and includes two walk-in closets and a privacy garden.

Rear View

3000 sq ft—4000 sq ft

Frank Betz Associates, Inc.

Brookmere — UDHFB01-3452 — 1-866-525-9374

© 1999 Frank Betz Associates, Inc.

Total Living	First Floor	Second Floor	Opt. Bonus	Bed	Bath	Width	Depth	Foundation	Price Category
3274 sq ft	2332 sq ft	942 sq ft	305 sq ft	4	3-1/2	60' 0"	64' 4"	Basement, Crawl Space or Slab	H

Design Features

- The kitchen overlooks a large breakfast area and cozy keeping room.

- This area is gently divided from the grand room, creating two separate spaces to entertain guests.

- Decorative columns and a furniture niche give the dining room that extra dose of character.

- A sitting area surrounded by a wall of windows overlooks the backyard from the master suite.

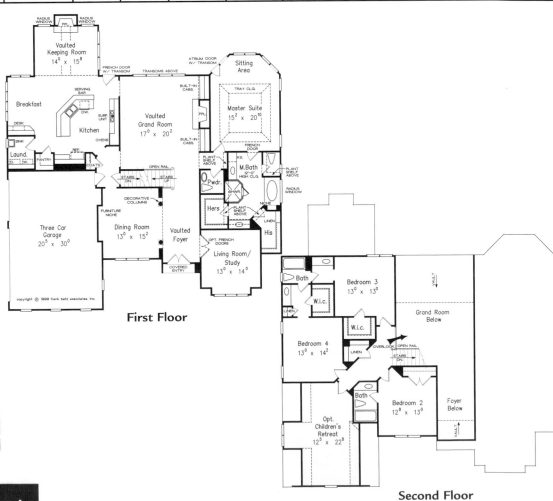

First Floor

Second Floor

Rear Elevation

Berkshire — UDHDG01-748-D — 1-866-525-9374

Total Living	First Floor	Second Floor	Bonus	Bed	Bath	Width	Depth	Foundation	Price Category
3281 sq ft	2065 sq ft	1216 sq ft	N/A	4	3-1/2	82' 2"	43' 6"	Hillside Walkout	G

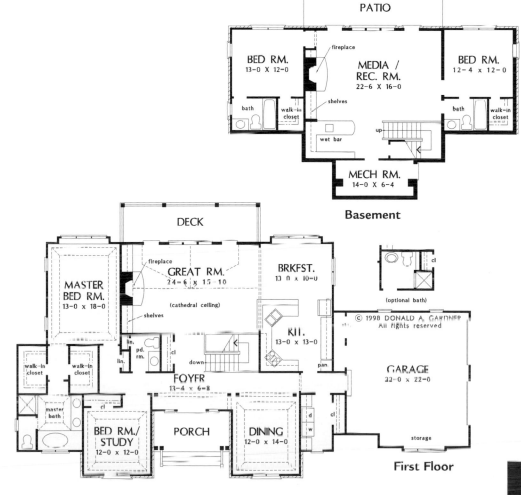

Basement

First Floor

Design Features

- Stone, siding and multiple gables combine beautifully on this walkout basement home.
- Capped by a cathedral ceiling, the great room features a fireplace and built-in shelves.
- Twin walk-in closets and a private bath infuse the master suite with luxury.
- The nearby powder room offers an optional full bath, allowing the study to double as a bedroom.
- Downstairs, a large media/recreation room with wet bar and fireplace separates two bedrooms.

Rear Elevation

Summerlyn — UDHFB01-3675 — 1-866-525-9374

© 2002 Frank Betz Associates, Inc.

Total Living	First Floor	Second Floor	Opt. Bonus	Bed	Bath	Width	Depth	Foundation	Price Category
3281 sq ft	1685 sq ft	1596 sq ft	N/A	5	4-1/2	51' 0"	66' 10"	Basement, Crawl Space or Slab	I

Design Features

- An attention-grabbing two-story turret is perhaps the most unique feature of the *Summerlyn's* façade.

- A sunken sunroom off the breakfast area shares a see-through fireplace with the family room where a bowed wall of windows illuminates the room.

- Upstairs, the master bath features decorative niches on each end of the tub for fun decorating opportunities.

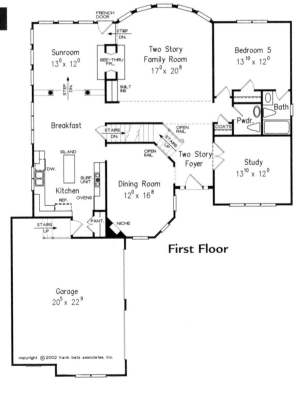

First Floor

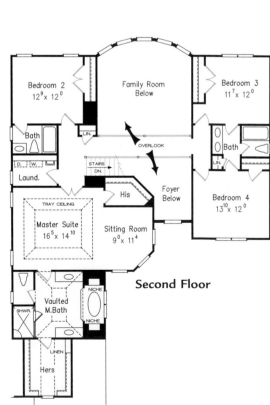

Second Floor

Rear Elevation

Frank Betz Associates, Inc.

Fenway — UDHFB01-3444 — 1-866-525-9374

Total Living	First Floor	Second Floor	Opt. Bonus	Bed	Bath	Width	Depth	Foundation	Price Category
3285 sq ft	2293 sq ft	992 sq ft	131 sq ft	4	3-1/2	71' 0"	62' 0"	Basement, Crawl Space or Slab	I

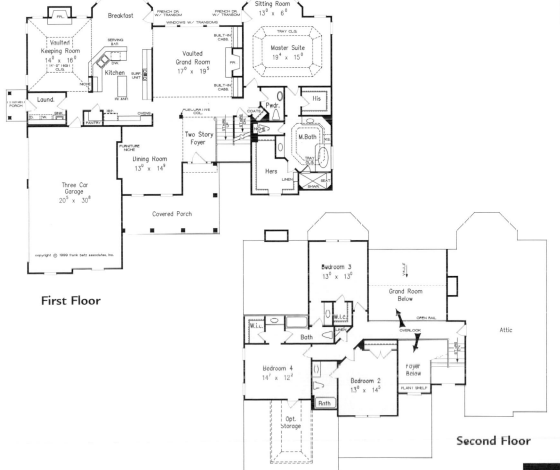

First Floor

Design Features

- A fire-lit keeping room borders the kitchen and breakfast area.

- Sunshine pours in through transom windows in the grand room.

- A buffet table or china cabinet will fit perfectly into the furniture niche in the dining room.

- Private lounging space has been incorporated into the master suite.

Second Floor

Rear Elevation

Les Anges — UDHDS01-6825 — 1-866-525-9374

© The Sater Design Collection, Inc.

Total Living	First Floor	Second Floor	Lower Level	Bed	Bath	Width	Depth	Foundation	Price Category
3285 sq ft	2146 sq ft	952 sq ft	187 sq ft	3	3-1/2	56' 0"	64' 0"	Island Basement	H

Design Features

- Built-in cabinetry and a massive fireplace anchor the central living space.

- The morning nook provides a bay window and fireplace view.

- A gourmet island kitchen serves the formal dining room.

- The secluded master wing enjoys a bumped-out window and twin walk-in closets.

- The upper level boasts a catwalk that connects two secondary suites.

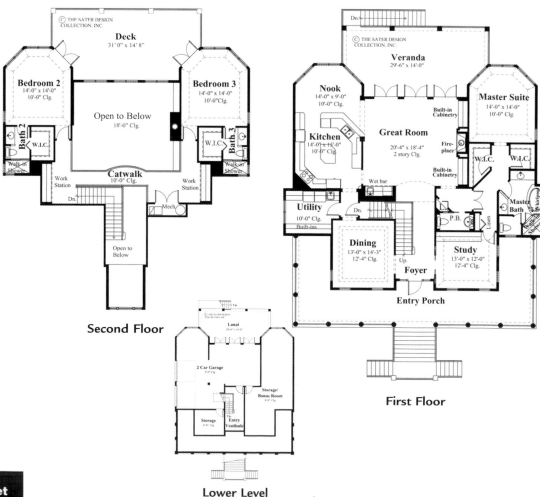

Rear Elevation

Adelaide — UDHDG01-866-D — 1-866-525-9374

Total Living	First Floor	Basement	Bonus	Bed	Bath	Width	Depth	Foundation	Price Category
3301 sq ft	2151 sq ft	1150 sq ft	N/A	4	3	83' 0"	74' 4"	Hillside Walkout	G

First Floor

BRKFST.
13-0 x 12-8
(vaulted ceiling)

DECK

DECK

MASTER BED RM.
14-0 x 16-0

master bath

KITCHEN
13-4 x 16-0

GREAT RM.
21-0 x 16-0
(cathedral ceiling)

fireplace

SCREEN PORCH
11-10 x 15-8
(cathedral ceiling)

walk-in closet

pan.

sto.

walk-in closet

DINING
13-0 x 12-4

FOYER
14-10 x 5-8

bath

down

w   d

UTIL.
9-8 x 8-0

storage

PORCH

BED RM./ STUDY
11-0 x 13-0

GARAGE
21-8 x 25-8

PATIO

storage

BED RM.
13-4 x 16-0

BED RM.
12-4 x 12-4

REC. RM.
20-0 x 16-0

fireplace

walk in closet

bath

up

storage

storage

Basement

Design Features

- Twin dormers, board-and-batten siding and stone add curb appeal to this charming Craftsman design.

- Two decks, a screened porch and spacious patio provide plenty of room for outdoor entertaining.

- Counters in the kitchen and utility room offer ample workspace.

- From decorative ceilings and columns to fireplaces and a shower seat, niceties are abundant.

Rear Elevation

Frank Betz Associates, Inc.

Benedict — UDHFB01-3768 — 1-866-525-9374

© 2002 Frank Betz Associates, Inc.

Total Living	First Floor	Second Floor	Opt. Bonus	Bed	Bath	Width	Depth	Foundation	Price Category
3301 sq ft	2355 sq ft	946 sq ft	275 sq ft	4	3-1/2	60' 0"	64' 4"	Basement or Crawl Space	I

Design Features

- Multiple gables, a cheery dormer and the classic combination of brick and siding make an impressive statement.

- The two-story foyer gives the perfect introduction to a vaulted grand room.

- Beyond the kitchen is a vaulted keeping room with radius windows and a fireplace.

- The master bedroom includes a secluded lounging area that overlooks the backyard.

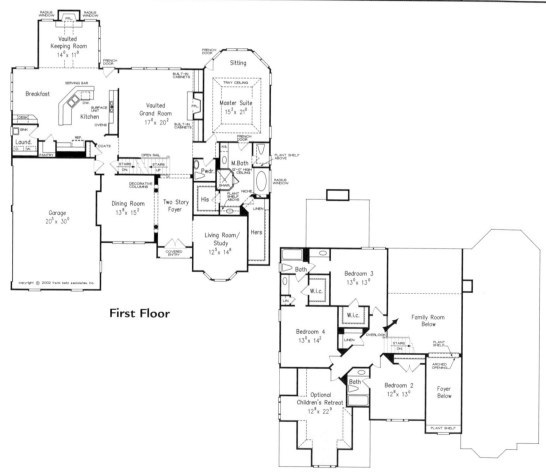

First Floor

Second Floor

Rear Elevation

© The Sater Design Collection, Inc.

Spring Hill Lane — UDHDS01-6661 — 1-866-525-9374

Total Living	First Floor	Bonus	Bed	Bath	Width	Depth	Foundation	Price Category
3301 sq ft	3301 sq ft	N/A	4 + Study	3-1/2	80' 0"	103' 8"	Slab	H

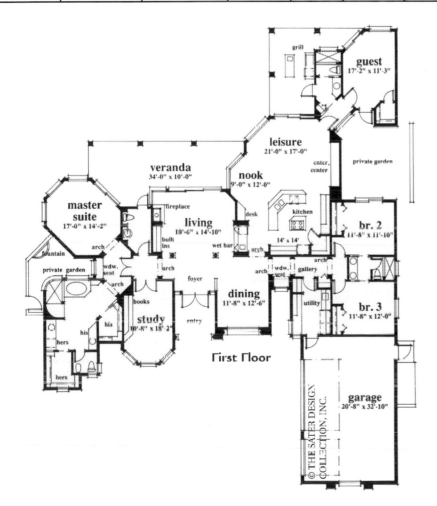

First Floor

© THE SATER DESIGN COLLECTION, INC.

Design Features

- A turret study and raised entry highlight the façade.

- The living room has built-ins and a fireplace.

- The kitchen is equipped with a center-island cooktop and built-in desk.

- The master bath has a curved glass shower and private garden views.

- An in-law suite off the rear of the home enjoys patio access.

Rear Elevation

Chadbryne — UDHDS01-8004 — 1-866-525-9374

© The Sater Design Collection, Inc.

Total Living	First Floor	Second Floor	Bonus	Bed	Bath	Width	Depth	Foundation	Price Category
3304 sq ft	2219 sq ft	1085 sq ft	404 sq ft	4	3-1/2	91' 0"	52' 8"	Slab or Basement	H

Design Features

- Fanlights, transoms and shapely balustrades highlight two bold turrets, which harbor a bay window and a wraparound portico.

- A fireplace, built-in cabinetry, access to the veranda and a two-story coffered ceiling enhance the great room.

- An open floor plan encourages a natural flow between the kitchen, breakfast nook and the dining and great room.

- Guests will enjoy the privacy of upper level bedrooms, each with its own bath and walk-in closet.

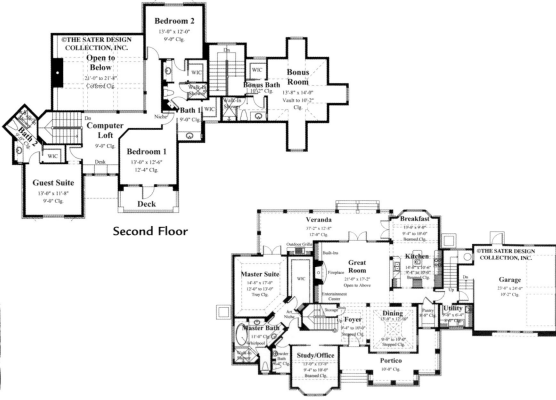

Second Floor

First Floor

Rear Elevation

© 2005 Frank Betz Associates, Inc.

Berkshire Pointe — UDHFB01-3955 — 1-866-525-9374

Total Living	First Floor	Second Floor	Opt. Bonus	Bed	Bath	Width	Depth	Foundation	Price Category
3306 sq ft	2278 sq ft	1028 sq ft	N/A	4	3-1/2	62' 0"	66' 0"	Basement or Crawl Space	I

Design Features

- Triple arches columns welcome you to the *Berkshire Pointe*. A front porch is the ideal place for rocking chairs.

- The breakfast room and kitchen offer an island that allows additional counter space, while the built-in desk helps keep clutter in its place.

- A cover porch and deck are accessible from the breakfast area and the master sitting room.

- An office in the front of the home is the perfect location for the busy stay-at-home mom or the telecommuter.

Second Floor

First Floor

Rear Elevation

Laycrest — UDHDG01-995-D — 1-866-525-9374

© 2002 Donald A. Gardner, Inc.

Total Living	First Floor	Basement	Bonus	Bed	Bath	Width	Depth	Foundation	Price Category
3320 sq ft	1720 sq ft	1600 sq ft	N/A	4	3-1/2	59' 0"	59' 4"	Hillside Walkout	G

Design Features

- With Arts-n-Crafts charm, this hillside design starts with an exterior of siding and stone.

- A rear clerestory frames the sky and places it under the great room's cathedral ceiling.

- Built-in cabinetry and fireplaces enhance the great room and rec room.

- An angled counter separates the kitchen from the dining room and great room.

- A wet bar, bay windows and tray ceilings add custom style.

Rear Elevation

First Floor

Basement

Walden Pond — UDHFB01-3927 — 1-866-525-9374

Total Living	First Floor	Second Floor	Opt. Bonus	Bed	Bath	Width	Depth	Foundation	Price Category
3325 sq ft	2348 sq ft	977 sq ft	N/A	4	4-1/2	66' 6"	60' 6"	Basement or Crawl Space	I

Second Floor

First Floor

Design Features

- The design of the *Walden Pond* must be seen to be believed.

- The vaulted family room offers a fireplace flanked by built-in cabinets.

- A guest suite is tucked behind the kitchen allowing guests a private bath.

- The combination of the kitchen, breakfast area and keeping room allow families plenty of room to congregation at the end of the day.

Rear Elevation

Sterling Heights — UDHFB01-3951 — 1-866-525-9374

© 2005 Frank Betz Associates, Inc.

Total Living	First Floor	Second Floor	Opt. Bonus	Bed	Bath	Width	Depth	Foundation	Price Category
3327 sq ft	2372 sq ft	955 sq ft	325 sq ft	4	3-1/2	61' 0"	66' 4"	Basement or Crawl Space	I

Design Features

- The many amenities in the *Sterling Heights* separate it from other comparable homes.

- The kitchen boasts an island with eat-in bar, a spacious breakfast area and a keeping room with a fireplace.

- The vaulted grand room offers a fireplace and built-in cabinets.

- A room in the front of the home can be used as a living room or a home office.

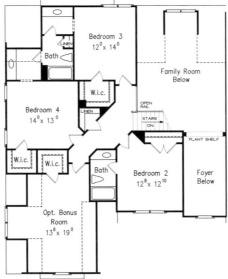

Second Floor

First Floor

Rear Elevation

Donald A. Gardner Architects, Inc.

Hollingbourne — UDHDG01-990 — 1-866-525-9374

Total Living	First Floor	Second Floor	Bonus	Bed	Bath	Width	Depth	Foundation	Price Category
3341 sq ft	2062 sq ft	1279 sq ft	386 sq ft	5	4-1/2	73' 8"	50' 0"	Crawl Space*	G

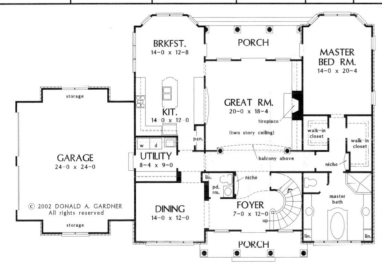

First Floor

Design Features

- Reminiscent of Old-World Manors, this stately home features a stone and stucco exterior.

- An elegant balustrade crowns the entryway, which is highlighted by columns and arches.

- A grand staircase leads to a balcony loft, which separates the two-story foyer and great room.

- Built-in cabinetry, a striking fireplace and French doors enhance the great room.

Second Floor

Rear Elevation

Shiloh — UDHDS01-6763 — 1-866-525-9374

© The Sater Design Collection, Inc.

Total Living	First Floor	Bonus	Bed	Bath	Width	Depth	Foundation	Price Category
3353 sq ft	3353 sq ft	N/A	3 + Study	2F/2H	84' 0"	92' 0"	Slab	H

Design Features

- This Adobe-style home features a floor plan that is perfect for entertaining.
- The wide-open living and dining area embraces rear views and is warmed by a wood-burning fireplace.
- The updated bedrooms are over-sized with walk-in closets.
- A veranda with outdoor grille and pool bath wraps the leisure, nook and kitchen area.

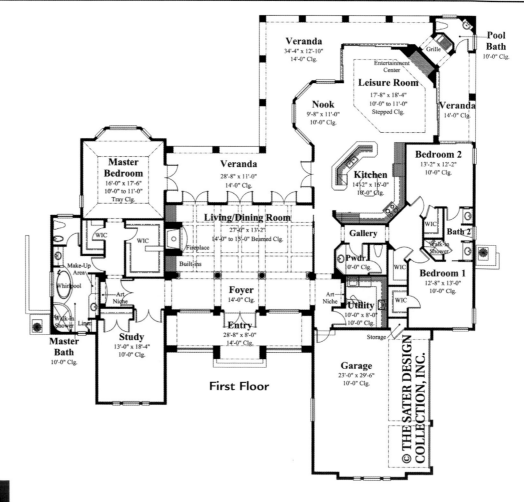

First Floor

Rear Elevation

© The Sater Design Collection, Inc.

Bellini — UDHDS01-8042 — 1-866-525-9374

Total Living	First Floor	Second Floor	Bonus	Bed	Bath	Width	Depth	Foundation	Price Category
3351 sq ft	3351 sq ft	N/A	N/A	3	2F/2H	84' 0"	92' 2"	Opt. Basement/Slab	H

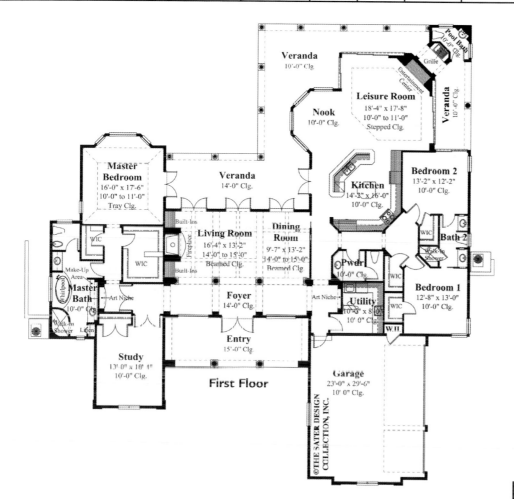

First Floor

Design Features

- An open gallery and a sculpted arcade announce the living/dining room—a welcoming space anchored by a massive fireplace and built-ins.

- A state-of-the-art kitchen overlooks a bumped-out morning nook and a media room with retreating glass walls to the veranda.

- A wraparound veranda boasts a pool bath and an outdoor grille.

- The owners' wing includes a pampering bath, an art niche, private study and a gallery hall.

Rear Elevation

Wellington — UDHDS01-8041 — 1-866-525-9374

© The Sater Design Collection, Inc.

Total Living	First Floor	Bonus	Bed	Bath	Width	Depth	Foundation	Price Category
3353 sq ft	3353 sq ft	N/A	3 + Study	2F/2H	84' 0"	92' 0"	Slab	H

Design Features

- This English Revival façade pairs its formal style with a welcoming front porch.

- The oversized kitchen is the hub for easy entertaining inside and out.

- Pocketing glass doors connect the leisure room and patio.

- An outdoor grill area is perfect for entertaining.

- A foyer with art niche secludes the master suite.

Rear Elevation

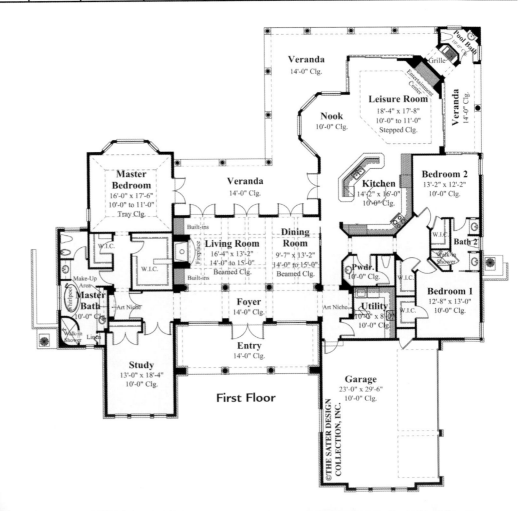

© The Sater Design Collection, Inc.

Sandusky — UDHDS01-7062 — 1-866-525-9374

Total Living	First Floor	Second Floor	Bonus	Bed	Bath	Width	Depth	Foundation	Price Category
3082 sq ft	2138 sq ft	944 sq ft	427 sq ft	3	3-1/2	77' 8"	64' 0"	Crawl Space/Opt. Basement	H

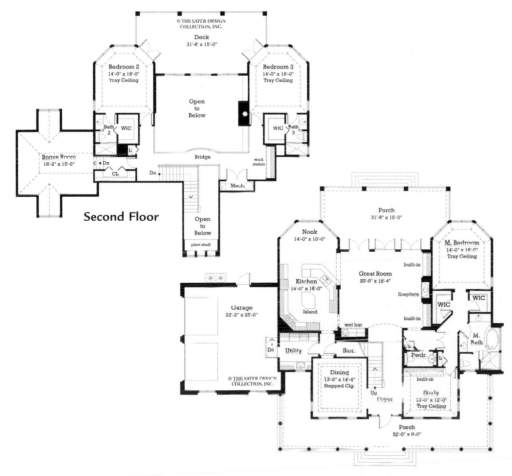

Second Floor

First Floor

Design Features

- A split-shake roof, columns, arches and mirrored stone chimneys add the finishing touch to the exterior.

- Built-in cabinetry, a massive fireplace and a host of French doors highlight the central living space.

- An island kitchen provides ample counter and storage space, a work island and easy access to the breakfast nook and great room.

- The upper level boasts a spacious deck that connects the two secondary suites.

Rear Elevation

McFarlin Park — UDHFB01-3808 — 1-866-525-9374

© 2003 Frank Betz Associates, Inc.

Total Living	First Floor	Second Floor	Opt. Bonus	Bed	Bath	Width	Depth	Foundation	Price Category
3397 sq ft	2434 sq ft	963 sq ft	N/A	5	4	64' 0"	62' 10"	Basement or Crawl Space	I

Design Features

- From the *Southern Living® Design Collection*

- The timeless façade of the *McFarlin Park* is a welcoming blend of stone and cedar shake.

- A vaulted keeping room adjoins the kitchen area, creating the perfect spot for lounging or entertaining guests.

- Unwind on the cozy screened porch, tucked away off the kitchen.

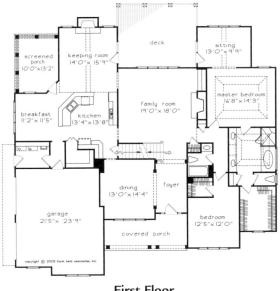

First Floor

Second Floor

Rear Elevation

© The Sater Design Collection, Inc.

Governor's Club — UDHDS01-6674 — 1-866-525-9374

Total Living	First Floor	Bonus	Bed	Bath	Width	Depth	Foundation	Price Category
3398 sq ft	3398 sq ft	N/A	3	3-1/2	121' 5"	96' 2"	Slab	H

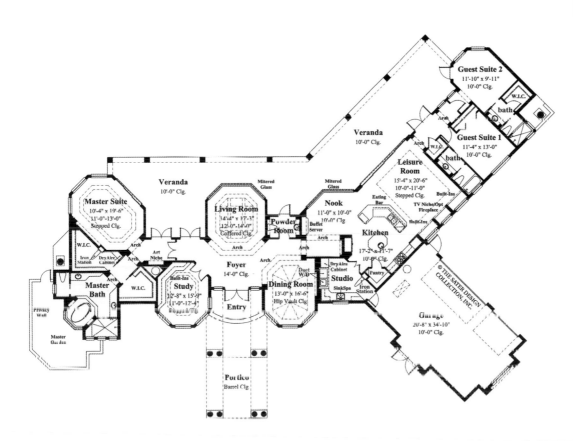

Design Features

- An elegant portico entry greets those who pass-by.

- Built-in cabinetry, optional fireplace, an eating bar connecting to the kitchen and retreating glass doors to the veranda make the leisure room the central hub of the home.

- To ensure privacy the master suite is tucked away from the main living areas and features a private garden, access to the veranda, two spacious walk-in closets and a luxurious bath.

- The kitchen offers ample counter space, a breakfast nook with a buffet server and a walk-in pantry.

Rear Elevation

Photographed home may have been modified from original construction documents.

3000 sq ft—4000 sq ft

Frank Betz Associates, Inc.

Crossville — UDHFB01-3938 — 1-866-525-9374

Total Living	First Floor	Second Floor	Opt. Bonus	Bed	Bath	Width	Depth	Foundation	Price Category
3399 sq ft	2272 sq ft	1127 sq ft	N/A	4	3-1/2	58' 0"	75' 4"	Basement or Crawl Space	I

Design Features

- Double front porches make quite a statement in this *Crossville* plan.

- The upper porch is accessible from an upstairs bedroom.

- This bedroom is adjacent to another bedroom. These bedrooms share a Jack-and-Jill bathroom and built-in desk.

- A fourth bedroom also boasts a private bath. All upstairs bedroom offer walk-in closets.

Rear Elevation

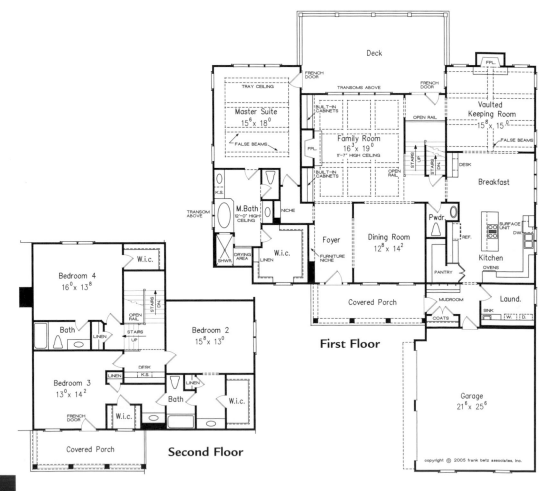

Yesterview — UDHDG01-1002 — 1-866-525-9374

Total Living	First Floor	Second Floor	Bonus	Bed	Bath	Width	Depth	Foundation	Price Category
3419 sq ft	2237 sq ft	1182 sq ft	475 sq ft	4	3-1/2	85' 4"	56' 4"	Crawl Space*	G

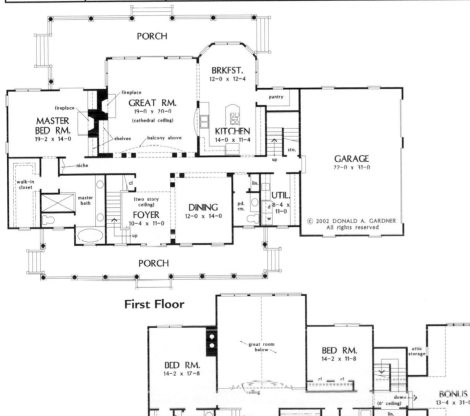

First Floor

Second Floor

Design Features

- An elegant exterior with country and traditional flair—surrounds a modern floor plan.

- Two spacious porches promote outdoor entertaining.

- Built-in cabinetry and fireplaces complement the great room and master bedroom.

- Two staircases, a large laundry room with sink and a guest suite create enjoyable living.

Rear Elevation

Frank Betz Associates, Inc.

Ingrams Mill — UDHFB01-3932 — 1-866-525-9374

Total Living	First Floor	Second Floor	Opt. Bonus	Bed	Bath	Width	Depth	Foundation	Price Category
3427 sq ft	2108 sq ft	1319 sq ft	340 sq ft	4	3-1/2	55' 0"	78' 0"	Basement or Crawl Space	I

Design Features

- The European design of the *Ingrams Mill* offers a beautiful stone turret to the elevation.

- The vaulted master suite has a beamed ceiling and a luxurious master bathroom.

- The keeping room and family room share a see-thru fireplace.

- Three bedrooms, an optional bonus and a loft complete the second floor.

Rear Elevation

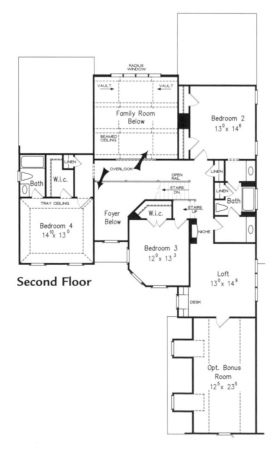

Second Floor

First Floor

Candace — UDHFB01-965 — 1-866-525-9374

Total Living	First Floor	Second Floor	Opt. Bonus	Bed	Bath	Width	Depth	Foundation	Price Category
3434 sq ft	2384 sq ft	1050 sq ft	228 sq ft	4	3-1/2	65' 8"	57' 0"	Basement, Crawl Space or Slab	I

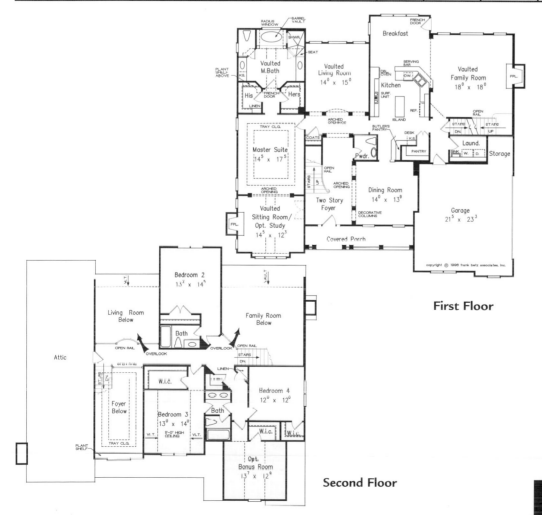

First Floor

Second Floor

Design Features

- The master suite has its own private sitting area.

- Decorative columns and arched openings serve as transitional points from various rooms.

- An optional bonus room upstairs has endless finishing possibilities.

- Plenty of volume in ceiling heights gives the entire first floor of this design a very spacious and roomy feeling.

Rear Elevation

Wentworth Trail — UDHDS01-6653 — 1-866-525-9374

© The Sater Design Collection, Inc.

Total Living	First Floor	Second Floor	Bonus	Bed	Bath	Width	Depth	Foundation	Price Category
3462 sq ft	2894 sq ft	568 sq ft	N/A	3	3-1/2	67' 0"	102' 0"	Slab	H

Design Features

- The foyer opens to a living room with corner pocketing doors.

- The kitchen has a walk-in pantry and cooktop island.

- The leisure room has a fireplace, bar and TV niche.

- The opulent master wing includes a study and sitting area.

- The loft has a wet bar and an observation deck.

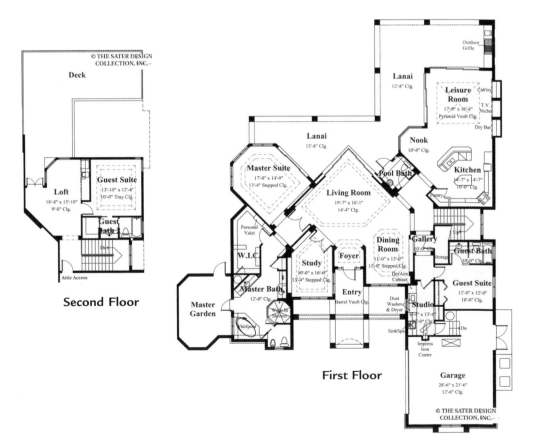

Second Floor

First Floor

Rear View

Photographed home may have been modified from original construction documents.

© 2005 Frank Betz Associates, Inc.

Westborough — UDHFB01-3917 — 1-866-525-9374

Total Living	First Floor	Second Floor	Opt. Bonus	Bed	Bath	Width	Depth	Foundation	Price Category
3467 sq ft	2550 sq ft	917 sq ft	736 sq ft	4	5	61' 6"	85' 0"	Basement, Crawl Space or Slab	I

Design Features

- The covered porch and courtyard entry welcome you to the *Westborough*.

- Inside the foyer leads to the vaulted family room that includes a fireplace, built-in cabinets and a rear wall of windows that allows views to the back yard.

- The master suite encompasses one wing of the home.

- A loft on the second floor has French doors that open to overlook the keeping room, adjacent to the kitchen.

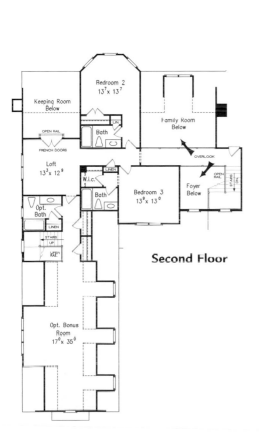

Second Floor

First Floor

Rear Elevation

Innsbrook Place — UDHDS01-6634 — 1-866-525-9374

© The Sater Design Collection, Inc.

Total Living	First Floor	Bonus	Bed	Bath	Width	Depth	Foundation	Price Category
3477 sq ft	3477 sq ft	N/A	3 + Study	3-1/2	95' 0"	88' 8"	Slab	H

Design Features

- An angled entry opens the home to formal areas with rear views.

- The living room and master share a double-sided fireplace.

- A grand ale wet bar serves the dining room and lanai.

- An octagon breakfast nook has panoramic views.

- The study has a peaked vaulted ceiling and cove lighting.

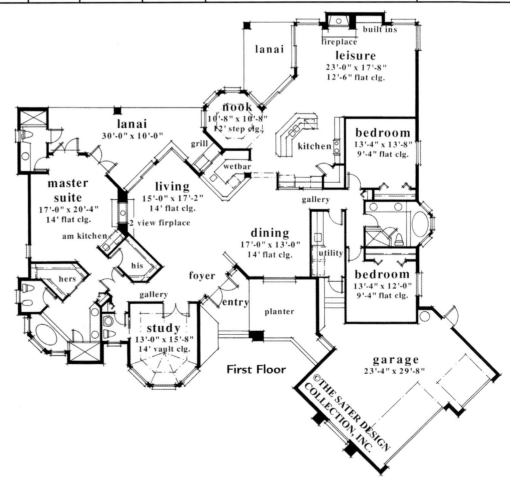

Rear Elevation

Photographed home may have been modified from original construction documents.

© The Sater Design Collection, Inc.

Salcito — UDHDS01-6787 — 1-866-525-9374

Total Living	First Floor	Second Floor	Bed	Bath	Width Bldg.	Width w/Garden	Depth	Foundation	Price Category
3473 sq ft	2357 sq ft	1116 sq ft	4	4-1/2	45' 0"	52' 2"	94' 0"	Slab	H

Second Floor

First Floor

Design Features

- This enchanting courtyard home features interesting spaces.

- Rooms open to a central loggia with fountain pool.

- The second level includes a study and two bedroom suites.

- Multiple upstairs decks have courtyard views.

- The main-floor leisure room has a two-story boxed-beamed ceiling.

Interior Courtyard

Kenthurst — UDHFB01-3755 — 1-866-525-9374

© 2002 Frank Betz Associates, Inc.

Total Living	First Floor	Second Floor	Opt. Bonus	Bed	Bath	Width	Depth	Foundation	Price Category
3482 sq ft	2461 sq ft	1021 sq ft	N/A	5	4-1/2	80' 0"	57' 0"	Basement or Crawl Space	I

Design Features

- A beautiful covered porch on the front of the home makes a wonderful entrance.

- A secondary covered entrance is placed near the garage bays and leads directly to the laundry room.

- A striking keeping room is connected to the kitchen, featuring a fireplace, built-in cabinetry and vaulted ceilings.

- Homeowners will appreciate the master bedroom's private sitting area when it comes time to rest for the evening.

First Floor

Second Floor

Rear Elevation

Churchdown — UDHDG01-867 — 1-866-525-9374

Total Living	First Floor	Second Floor	Bonus	Bed	Bath	Width	Depth	Foundation	Price Category
3499 sq ft	2755 sq ft	744 sq ft	481 sq ft	3	3-1/2	92' 6"	69' 10"	Crawl Space*	G

Design Features

- The master suite features two walk-in closets, sitting area and a private porch.

- In addition to the living room, this plan also has a family room with a cathedral ceiling.

- Built-in shelves enhance the private study.

- Secondary bedrooms, two full bathrooms, a library and bonus room complete the second level.

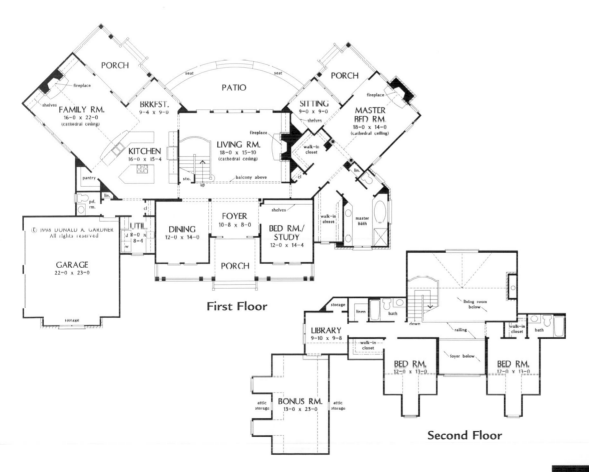

First Floor

Second Floor

Rear Elevation

*Other options available. See page 513.

New Brunswick — UDHDS01-8021 — 1-866-525-9374

© The Sater Design Collection, Inc.

Total Living	First Floor	Second Floor	Bonus	Bed	Bath	Width	Depth	Foundation	Price Category
3501 sq ft	2232 sq ft	1269 sq ft	N/A	4	4-1/2	80' 0"	63' 9"	Opt. Basement/Slab	I

Design Features

- This wonderful floor plan is centralized around a great room.

- The rear garage has a large bonus room/guest suite above.

- French doors open the great room to a wide veranda.

- The kitchen and nook open to a covered veranda with grille.

- The secluded master suite has private veranda access.

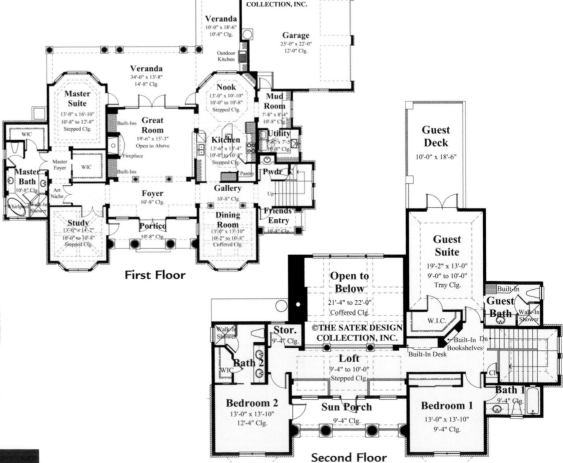

First Floor

Second Floor

Rear Elevation

© The Sater Design Collection, Inc.

Vienna — UDHDS01-8020 — 1-866-525-9374

Total Living	First Floor	Second Floor	Bonus	Bed	Bath	Width	Depth	Foundation	Price Category
3477 sq ft	2232 sq ft	1245 sq ft	N/A	4	4-1/2	63' 8"	80' 0"	Opt. Basement/Slab	I

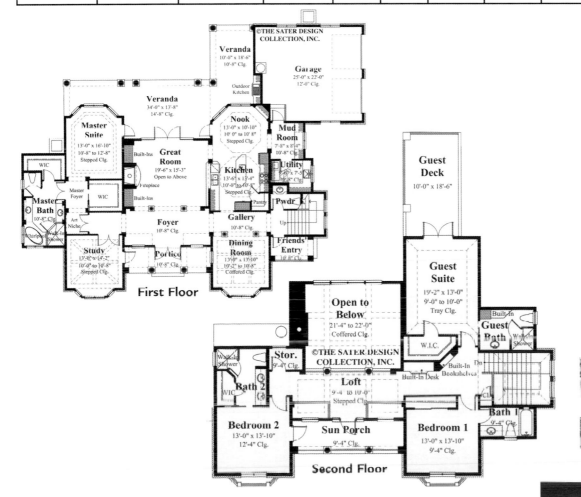

First Floor

Second Floor

Design Features

- Rugged stone walls, rough hewn wood shutters and a grand portico grace the front exterior.

- Wraparound counters, a walk-in pantry and extensive shelf space enhance the kitchen.

- A luxurious bath, access to the verandah and a private foyer promise rest and relaxation in the master suite.

- A forward sun porch on the upper level extends natural light to the balcony loft.

Rear Elevation

Wellingley — UDHDG01-943 — 1-866-525-9374

Total Living	First Floor	Second Floor	Bonus	Bed	Bath	Width	Depth	Foundation	Price Category
3573 sq ft	2511 sq ft	1062 sq ft	465 sq ft	4	3-1/2	84' 11"	55' 11"	Crawl Space*	H

Design Features

- Dormers echo the angles found in the gables, which provide a great contrast to the hip roof.

- A balcony overlooks, while fireplaces highlight, the two-story great room.

- The breakfast nook is expanded by a gentle curve.

- The sitting room off the master suite makes a perfect reading area or private study.

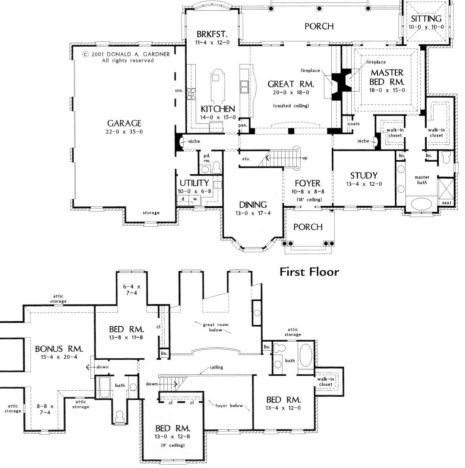

First Floor

Second Floor

Rear Elevation

*Other options available. See page 513.

© 2005 Frank Betz Associates, Inc.

Havenbrooke — UDHFB01-3924 — 1-866-525-9374

Total Living	First Floor	Second Floor	Opt. Bonus	Bed	Bath	Width	Depth	Foundation	Price Category
3574 sq ft	1737 sq ft	1837 sq ft	N/A	5	4	55' 0"	50' 6"	Basement or Crawl Space	I

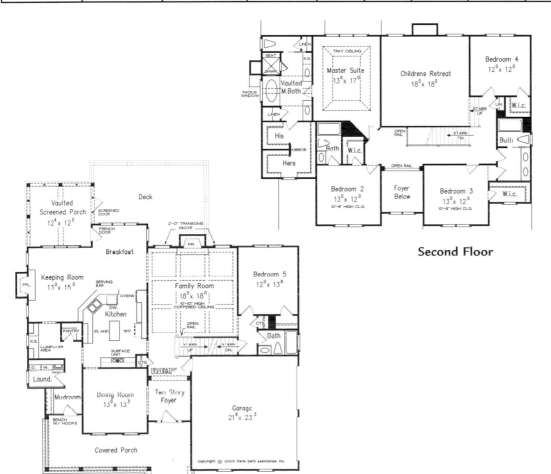

Second Floor

First Floor

Design Features

- Dual entries are just a hint of the special features found in the *Havenbrooke*.

- Inside the front door, decorative columns welcome visitors into the family room complete with a coffered ceiling.

- An additional door allows friends and family into a mudroom that offers a built-in bench and coat hooks.

- The laundry room, computer area and walk-in pantry are all tucked behind the kitchen keeping clutter in its place.

Rear Elevation

Bellamy — UDHDS01-8018 — 1-866-525-9374

© The Sater Design Collection, Inc.

Total Living	First Floor	Second Floor	Bonus	Bed	Bath	Width	Depth	Foundation	Price Category
3610 sq ft	2483 sq ft	1127 sq ft	332 sq ft	4	3-1/2	83' 0"	71' 8"	Opt. Basement/Slab	I

Design Features

- The two-story foyer leads past columns and archways to the living and dining rooms.

- A fireplace is shared by the leisure room and study.

- The master suite enjoys a morning kitchen.

- An upstairs guest suite has an outdoor balcony.

- A second-floor common area offers a built-in computer desk.

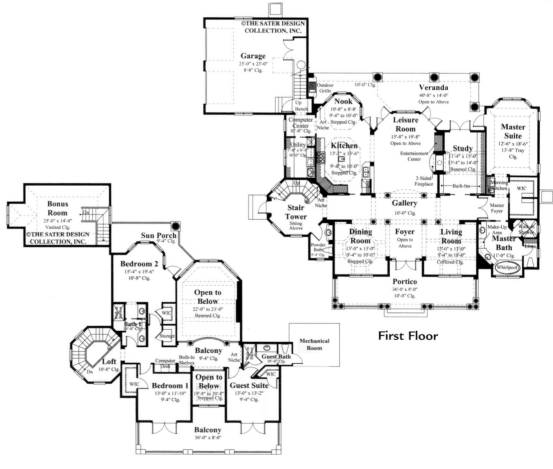

First Floor

Second Floor

Rear Elevation

© The Sater Design Collection, Inc.

Les Tourelles — UDHDS01-8017 — 1-866-525-9374

Total Living	First Floor	Second Floor	Bonus	Bed	Bath	Width	Depth	Foundation	Price Category
3613 sq ft	2481 sq ft	1132 sq ft	332 sq ft	4	3-1/2	83' 0"	71' 8"	Opt. Basement/Slab	I

First Floor

Second Floor

Design Features

- Double columns, simple balustrades, dormers, artful porticos and a thoughtfully placed turret impress those who pass-by.

- The kitchen features ample storage space, stepped ceiling, an island workstation and access to the nook and leisure room.

- It's all in the details—an art niche in the breakfast nook, outdoor grill on the verandah and built-in shelves and computer desk in the upper balcony.

Rear Elevation

Greywell — UDHFB01-3914 — 1-866-525-9374

© 2004 Frank Betz Associates, Inc.

Total Living	First Floor	Second Floor	Opt. Bonus	Bed	Bath	Width	Depth	Foundation	Price Category
3629 sq ft	2499 sq ft	1130 sq ft	N/A	5	4	67' 6"	69' 10"	Basement, Crawl Space or Slab	I

Design Features

- The kitchen overlooks a gracious breakfast area, as well as a fire-lit keeping room.

- A screened porch is accessed off this area as well, providing the perfect opportunity to take the party outside.

- Coffered ceilings and built-in cabinetry make the family room extra special.

- A children's retreat upstairs can be used as the perfect playroom, as a fourth bedroom or guest suite.

First Floor

Second Floor

Rear Elevation

© 1999 Frank Betz Associates, Inc.

Witherspoon — UDHFB01-3462 — 1-866-525-9374

Total Living	First Floor	Second Floor	Opt. Bonus	Bed	Bath	Width	Depth	Foundation	Price Category
3618 sq ft	2384 sq ft	1234 sq ft	344 sq ft	5	4-1/2	64' 6"	57' 10"	Basement, Crawl Space or Slab	I

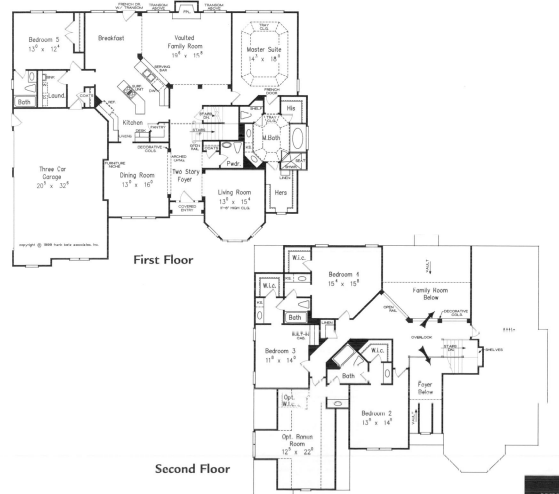

First Floor

Second Floor

Design Features

- A handy built-in message center and double ovens are included in the kitchen.

- Distinctive and elegant, tray ceilings enhance the master suite.

- A seated shower, double sinks and his-and-her closets make for an enviable master bath.

- Decorative columns and a furniture niche add charm to the formal dining room.

Rear Elevation

Willingham Manor — UDHFB01-3957 — 1-866-525-9374

© 2005 Frank Betz Associates, Inc.

Total Living	First Floor	Second Floor	Opt. Bonus	Bed	Bath	Width	Depth	Foundation	Price Category
3644 sq ft	2458 sq ft	1186 sq ft	366 sq ft	4	3-1/2	73' 0"	72' 6"	Basement, Crawl Space, or Slab	I

Design Features

- A rocking chair front porch welcomes guests to the *Willingham Manor.*

- Inside more treasures await. Coffered and beamed ceiling are an example of the attention to detail this plan offers.

- The pantry and built-in desk are conveniently located behind the kitchen to keep clutter in its place.

- Arched openings and built-in cabinets are found on either side of the family room.

First Floor

Second Floor

Rear Elevation

Cedar Ridge — UDHDG01-1125-D — 1-866-525-9374

Total Living	First Floor	Basement	Bonus	Bed	Bath	Width	Depth	Foundation	Price Category
3678 sq ft	2405 sq ft	1273 sq ft	679 sq ft	3	4	62' 10"	64' 2"	Hillside Walkout	O

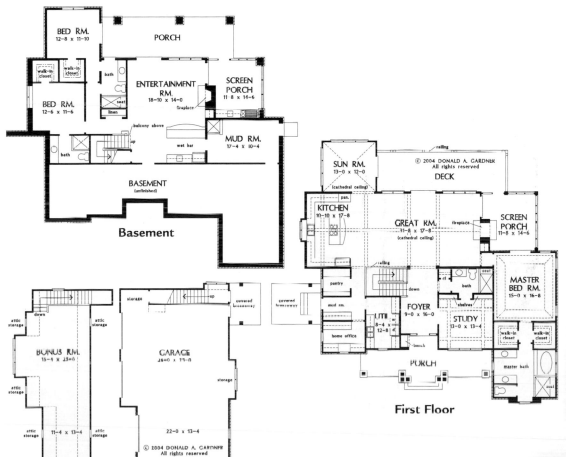

Basement

Bonus Room

First Floor

Design Features

- This gorgeous Craftsman home exposes rich detail throughout.

- A sunroom, rear deck and screened porch are all on the main level.

- The lower level boasts a screened porch with summer kitchen and a second covered porch.

- Multiple mud rooms, a large pantry and utility room provide abundant storage space.

Rear Elevation

Rosewood Court — UDHDS01-6733 — 1-866-525-9374

© The Sater Design Collection, Inc.

Total Living	First Floor	Second Floor	Bonus	Bed	Bath	Width	Depth	Foundation	Price Category
3688 sq ft	3688 sq ft	N/A	N/A	3	3-1/2	101' 8"	128' 4"	Slab	O

Design Features

- A bay turret, transom windows and an elegant recessed arch entry enhance the front façade.

- The kitchen provides counter-style seating and a food-prep island.

- The master retreat features a private foyer with an art niche, two walk-in closets and a spacious bath.

- Guests will enjoy spacious suites that include walk-in closets, private baths and patio access.

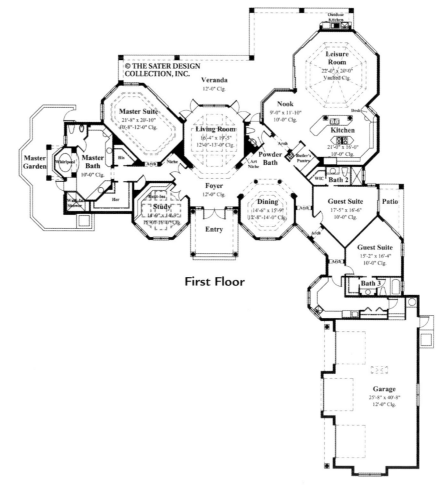

First Floor

Rear View

Photographed home may have been modified from original construction documents.

© The Sater Design Collection, Inc.

Salina — UDHDS01-8043 — 1-866-525-9374

Total Living	First Floor	Bonus	Bed	Bath	Width	Depth	Foundation	Price Category
3743 sq ft	3743 sq ft	N/A	4 + Study	3-1/2	80' 0"	104' 8"	Slab or Opt. Basement	I

First Floor

Optional 4th Bedroom

Design Features

- Beamed and coffered ceilings highlight the interior.

- The kitchen has cutting-edge culinary appliances.

- A stand-alone media center divides the leisure and game rooms.

- A vestibule links the master retreat with a study.

- Guest quarters include a cabana-style bath.

Rear Elevation

Manhasset — UDHFB01-3929 — 1-866-525-9374

© 2005 Frank Betz Associates, Inc.

Total Living	First Floor	Second Floor	Opt. Bonus	Bed	Bath	Width	Depth	Foundation	Price Category
3761 sq ft	2308 sq ft	1453 sq ft	N/A	4	3-1/2	78' 0"	52' 0"	Basement, Crawl Space or Slab	I

Design Features

- The open floor plan of the *Manhasset* allows for easy flow from room to room.

- The family room has a coffered ceiling and a fireplace flanked by built-in cabinets.

- A bedroom on the second floor has a window seat and built-in bookshelves.

- The kitchen offers both an island and a serving bar, perfect for the chef and for impromptu meals.

First Floor

Second Floor

Rear Elevation

© The Sater Design Collection, Inc.

Demetri — UDHDS01-8045 — 1-866-525-9374

Total Living	First Floor	Second Floor	Bonus	Bed	Bath	Width	Depth	Foundation	Price Category
3764 sq ft	3764 sq ft	N/A	N/A	4	3-1/2	80' 0"	108' 0"	Opt. Basement/Slab	I

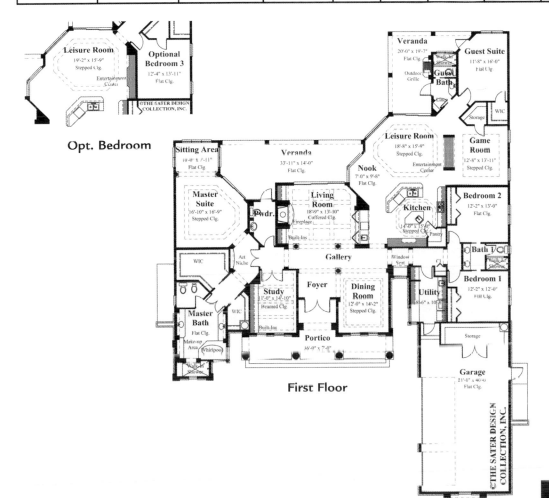

Opt. Bedroom

First Floor

Design Features

- A hipped roofline, pilasters, Corinthian columns and a trio of pediments set off this revival façade.

- The living room sits under a coffered ceiling and features a fireplace, built-ins and a wall of glass that opens to the verandah.

- The main living area of the home enjoys an open flow between the kitchen, nook, leisure and game room.

- The master suite features an art niche in the private foyer, a sitting area and glass doors to the veranda.

Rear Elevation

Sonora — UDHDS01-6764 — 1-866-525-9374

© The Sater Design Collection, Inc.

Total Living	First Floor	Bonus	Bed	Bath	Width	Depth	Foundation	Price Category
3790 sq ft	3790 sq ft	N/A	4 + Study	3-1/2	80' 0"	107' 8"	Slab	I

Design Features

- A keystone portico leads to an open foyer and column-lined gallery.

- The living room has an inviting fireplace and convenient wet bar.

- A unique kitchen has easy access to the game room, leisure room and nook.

- An entertainment center divides the leisure and game rooms.

- The rear guest suite offers veranda access.

Rear Elevation

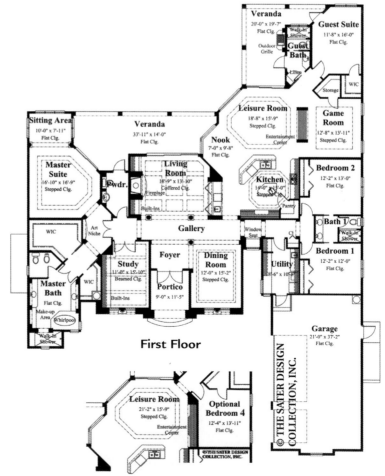

First Floor

Optional 4th Bedroom

© 2005 Frank Betz Associates, Inc.

Avignon — UDHFB01-3941 — 1-866-525-9374

Total Living	First Floor	Second Floor	Opt. Bonus	Bed	Bath	Width	Depth	Foundation	Price Category
3853 sq ft	2598 sq ft	1255 sq ft	401 sq ft	5	4-1/2	71' 6"	61' 0"	Basement or Crawl Space	I

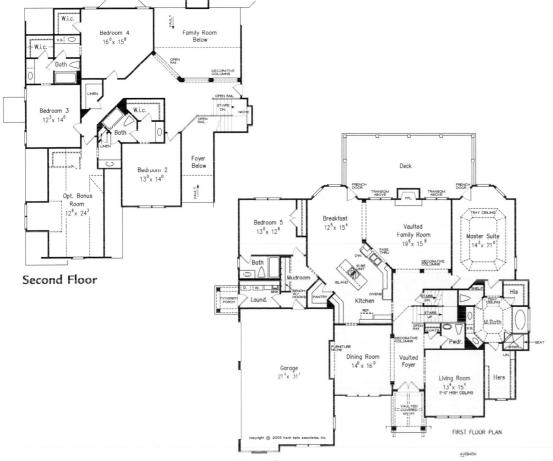

Second Floor

First Floor

Design Features

- Traditional appeal abounds from the *Avignon*.

- Covered side entry was designed allowing children and guests a place to put their coats, shoes and book bags. The built-in coat hooks and bench are a convenient addition.

- The master bedroom and a guest room occupy the main level.

- Three bedrooms and an optional bedroom can be found on the second floor.

Rear Elevation

Starwood — UDHDS01-6911 — 1-866-525-9374

© The Sater Design Collection, Inc.

Total Living	First Floor	Bonus	Bed	Bath	Width	Depth	Foundation	Price Category
3877 sq ft	3877 sq ft	N/A	3 + Study	3-1/2	102' 4"	98' 10"	Slab	O

Design Features

- The triple-arch entry announces the classic Mediterranean-style of this home.

- A rambling covered veranda enhances outdoor living.

- Curved walls of glass provide views from the nook.

- Arches and columns define the living and dining rooms.

- The secluded master suite has private garden views.

Pool & Veranda View

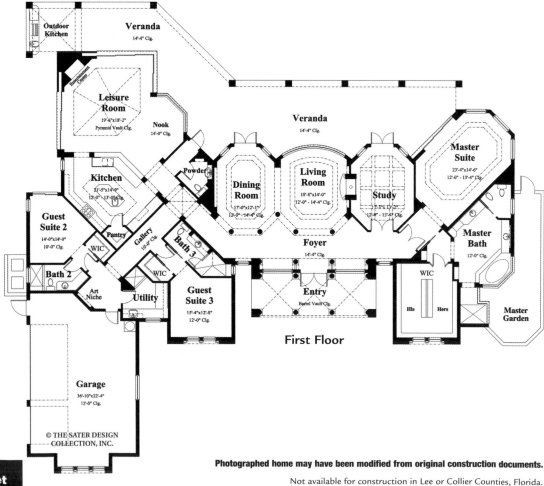

First Floor

© THE SATER DESIGN COLLECTION, INC.

Photographed home may have been modified from original construction documents.

Not available for construction in Lee or Collier Counties, Florida.

© 1997 Frank Betz Associates, Inc.

Flanagan — UDHFB01-1058 — 1-866-525-9374

Total Living	First Floor	Second Floor	Opt. Bonus	Bed	Bath	Width	Depth	Foundation	Price Category
3877 sq ft	2060 sq ft	1817 sq ft	N/A	5	4-1/2	54' 0"	78' 4"	Basement, Crawl Space or Slab	J

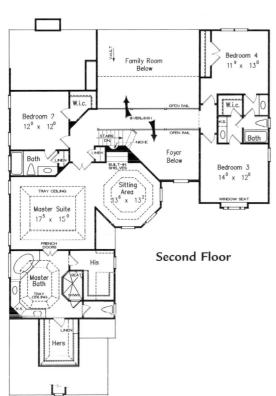

Second Floor

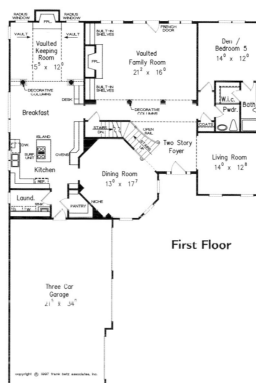

First Floor

Design Features

- A stunning stone turret gives this plan eye-catching curb appeal.

- A vaulted keeping room—accentuated by decorative columns—adjoins the kitchen area.

- The master suite earns its name, featuring a uniquely shaped sitting area

- A main-floor bedroom can be easily converted into a den or home office.

Rear Elevation

Northfield Manor — UDHFB01-3921 — 1-866-525-9374

© 2005 Frank Betz Associates, Inc.

Total Living	First Floor	Second Floor	Opt. Bonus	Bed	Bath	Width	Depth	Foundation	Price Category
3878 sq ft	2745 sq ft	1133 sq ft	649 sq ft	4	4-1/2	69' 0"	85' 6"	Basement, Crawl Space or Slab	J

Design Features

- The *Northfield Manor* offers a rear entry garage, which is perfect for a corner lot.

- A mudroom is accessible through the garage making sure coats, shoes and book bags stay in their place.

- A keeping room is an extension of the breakfast area, allowing family members to congregate at the end of the day.

- Three bedrooms and a very large bonus room occupy the second floor.

Rear Elevation

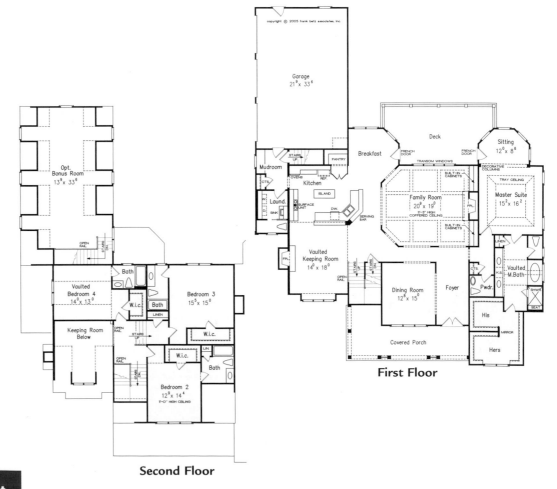

Second Floor

First Floor

© The Sater Design Collection, Inc.

Cardiff — UDHDS01-6750 — 1-866-525-9374

Total Living	First Floor	Bonus	Bed	Bath	Width	Depth	Foundation	Price Category
3883 sq ft	3883 sq ft	N/A	3 + Study	3-1/2	101' 4"	106' 0"	Slab	O

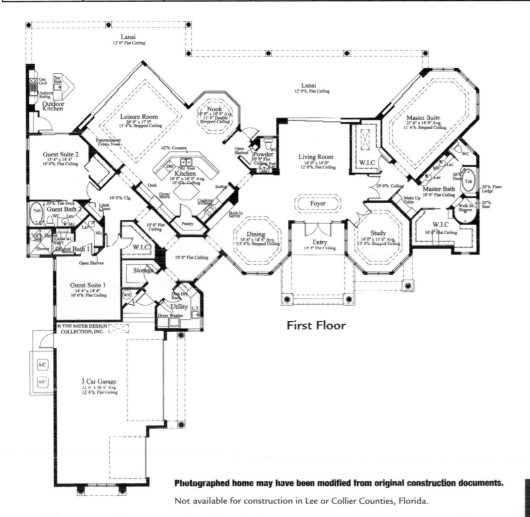

First Floor

Design Features

- The elegant gabled entry and tapered columns define the front façade of this contemporary Mediterranean-style home.

- The octagonal study has a thirteen-foot tray ceiling.

- The leisure room has a carved nook for an entertainment center.

- The living room opens to the rear through pocketing-glass doors.

- The kitchen holds center-stage in the casual zone of the plan.

Pool & Lanai View

Photographed home may have been modified from original construction documents.

Not available for construction in Lee or Collier Counties, Florida.

3000 sq ft—4000 sq ft

The Sater Design Collection, Inc.

Fiddler's Creek — UDHDS01-6746 — 1-866-525-9374

© The Sater Design Collection, Inc.

Total Living	First Floor	Second Floor	Bonus	Bed	Bath	Width	Depth	Foundation	Price Category
3893 sq ft	2841 sq ft	1052 sq ft	N/A	4	3-1/2	85' 0"	76' 2"	Opt. Basement/Slab	I

Design Features

- Inside the foyer, columns frame a living room with a fireplace.
- A column-lined gallery hall leads down each wing.
- The kitchen has a walk-in pantry and counter to the veranda.
- The leisure room has a fireplace and French doors to the lanai.
- A balcony overlook leads to three upstairs bedrooms.

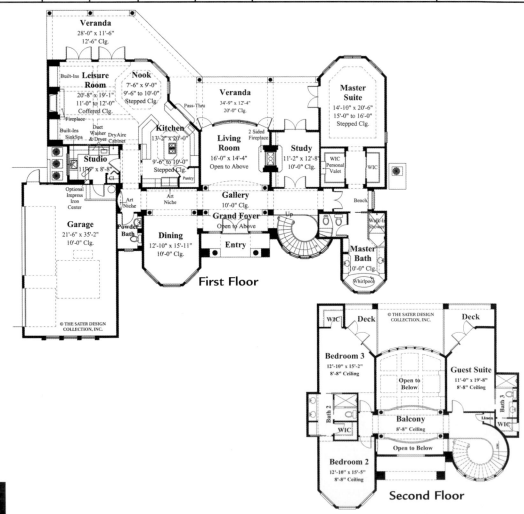

Rear Elevation

© 2003 Frank Betz Associates, Inc.

Hazelwood Ridge — UDHFB01-3812 — 1-866-525-9374

Total Living	First Floor	Second Floor	Opt. Bonus	Bed	Bath	Width	Depth	Foundation	Price Category
3830 sq ft	2786 sq ft	1044 sq ft	319 sq ft	4	3-1/2	76' 0"	66' 6"	Basement or Crawl Space	I

Design Features

- From the *Southern Living® Design Collection*

- It's the added extras of the *Hazelwood Ridge* that make it one of a kind.

- The sizeable kitchen includes an island for easy meal preparation and a vaulted keeping room - great for entertaining or family time.

- A handy grilling porch is directly accessible from the kitchen and breakfast areas.

First Floor

Second Floor

Rear Elevation

Southerland Place — UDHFB01-3950 — 1-866-525-9374

© 2005 Frank Betz Associates, Inc.

Total Living	First Floor	Second Floor	Opt. Bonus	Bed	Bath	Width	Depth	Foundation	Price Category
3931 sq ft	2641 sq ft	1290 sq ft	399 sq ft	4	3-1/2	71' 0"	72' 4"	Basement or Crawl Space	J

Design Features

- This home offers four bedrooms and an optional bonus room that can be used as a fifth bedroom.

- A keeping room with a beamed ceiling and a fireplace is the perfect place to end the day.

- The dining room has a convenient furniture niche to add additional space to the room.

- Outside the screened porch and deck ensure that the outdoors can be enjoyed in all types of weather.

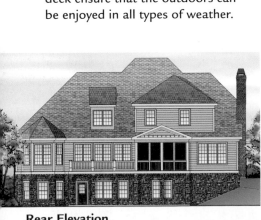

Rear Elevation

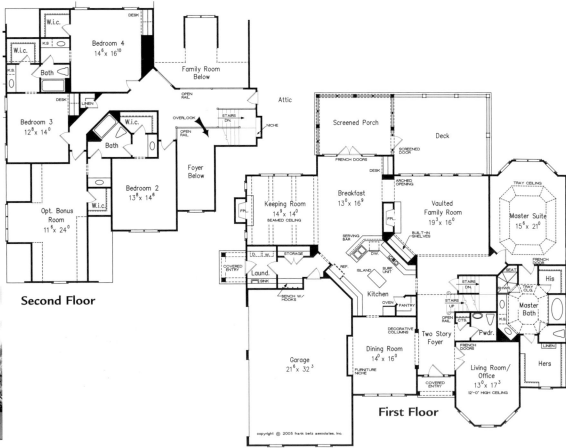

Second Floor

First Floor

© The Sater Design Collection, Inc.

Winthrop — UDHDS01-8034 — 1-866-525-9374

Total Living	First Floor	Bonus	Bed	Bath	Width	Depth	Foundation	Price Category
3954 sq ft	3954 sq ft	N/A	3 + Study	4	83' 10"	106' 0"	Slab	I

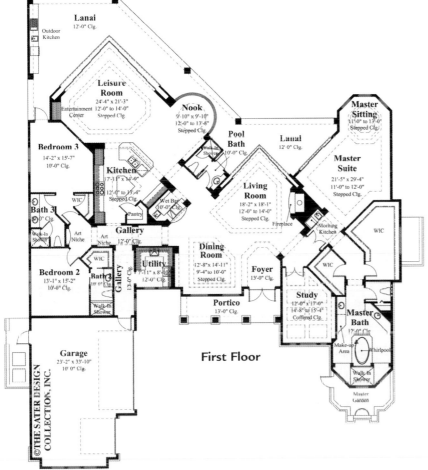

First Floor

Design Features

- Triple arches announce the entry to this Mediterranean-style country villa.

- The interior is enhanced by coffered and stepped ceiling treatments.

- The living room, dining room and foyer open to views of the lanai.

- The leisure room walls roll away to reveal an outdoor-kitchen and dining area.

Pool & Lanai View

Photographed home may have been modified from original construction documents.

Alessandra — UDHDS01-8003 — 1-866-525-9374

© The Sater Design Collection, Inc.

Total Living	First Floor	Second Floor	Bonus	Bed	Bath	Width	Depth	Foundation	Price Category
3945 sq ft	2815 sq ft	1130 sq ft	N/A	4	3-1/2	85' 0"	76' 8"	Opt. Basement/Slab	I

Design Features

- Impressive square columns, portico, turrets and a pediment window above the entry adorn the front elevation.

- The spacious kitchen features ample storage space and opens up to the breakfast nook and great room.

- The great room welcomes guests with a warm fireplace, built-ins, a coffered ceiling and two French doors that open to the veranda.

- The master suite indulges with a private entry, spacious walk-in closets, and a luxurious bath.

Second Floor

First Floor

Rear Elevation

© 2003 Frank Betz Associates, Inc.

Hartford Springs — UDHFB01-3824 — 1-866-525-9374

Total Living	First Floor	Second Floor	Opt. Bonus	Bed	Bath	Width	Depth	Foundation	Price Category
3971 sq ft	2504 sq ft	1467 sq ft	N/A	4	3-1/2	73' 0"	66' 10"	Basement or Crawl Space	I

Design Features

- From the *Southern Living® Design Collection*

- Two decks are situated on the back of the home.

- A crackling fire is the backdrop for family time spent in the vaulted keeping room.

- The master suite includes a roomy sitting area with access to the deck.

Second Floor

First Floor

Rear Elevation

Elise — UDHDS01-8012 — 1-866-525-9374

© The Sater Design Collection, Inc.

Total Living	First Floor	Second Floor	Bonus	Bed	Bath	Width	Depth	Foundation	Price Category
4022 sq ft	2867 sq ft	1155 sq ft	371 sq ft	4	4-1/2	71' 6"	82' 2"	Opt. Basement/Slab	J

Design Features

■ A sculpted recessed entry combines with multiple gables, decorative sunburst transoms, shutters and bay window to create a memorable front exterior.

■ An airy indoor/outdoor relationship is prevalent in the shared space of the leisure room, morning nook and kitchen.

■ The master retreat is the right wing of the main level, complete with a garden bath, spacious dressing area and a private sitting area.

Rear Elevation

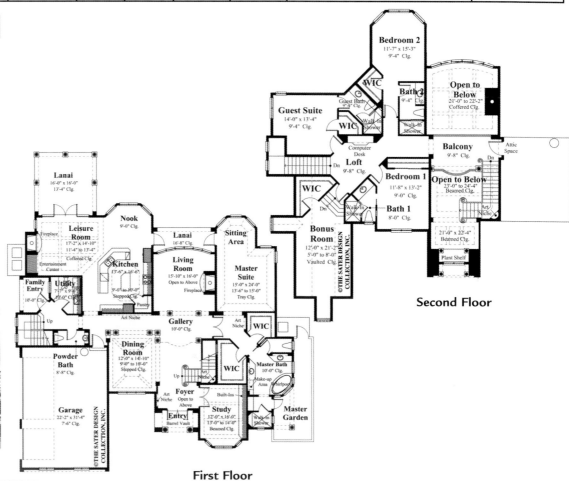

Second Floor

First Floor

Wedgewood Place — UDHFB01-3931 — 1-866-525-9374

Total Living	First Floor	Second Floor	Opt. Bonus	Bed	Bath	Width	Depth	Foundation	Price Category
4024 sq ft	2430 sq ft	1594 sq ft	405 sq ft	4	4-1/2	81' 0"	77' 0"	Basement, Crawl Space or Slab	J

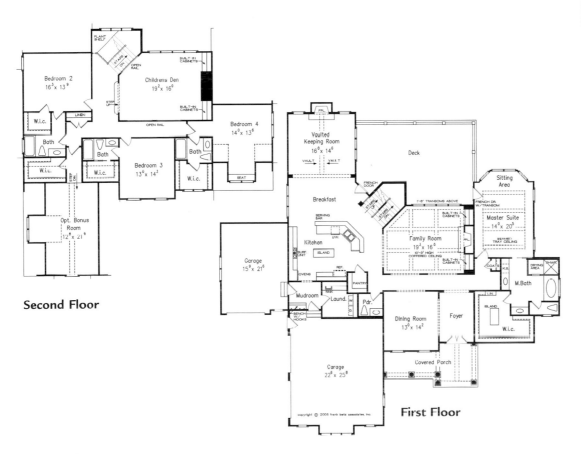

Second Floor

First Floor

Design Features

- The brick siding exterior of the *Wedgewood Place* is a welcoming sight. The inside is just as amazing.

- The family room boasts a coffered ceiling with a fireplace and built-in cabinets.

- A keeping room adjacent to the breakfast area is accented by a fireplace.

- The master suite offers a large walk-in closet with an island for added convenience.

Rear Elevation

Plantation Pine — UDHDS01-6735 — 1-866-525-9374

© The Sater Design Collection, Inc.

Total Living	First Floor	Guest Suite	Bed	Bath	Width	Depth	Foundation	Price Category
4282 sq ft	4282 sq ft	331 sq ft	4 + Study	5	88' 0"	133' 0"	Slab	J

Design Features

- The living and dining rooms share triple French doors to the lanai.

- A private detached guest suite is a favorite family option.

- An arched hallway leads to sunny family areas.

- The kitchen boasts an island and walk-in pantry.

- The leisure room has a fireplace and entertainment center.

- A computer center and bonus room are wonderful extras.

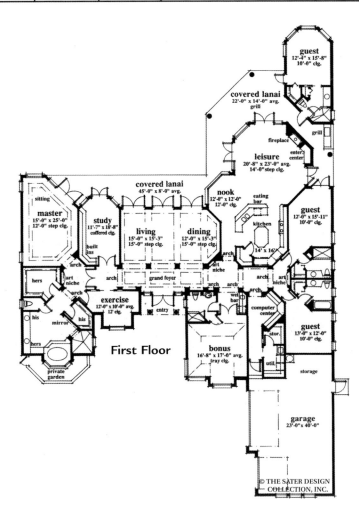

First Floor

Rear Elevation

© 2002 Frank Betz Associates, Inc.

Clarendon — UDHFB01-3685 — 1-866-525-9374

Total Living	First Floor	Second Floor	Opt. Bonus	Bed	Bath	Width	Depth	Foundation	Price Category
4317 sq ft	2635 sq ft	1682 sq ft	114 sq ft	4	4-1/2	79' 0"	74' 5"	Basement or Crawl Space	J

First Floor

Second Floor

Design Features

- Soaring white columns against striking red brick create a time-honored façade that takes you back in time.

- An impressive foyer has a curved staircase and furniture niche. A library—with a massive wall of bookshelves—overlooks the entry.

- The well-appointed kitchen opens to a breakfast area, two-story keeping room and covered porch.

Rear Elevation

Donald A. Gardner Architects, Inc.

The Oak Abbey — UDHAL01- 5003 — 1-866-525-9374

Total Living	First Floor	Basement	Bonus	Bed	Bath	Width	Depth	Foundation	Price Category
4547 sq ft	3006 sq ft	1541 sq ft	480 sq ft	4	4.5	93' 11"	80' 9"	Hillside Walkout	O

Design Features

- This hillside walkout features an open floor plan and plenty of outdoor living areas.

- Cathedral ceilings top the great room, master bedroom and screened porch.

- Three fireplaces, wet-bar, built-in cabinetry and an art niche add custom touches.

- Downstairs, each bedroom has its own walk-in closet and bath.

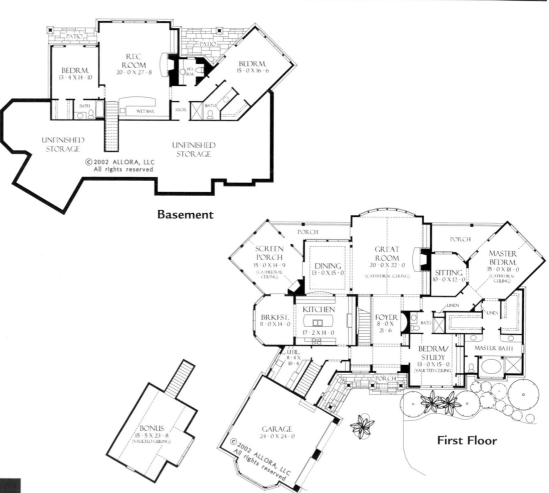

Basement

First Floor

Rear Elevation

© 1994 Frank Betz Associates, Inc.

Castlegate — UDHFB01-790 — 1-866-525-9374

Total Living	First Floor	Second Floor	Bonus	Bed	Bath	Width	Depth	Foundation	Price Category
4362 sq ft	2764 sq ft	1598 sq ft	N/A	4	3-1/2	74' 6"	65' 10"	Basement, Crawl Space or Slab	J

Design Features

- Your castle awaits.....A portico entry leads into a breathtaking two-story foyer with a curved staircase.

- The master suite is appropriately named, with its vaulted sitting room and luxurious bath.

- An art niche, built-in cabinetry and bookshelves, coffered ceilings and decorative columns are pleasant surprises as you wander the home.

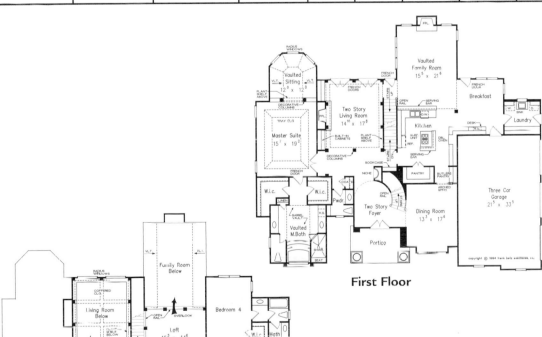

First Floor

Second Floor

Rear Elevation

Coach Hill — UDHDS01-8013 — 1-866-525-9374

© The Sater Design Collection, Inc.

Total Living	First Floor	Second Floor	Bonus	Bed	Bath	Width	Depth	Foundation	Price Category
4664 sq ft	3025 sq ft	1639 sq ft	294 sq ft	4	4-1/2	70' 0"	100' 0"	Slab/Opt. Basement	J

Design Features

- The foyer surrounds a staircase enhanced with a dome ceiling.

- A stepped ceiling and arched columns define the living room.

- The great room features a two-story bow window and two-sided fireplace.

- French doors open the master suite to a private veranda.

- The owners' bath has access to an outdoor garden.

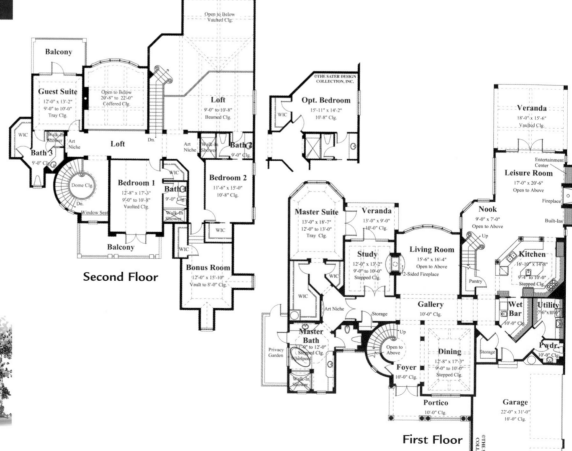

Second Floor

First Floor

Rear Elevation

© The Sater Design Collection, Inc.

Stonehaven — UDHDS01-8032 — 1-866-525-9374

Total Living	First Floor	Second Floor	Bonus	Bed	Bath	Width	Depth	Foundation	Price Category
4465 sq ft	2163 sq ft	2302 sq ft	N/A	5	5-1/2	58' 0"	65' 0"	Slab/Opt. Basement	J

Second Floor

First Floor

Design Features

■ This grand plan has a host of windows and outdoor places.

■ Views fill the home through a wall of glass to the rear.

■ A retreating-glass wall in the leisure room brings in the outdoors.

■ A wraparound loft leads to a master suite and child's suite.

■ Two secondary suites, perfect for teenagers, are also upstairs.

Rear Elevation

Hillcrest Ridge — UDHDS01-6651 — 1-866-525-9374

© The Sater Design Collection, Inc.

Total Living	First Floor	Second Floor	Bonus	Bed	Bath	Width	Depth	Foundation	Price Category
4759 sq ft	3546 sq ft	1213 sq ft	N/A	4	3-1/2	95' 4"	83' 0"	Basement	L

Design Features

- An arched gallery hallway leads to the family areas.

- The expansive kitchen has a cooktop island and pass-thru to the veranda.

- Three sets of French doors open the leisure and living rooms to the rear.

- The owner's wing includes a study perfect for an office.

- Upstairs, two bedroom have private balconies, and a third has a bayed sitting space.

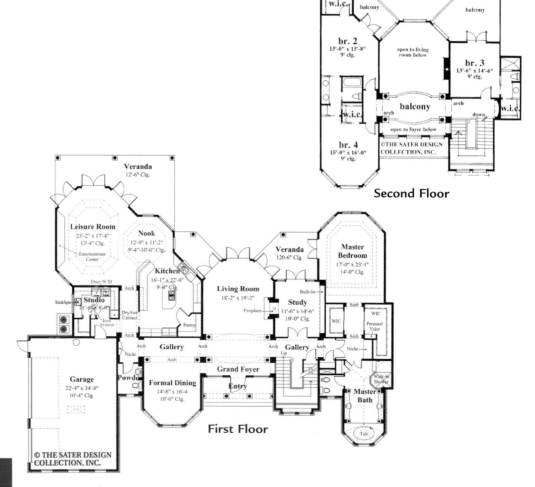

Second Floor

First Floor

© THE SATER DESIGN COLLECTION, INC.

Rear Elevation

© The Sater Design Collection, Inc.

Sherbrooke — UDHDS01-6742 — 1-866-525-9374

Total Living	First Floor	Second Floor	Bonus	Bed	Bath	Width	Depth	Foundation	Price Category
4771 sq ft	3933 sq ft	838 sq ft	N/A	4	4-1/2	91' 4"	109' 0"	Slab	O

Second Floor

First Floor

Design Features

- The master suite has walk-in closets and a pampering bath.

- With an extended stonewall mantle and an art niche, the living room exudes detail.

- The patio is perfect for entertaining and includes an outdoor kitchen.

- The formal dining room features a high domed ceiling.

- Designed for convenience, the kitchen has plenty of counter space and double ovens.

Rear View

Trevi — UDHDS01-8065 — 1-866-525-9374

© The Sater Design Collection, Inc.

Total Living	First Floor	Second Floor	Bonus	Bed	Bath	Width	Depth	Foundation	Price Category
4837 sq ft	3581 sq ft	1256 sq ft	N/A	4	3-1/2	95' 0"	84' 0"	Opt. Basement/Slab	J

Design Features

- A massive turret and a rusticated gable frame the entry arcade of this magnificent manor.

- The gourmet kitchen features an island workspace, ample counter and storage space, an eating bar and easy access to the nook and leisure room.

- A splendid owners' retreat features stepped ceilings, access to the verandah, walk-in closets and a spacious bath that includes a bumped-out oval tub and deck, with a garden view.

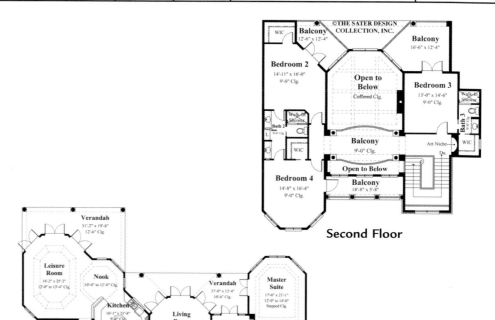

Second Floor

First Floor

Rear Elevation

Crowne Canyon — UDHDG01-732-D — 1-866-525-9374

Total Living	First Floor	Basement	Bonus	Bed	Bath	Width	Depth	Foundation	Price Category
4776 sq ft	3040 sq ft	1736 sq ft	N/A	5	4-1/2	106' 5"	104' 2"	Hillside Walkout	J

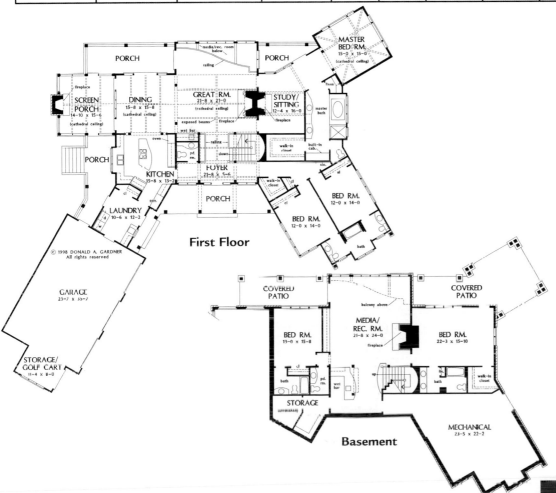

First Floor

Basement

Design Features

- Exposed wood beams enhance the cathedral ceilings through several of the rooms.

- The great room takes in scenic rear views through a wall of windows shared by the media/rec room.

- Fireplaces add warmth to the great room, media/rec room, screened porch and master suite's study/sitting.

- The kitchen is complete with its center island pantry, and ample room for two or more cooks.

Rear Elevation

The Sater Design Collection, Inc.

St Regis Grand — UDHDS01-6916 — 1-866-525-9374

© The Sater Design Collection, Inc.

Total Living	First Floor	Second Floor	Bonus	Bed	Bath	Width	Depth	Foundation	Price Category
5265 sq ft	4784 sq ft	481 sq ft	N/A	4	6-1/2	106' 6"	106' 0"	Slab	O

Design Features

- Gently pitched roofs, stone trim work and a turret capped with a trio of transoms enhance the front façade.

- The gourmet kitchen includes a centered food-preparation island with a sink, and a snack counter that overlooks the leisure room.

- A separate segment of the lanai provides an outdoor kitchen that handles crowd-size gatherings or more intimate meals by the fireplace in the courtyard.

Rear View

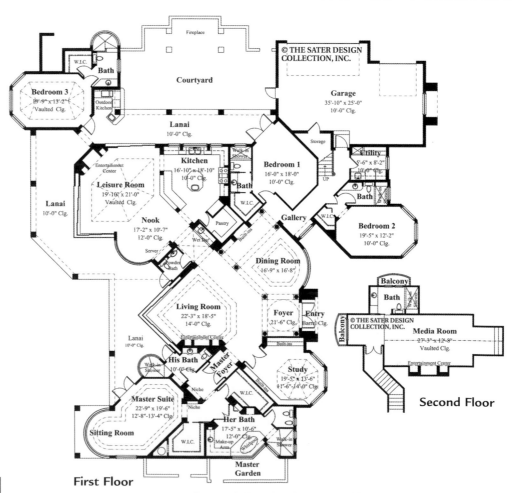

First Floor

Second Floor

Photographed home may have been modified from original construction documents.

© The Sater Design Collection, Inc.

Gambier Court — UDHDS01-6948 — 1-866-525-9374

Total Living	First Floor	Second Floor	Bonus	Bed	Bath	Width	Depth	Foundation	Price Category
4951 sq ft	3758 sq ft	1193 sq ft	N/A	4	4-1/2	93' 10"	113' 8"	Slab	O

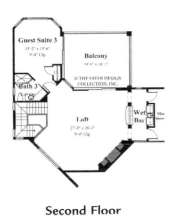

Second Floor

First Floor

Design Features

- A cozy courtyard features an extraordinary fireplace.

- The leisure room has a coffered ceiling and disappearing-glass walls to the courtyard.

- The kitchen has an extended serving counter and center island.

- The large master retreat includes a cozy sitting area.

- A center garden tub and walk-in shower make the bath luxurious.

Rear View

Sterling Oaks — UDHDS01-6914 — 1-866-525-9374

© The Sater Design Collection, Inc.

Total Living	First Floor	Second Floor	Bonus	Bed	Bath	Width	Depth	Walls/Foundation	Price Category
5816 sq ft	4385 sq ft	1431 sq ft	N/A	5	5-1/2	88' 0"	110' 1"	Slab	O

Design Features

- A dramatic entry under a porte-cochere leads to a living room with a bowed window.

- Bedrooms are cozily sequestered and have full baths.

- Two gallery areas lead to a grand master bedroom.

- Multiple outdoor spaces include a winding verandah with kitchen.

- The second floor features a loft, two guests suites and two decks.

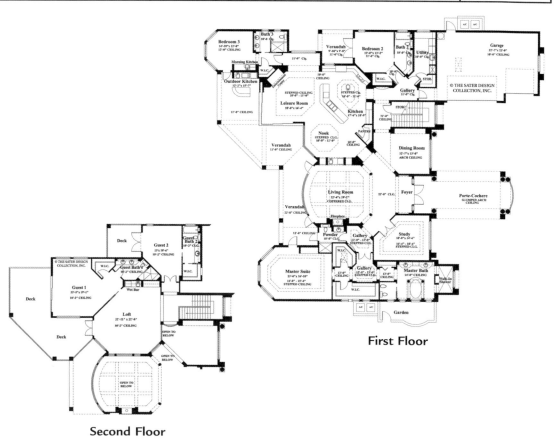

First Floor

Second Floor

Rear View

Photographed home may have been modified from original construction documents.

© 1998 Frank Betz Associates, Inc.

Brookshire Manor — UDHFB01-1184 — 1-866-525-9374

Total Living	First Floor	Second Floor	Opt. Bonus	Bed	Bath	Width	Depth	Foundation	Price Category
5466 sq ft	2732 sq ft	2734 sq ft	N/A	5	5-1/2	85' 0"	85' 6"	Basement, Crawl Space or Slab	J

Design Features

- Class, style, tradition and every creature comfort imaginable — the *Brookshire Manor* grants every wish!

- Relax and unwind by the fire in the cozy hearth room adjoining the kitchen.

- The master suite earns its name, featuring a personal lounging room with a fireplace and a lavish master bath with private dressing area and direct access to the exercise room.

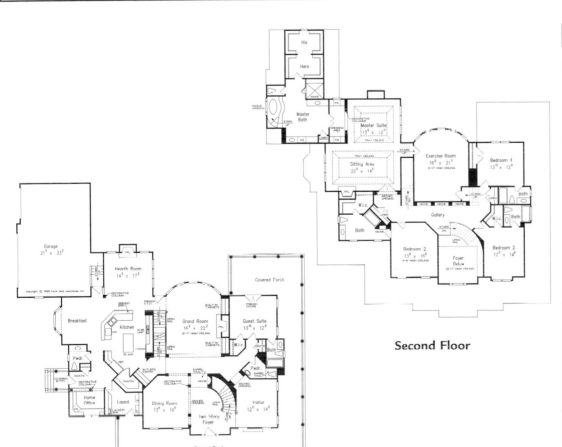

Second Floor

First Floor

Rear Elevation

Port Royal Way — UDHDS01-6635 — 1-866-525-9374

© The Sater Design Collection, Inc.

Total Living	First Floor	Second Floor	Bonus	Bed	Bath	Width	Depth	Foundation	Price Category
6312 sq ft	4760 sq ft	1552 sq ft	N/A	5	6-1/2	98' 0"	103' 8"	Slab	M

Design Features

- Columns and archways grace the view through the formal spaces.

- A two-story ceiling, fireplace and French doors add drama to the living room.

- The family room pleases with a media center and corner wet bar.

- An enormous master wing has a personal valet and center whirlpool tub.

- Multiple verandas and second-floor decks offer limitless outdoor living.

Rear Elevation

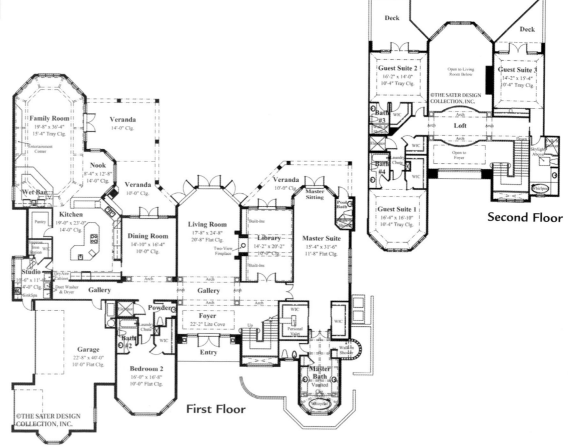

© The Sater Design Collection, Inc.

Fiorentino — UDHDS01-6910 — 1-866-525-9374

Total Living	First Floor	Second Floor	Bonus	Bed	Bath	Width	Depth	Foundation	Price Category
6273 sq ft	4742 sq ft	1531 sq ft	N/A	4	4F/2H	96' 0"	134' 8"	Slab	O

Second Floor

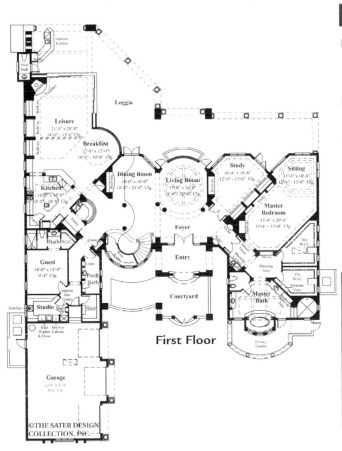

First Floor

Design Features

- The guest quarters and family spaces shares a wet bar with the formal rooms.

- The kitchen has a food-prep island and a serving counter.

- The leisure room has a fireplace and retreating-glass walls to the loggia.

- The master suite is secluded, with a spa tub viewing a private garden.

- On the upper level, a computer loft overlooks the living room.

Rear View

Photographed home may have been modified from original construction documents.

PLAN INDEX

PLAN INDEX

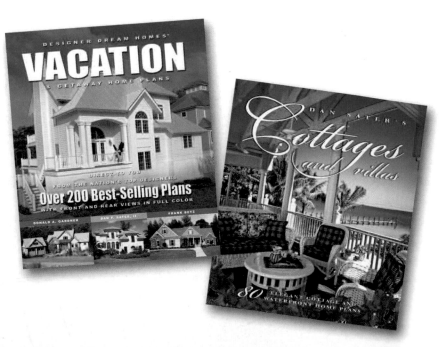